News in a Globalized Society

Edited by Stig Hjarvard

Globalized News in a Society

NORDICOM

News in a Globalized Society
Edited by Stig Hjarvard

ISBN 91-89471-05-9

Cover: *Torben Lundsted*
Printed in Sweden by
Grafikerna Livréna i Kungälv AB 2001

NORDICOM
Göteborg university
Box 713
SE-405 30 Göteborg
http://www.nordicom.gu.se
phone +46 31-773 10 00, fax +46 31-773 46 55

Contents

Introduction

Stig Hjarvard

Since the late 1980s a new agenda for research on the relationship between media and society has gradually emerged. The revolutionary changes in the former Soviet Union and Eastern Europe and the Gulf War were the first and very prominent indicators of major changes in media as well as in society. Apart from being significant in their own right, the way these events unfolded also related a strong feeling that developments in national and international politics were somehow connected to – perhaps interdependent with – changes within the media sector. The media – and the news media in particular – not only reported on these major social changes, but were somehow implicated in them and perhaps partly constitutive of them, at least to the extent that media influenced certain key decisions and events and favored certain paths of development over others. It was not without reasons that phrases like "television revolution" and "media war" were used to describe the breakdown of communism and the war between Irak and the multilateral alliance.

Not least in the broadcast news industry these events had a very strong impact. Broadcasters acquired a new sense of the media's potential during such events and they came under pressure for renewing the kind of news services they traditionally provided. The head of the news working party of the European Broadcasting Union, Jacques Vandersichel, stated in a EBU publication from 1991 with the telling title *Actors or Spectators?* that

> after the orgy of the Gulf coverage, television newsrooms will be faced with a
> new challenge, whether they want it or not. [...] our audience will expect more
> than ever from now on. They will expect television news to be there, and show
> them all that is happening, as it is happening. (EBU, 1991: 4-5)

And news media did change. Broadcast news proliferated during the 1990s. News bulletins expanded to the entire day providing continuous updates on both local and global events from early morning to late in the night. Several satellite news services gained access to every major satellite platform and cable distributor around the globe. News diversified into many subgenres like business news, entertainment news, sports news, medical news etc., and the rise of the

Internet media provided a new platform for an even greater expansion in the geographical reach and volume of news output. Newspapers, broadcasters, news agencies, and other media actors began to distribute news on the Internet. News increasingly became available in real-time and across national boundaries.

The role of media in the historical events and social changes from the late 1980s and onwards gradually began to be reflected in theoretical thinking in the social and political sciences. The German social theorist Jürgen Habermas, who in the 1960s announced the demise of the public sphere not least as a consequence of the spread of popular media, began in 1990 to talk about the formation of a world public sphere. He labeled the changes in eastern and central Europe and the Gulf War "the first *world-political* events in a strict sense" (Habermas, 1996: 514, Habermas' emphasis):

> Through the electronic media, these events were brought instantaneously before a ubiquitous public sphere. In the context of the French Revolution, Kant made reference to the reactions of a participatory public. At that time, he identified the phenomenon of a world public sphere, which today is becoming political reality for the first time in a cosmopolitan matrix of communication (Habermas, 1996: 514).

Globalization became the key concept by which social changes during the post-communist era were analyzed and interpreted in the 1990s. Although globalization has frequently been criticized and even rejected as a proper concept because of its at once all-embracing character and vague contours, it nevertheless established a new agenda in disciplines like social theory, international politics, cultural studies etc. (e.g., Bauman, 1998; Giddens, 1999; Held, 1995; Held et al., 1999; Tomlinson, 1999).

Media studies were also influenced by the new agenda of globalization. Media studies have had a long tradition for research on media flows between nations, including the impact of foreign media flows on national cultures etc. but such studies were previously confined to sub-disciplines like international communication or development communication. The implicit, yet crucial, assumption behind these disciplines was the notion that the nation state is the key unit of analysis. Thus, media flows were studied as flows between nations, media development was very often measured by comparing levels of national development, and international media were understood as something foreign that penetrated into the national environment. Dependency theory as well as media and cultural imperialism constituted the critical framework that guided this nation-centered understanding of an international media system. For media researchers and the general public alike, foreign media were something that only became visible, of social importance – and possible to study – when they crossed the national border, or you would have to travel a long way – preferably to US – in order to experience or study them.

The globalization agenda challenged this nation-centeredness. Today, the nation is still an important unit of analysis, but it is increasingly one among several other social entities defined by cultural, economic or political characteristics, ethnicity, class, religion, age etc., all of which transcend national borders. Globalization entails a new social geography with several interconnected and overlapping social spaces of which the national realm is only one. In order to examine and explain the distribution and consumption patterns of media flows in this new geography, levels of urbanization and education, the nature and size of language communities, and the spread of ethnic groups within larger regions may have more explanatory power than do differences between nations. As a result, the study of "foreign" media is no longer the exclusive property of specialists in international communication, but has increasingly become an important element of media studies in general. In order to understand the development of media production concepts and routines, or to explain changes in genres, formats and audience preferences, the global context of media must be taken into consideration. Even local media are rarely local in the strict sense of the word. They are very often affiliates of transnational media companies and part of their regional strategy – and as such they must be analyzed. Thus, the globalization agenda has not only changed the framework of international communication studies, but also functioned as a lever for a de-nationali _Globalisation_ general.

Globalization not only entails a change in the socia analyze globalization in media studies implies a double-sided approach that takes into account both the influence of globalization on media and the impact of globalized media on society. Although social theory often stresses the key role of communication media in processes of globalization, conceptualization and studies of this role in the social sciences are very few. Therefore, the field of media studies cannot restrict itself to the study of the globalization of media alone. It must also contribute to a cross-disciplinary understanding of how media contributes to the globalization of society.

As a starting point, we can distinguish between three different ways in which communication media contribute to processes of globalization: as *channels* of communications, as *messengers* of a world beyond the local, and as providers of a new social *infrastructure*. As channels of communication, media in general and electronic media in particular have been the necessary condition for globalization of other social institutions. Without the development and proliferation of the telephone, telegraphy, radio, television, communication satellites, computers, Internet etc., the globalization of industry, finance, military, culture etc. would simply not have taken place. The global scope of the stock market, the advance of post-Fordist transnational production regimes, the development of high-tech warfare capabilities with a global reach, and the explosion in transport of passengers and manufactured goods around the globe all rely on communication media to coordinate activities in real-time across vast distances. The media are to a very large extent responsible for a key feature of globalization: the increased *interconnectedness* of social institutions and actors.

Not least through media, globalization also becomes a *psychological* reality. The increased availability and penetration of media originating from many parts of the world makes it obvious for any culture that it is not alone. Some decades

9

ago, it was still possible for a culture and a society to develop in an at least fairly autonomous way with limited communication with the outside world (the Soviet block, China, and several 3rd world countries are all examples of such partially independent paths of development). Such independent development is no longer possible. Today, each culture must develop itself against the backdrop of other cultures. The visibility of other cultures within ones own creates a cultural and social *reflexivity*, making each cultural choice a relative one. No cultural path is natural or self-evident any longer. Being traditional is today a conscious cultural choice among – and often against – other possibilities that have acquired local presence and salience through media. As such, globalization is as much a psychological phenomenon as it is an economic or political reality. Not least because of the flow of media images, texts and sounds from all corners of the world, globalization entails both an increased awareness of other cultures often in competition with one's local culture and a much more immediate experience of the world as a whole.

Because media facilitate social communication and interaction, the structure and control of media systems are important factors for the distribution of power in society. Due to deregulation policies during the last decades, communication media have become increasingly disembedded from national political and cultural institutions and have become independent institutions governed by their own "media logic". The increased significance of transnational and regional media conglomerates and the emergence of a truly global media like the Internet facilitate a redistribution of power in politics, culture and commerce, and favor certain actors and social logics (not least the law of the market) at the expense of others. The structure and control of media systems imply both new patterns of inclusion/exclusion, and new dependencies. Thus, globalization of the media infrastructure entails a redistribution of social power that can both enable and weaken communication and interaction among social actors.

This book is concerned with the role of news media in an increasingly globalized society. Because of the strong interdependence between news and political institutions, a recurrent theme in all of the articles is the impact of globalization on the role of news for the viability of public debate, information supply and the exercise of democracy. The book tries to unravel how news as an institution and a genre is both affected by globalization and itself an agent of globalization. It examines, although not in the above-mentioned schematic order, how news media – both as information channels, as messengers of a world outside, and as providers of a social infrastructure – contribute to a disembedding of politically relevant information and discourse from extant social institutions, but also how such information and discourses become reembedded in new – globalized – social structures.

The articles are organized around four themes: 1. Globalization and the role of news media; 2. New media, global news, and democracy; 3. Regionalization and domestication of global news, and 4. War news in global media. The two articles in the first theme provide an overview of the relationship between the concept of globalization and key issues in media studies. *Stig Hjarvard* discusses the different ways in which the concept of a global public sphere has been used in recent media studies and suggests – as an alternative – that the concept of deterritorialization may be useful for the reinterpretation of a globalized public sphere as a process rather than a single entity. A global public sphere should not be conceptualized as a larger, extended version of the national public sphere. Instead, it must be understood as a process through which public communication becomes restructured and disembedded from national political and cultural institutions. He then provides an overview of recent changes in the international news business in order to discuss how these changes in media structures influence this restructuration of public space. *Daniel Biltereyst* takes as his point of departure the paradox that the immense increase in capacity to produce and distribute news around the globe seems to coincide with a general decline in audiences' interest in and actual consumption of foreign news. Through a careful examination of existing analyses of foreign news audiences, he discusses the role of citizenship in relation to foreign news and suggests a need for a more multifaceted approach to the concept of citizenship. Globalization as well as recent changes in the overall "news ecology" imply a new notion of citizenship and, on the basis of this, he puts forward a new framework for both quantitative and qualitative audience research

The second theme about new media, global news, and democracy opens with *Ingrid Volkmer's* discussion of the significance of new media for international communication theory. The challenge for communication theory today, she argues, is to understand the extension of the public sphere into the global arena, an enlargement that has created a substantial new extra-societal sphere. Taking the program CNN World Report as an early example and the Internet as a current example, she demonstrates how this new sphere of mediation is not a homogenous one, but involves different types of communication environments. *Chris A. Paterson's* article is focused on the industrial and economic aspects of news on the Internet. In particular he examines how the major news agencies are now rapidly moving into cyberspace and have consolidated themselves as major wholesale news providers on the Internet. The big agencies like Reuters and Associated Press have not only continued their dominant role as news providers for the Internet services of newspapers and broadcasters, but are also major news contributors to non-journalistic media like Internet gateways, portals, malls etc. The actual patterns of supply and demand of news on the Internet, he concludes, do not confirm the widespread assumption that the Internet is more, diverse, pluralistic, or original in terms of news content.

Klaus Bruhn Jensen's theoretical contribution takes Michael Schudson's recent article "Why Conversation is Not the Soul of Democracy" as point of departure. Adopting Schudson's critique of "the romance of conversation", he submits a reinterpretation of the impact of the virtuality of new media on democratic communication. Communication in new media is often performed through artificial or constructed roles and contexts (like in Internet games and chat rooms), but instead of considering this a loss or a source of alienation compared to direct face-to-face interaction, it may instead be understood as a civilizing potential that makes the virtual aspect of all communication, face-to-face as well as medi-ated, apparent. Thus, virtuality may be interpreted as a further step in the devel-opment of modernity, allowing us to see that not only is conversation *not* the soul of democracy, but democracy is a modern and secular enterprise and con-sequently has no soul.

The third theme on regionalization and domestication of global news begins with two articles on the production of foreign news. *Hans-Henrik Holm's* study of the effect of globalization on the selection of news is based on the premise that it is necessary to distinguish between various levels of impact. Through participant observation of the actual choice of foreign news at five newspapers, two tv stations and one radio station in Denmark, he concludes that globalization has had a profound impact on the media structure and media policy and, albeit to a lesser extent, also provoked changes in the internal editorial structure of news production. For instance, foreign news is no longer as isolated and independent a news desk as it used to be, but is gradually merging with other areas of reporting like economy and culture. So far, however, little impact is discernable at the level of usage of journalistic news criteria.

Tore Slaatta's study of Norwegian correspondents on the Brussels beat is concerned with the influence of transnational political structures on national reporting on EU politics. The study covers a period after the referendum in Norway, which left the country outside the EU. However, the EEA Agreement (European Economic Area) was an important framework for transnational politics between Norway, EFTA and the EU, and consequently, there was a continuing need for news coverage and media debate on Norwegian relations to the EU. Because of Norway's non-membership, the sources at the Brussels beat treated Norwegian reporters as outsiders, and access to and the information flow from politicians and bureaucrats were considerably reduced.

The parallel process of regionalization and domestication is the topic of *Norbert Wildermuth's* article about the profound changes in tv news and current affairs programming in India. During the 1990s India has experienced an explosion in both supply and consumption of satellite television, and the Murdoch controlled Star TV platform has been one of the major challengers of the former state monopoly broadcaster Doordarshan. News and current affairs on Star TV have been very successful in addressing the upper middle classes in the urban areas by combining professional standards of a western (BBC) model with extensive coverage of Indian affairs by journalists who had already acquired a reputation and trustworthiness during the period of state broadcasting hegemony.

The relationship between the pan-regional and the national level is also the topic of *Claes de Vreese's* cross-national study of tv coverage of the introduction of the Euro currency. The theoretical perspective is based on framing theory, and he begins the article with an overview of previous studies of frames in news. The empirical study compares the framing of the introduction of the Euro in Britain, Denmark and the Netherlands in January 1999. The study confirms that certain news frames seem to be generic to political and economic reporting across countries. At a general level, a similar frame, "the economic consequences" frame, was used in the reporting on the Euro in all three countries, but the application of this frame showed clear differences between countries and reflected an effort to domesticate a European issue.

The fourth and final theme on war news in global media is concerned with the news agenda and ideological framing of the Gulf War and the Kosovo War considered in light of the intricate relationships between military censorship and propaganda, media organizations, and national politics. *Stig A. Nohrstedt and Rune Ottosen* report on a major comparative study of news coverage of the Gulf War in four different media in five countries: Finland, Germany, Norway, Sweden and the US. In general, the US dominance in the military alliance was mirrored in the media coverage, since media reporting on the Gulf War was largely a question of conveying information about US policy to a global audience. The US global leadership was, however, not interpreted identically across nations but became domesticated through the narrative strategies of national newsrooms. One important explanatory factor for differences in news reporting was the historical ties between the homeland and the US as regards foreign or defense policies. Finally they compare the Gulf War media experience with the 1999 war in Kosovo. *Daya Kishan Thussu* focuses on the ability of a major Western news provider, the CNN, to set the media agenda for coverage of NATO's war in Kosovo. Based on an in-depth study of CNN's current affairs program's ("Insight") focus on NATO (from April 1999), whose 50 years anniversary and first out-of-area warfare coincided, he argues that CNN framed NATO's warfare as a humanitarian intervention and did not give adequate attention to the crucial and problematic issue of NATO's new role in a post-communist order. Because CNN also influenced other media's reporting on the war, the coverage tended to follow the news agenda set by NATO and downplayed other views.

The articles in this book were first presented at the seminar "News in a Global Culture" in December 1999 in Skodsborg, organized by the research program "Global Media Cultures" and financed by the Danish Research Council for the Humanities. This book owes a great deal to the friendly, and yet critical, spirit of the seminar. Finally, I would like to thank my colleagues Karsten Fledelius and Klaus Bruhn Jensen for valuable comments on chapter eleven and one, respectively. I would also like to acknowledge the readiness of Ulla Carlsson from Nordicom to support this publication, and last but not least thanks to Karen Williams for proofreading several of the manuscripts.

November 2000

Stig Hjarvard

References

Bauman, Zygmunt (1998) *Globalization. The Human Consequences*. Cambridge: Polity Press.

EBU (1991) *Actors or Spectators? The Media Look Back on Their Role in the Gulf War*. Geneva: EBU.

Giddens, Anthony (1999) *Runaway World. How Globalisation Is Reshaping Our World*. London: Profile Books.

Habermas, Jürgen (1996) *Between Facts and Norms*. Cambridge: Polity Press. (The quoted part of the text is originally from 1990.)

Held, David (1995) *Democracy and the Global Order. From the Modern State to Cosmopolitan Governance*. Cambridge: Polity Press.

Held, David; McGrew, Anthony; Goldblatt, David & Perraton, Jonathan (1999) *Global Transformations. Politics, Economics and Culture*. Cambridge: Polity Press.

Tomlinson, John (1999) *Globalization and Culture*. Cambridge: Polity Press.

Globalization and the Role of News Media

News Media and the Globalization of the Public Sphere

The aim of this article is to provide a critical discussion of the concept of a global public sphere and the ways in which this concept has been used in recent media studies. It puts forward the argument, that a global public sphere should not be conceptualized as a larger, extended version of the national public sphere as has often been the case. Instead, it is suggested that the concept of deterritorialization may be used for reinterpreting a globalized public sphere as a process rather than a single entity. The globalization of the public sphere must be understood as a process through which public communication becomes restructured and partly disembedded from national political and cultural institutions. In order to discuss how changes in media systems influence a restructuration of public space, recent changes in the international news industry are examined. Changes in the news media environment create a series of tensions in the public sphere, because they induce both fragmentation and interconnectedness.

Icons of Globalization

In both scholarly work and public debate on globalization, the influence of media and particularly electronic media on social change is considered to be of prime importance. In sociological and cultural analyses of globalization (e.g., Giddens, 1999; Tomlinson, 1999), media such as satellite television, the Internet, computers, mobile phones etc. are often thought to be among the primary forces behind current restructurations of social and cultural geography. Electronic media facilitate an increased interconnectedness across vast distances and a temporal flexibility in social interaction. Furthermore, a handful of media enterprises and media moguls such as Time-Warner-AOL, Disney, Rupert Murdoch, and Bill Gates have become icons of globalization. These media companies and actors both have ambitions of global market domination and serve as the messengers of a new global era. Particularly the transnational news services with a global or

17

regional reach, such as CNN, BBC World, Euronews, Sky News, and Star News, have come to be regarded as the town criers of the global village. Their continuous, on-line, and live distribution of news to all corners of the world has become emblematic of a world in which place and time mean less and less.

Parallel to the emergence of this globalized media environment, a gradual change in the social geography of public and political communication has taken place. The national embeddedness of the public sphere and public opinion no longer goes unquestioned. Increasingly, the formation of public opinion also takes place across national boundaries. The "opinion of the international community" no longer refers unambiguously to the opinions of assemblies of state leaders or the cosmopolitan elite, but increasingly to a less tangible, phantomlike, and much more volatile phenomenon emerging from extensive media coverage of world events. At least on certain special occasions, a transnational, if not global public sphere has emerged as a forum for political discussion and opinion formation. A series of international events during the last decade bear witness to the transnationalization of the public sphere and public opinion formation: Shell's plan to dump the Brent Spar oil platform in the North Sea, French nuclear testing in the Pacific Ocean, the suppression of student demonstrations in China, UN conferences on the environment, women, social development etc., the death of Lady Diana, Jörg Haider's Freedom Party's participation in Austria's government etc., etc.

During events like these, a series of interactions in different countries are activated and connected to each other partly as a result of intense media coverage. Actions by governments, corporate business interests, NGOs, and the civil society in general (demonstrations, appeals, strikes etc.) feed into a transnational public sphere and incite reactions and discursive responses in different regions and countries. The aggregation of public opinion during this process takes place both nationally and transnationally, and the media representation of this transnational public opinion acquires its own momentum. Although political leaders are still most sensitive to public opinion articulated within their own national boundaries, they cannot afford to ignore the public opinion articulated through the global media. This transnational public opinion represents a political force in its own right, and it has the ability to influence national opinions and, thus, to change the national political basis of power.

Under special circumstances, the power of such globalized public opinion poses a severe problem for even the mightiest nations, because public opinion demands political action that either contradicts national policies or outstrips the diplomatic, economic or military power of the nations involved. The intensive coverage by CNN and other global news media of the student demonstrations in China in 1989 created an urgent call for action by the international community, but the reality was that the major powers' political will and ability to act were quite limited. As a senior official from the US State Department said in reaction to the intensive media coverage of the Chinese authorities' violent suppression of protesters in Tiananmen Square: "It demanded a solution we couldn't provide. We were powerless to make it stop"[1]. In some cases, the rise of an internationally mediated public opinion does make a difference, even in terms of subsequent political action. The killing of Brazilian street children became an international media story, and this had a profound impact on national politics in Brazil (Serra, 2000).

It is important to stress, however, that although transnational public opinion can be very forceful during events with intensive media coverage, it is most often the case that political, economic or military decisions and actions concerning transnational or global matters take place without intense public attention. The routine, day-to-day decisions and actions related to international politics may often receive news coverage, but rarely do they induce a transnational dialogue involving people other than cosmopolitan elites such as diplomats, government officials, NGO experts, transnational business executives and information officers etc. On most occasions, a broader public debate about international issues rarely extends beyond this political elite, and if it does, it is confined to the framework of the national public sphere.

Although news media increasingly transcend national borders, this does not in itself create a public sphere at a transnational or global level. In fact, it can be argued that the development of the public sphere has increasingly become out of sync with the globalization of economy, governance, and culture. As regards industrial production and financial transactions, the world is becoming more and more interconnected and interdependent, and the flows of cultural products and symbols across borders have intensified. Similarly, political governance increasingly transcends the nation-state, as in the case of the EU. This does not imply, however, that the nation-state is necessarily losing power, but rather that it is acquiring a new role as the mediator of political governance between local, national and supranational levels. The globalization of economy, governance, and culture has not been accompanied by a similar globalization of the public sphere. Opinion formation is still very much tied to the level of national political institutions.

As a starting point, the following paradox can be observed regarding the relationship between the development of the news media and the public sphere: Due to the growth in transnational and global news media, public opinion formation occasionally transcends national borders and acquires a political momentum of its own at a global level. However, compared to the globalization of politics, economy and culture, the public sphere and the formation of public opinion are still very much tied to a national level and oriented toward national political institutions. This seemingly contradictory development has provided support for very different interpretations of current media changes. The idea that the rise of global media has instituted a global public sphere has both been proclaimed and denounced by media scholars, and both sides have actually been able to provide some empirical support for their interpretations. However, the apparent inextricability of these opposing viewpoints may – at least to some extent – be due to a lack of theoretical consideration of how current transformations in the social geography of media may be conceptualized.

A Global Public Sphere?

In an overview of current globalization theories, Held et al. (1999) distinguish between the hyperglobalizers, on the one hand, and the sceptics, on the other, and this rough categorization can also be applied to the different interpretations of public sphere globalization and of the media's role in this process.

The *hyperglobalizers* state that a global public sphere has already emerged, and subsequently that the national public sphere has either disappeared or that its borders have become permeable or fuzzy, open to influences from both local and global media. This argument is clearly supported by the marketing activities of the global media conglomerates themselves and frequently given anecdotal support by statements from American presidents. Consider the words of George Bush, "I learn more from the CNN than I do from the CIA," and Jimmy Carter, "CNN has done more to close gaps of misunderstanding between the world's people than any enterprise in recent memory"[2]. But certain academic studies of the CNN phenomenon also tend to take this position. In particular, CNN programs like "World Report" – with its mix of contributions from broadcasters all over the world – have been taken as evidence of the emergence of a truly global media system (Flourney, 1992; Flourney & Stewart, 1997).

The hyperglobalization position has also been put forward from a more theoretically reflected position. Thus, Volkmer (1999) interprets current developments not only as a geographical expansion of the public sphere, but also in terms of a changing relationship between the public, the media and the state:

 It can be argued that because of global communication, the public and its opinion is no longer a substantial element of the political system of a society but has turned into a more or less autonomous global public sphere which can only be considered not as a space between the 'public' and the state but between the state and an extra-societal, global community. (Volkmer, 1999: 119).

According to Volkmer (1999), the public sphere no longer fulfills the function as a forum for representation of publicity between the public (the political citizens) and the political power (the state). Instead, the new global public sphere is to be understood as an imaginary space made possible by global communication media, and the public produced by this space no longer has "recourse to rational opinions, to reasoning and discursive agreement" (Volkmer, 1999: 123). Because the public sphere loses its deliberative function, Volkmer suggests that the concept of a "global public sphere" be replaced by the concept of "global mediation". Through this global and mediated publicity, the social and cultural values of society become externalized; they do not arise from inside the national community as a basis for or a result of deliberation, but are increasingly delivered from the outside through global media.

Among the globalization *sceptics*, it is possible to discern two different lines of criticism. First, a critique of media globalization based on the political economy tradition (e.g., Schiller, 1993; Sparks, 1998), and second, a critique based on cultural and institutional analyses of current transnationalization processes in

Stig Hjarvard

Europe (e.g., Collins, 1994, 1996 & 1998; Schlesinger, 1993 & 1999). Both lines of criticism have as a mutual starting point a fundamental reservation about the actual global impact of so-called global media. According to their views, most transnational media have only a regional reach and even within their primary region, they do not have universal penetration. Global media like CNN and BBC World may technically have a near global reach, but the actual audience figures tell quite a different story. Compared to the consumption of nationally based media, that of CNN and BBC World is very limited. In most countries, these channels are only used as a supplement to the national news media diet, and usage is generally restricted to the well-educated social strata and the political and business elite. During major world events, these channels may enjoy a rapid rise in viewing figures, but this is only short-lived. As audience studies have shown, CNN – even during the Gulf War, its biggest television success – was not able to keep high audience figures for more than a very limited period (Gutstadt, 1993). Thus, according to this line of criticism, the very label "global media" and its regional counterparts such as "European media" are in fact misleading. Audiences do not attend to the same global media at the same time, and consequently the media do not give rise to the formation of a global or European public sphere.

Criticism in the political economy tradition, however, holds that global media conglomerates do play an increasingly important role in that they actually dominate media industries all over the world. Transnational and particularly American media industries dominate the worldwide production and distribution of motion pictures, video, computer games, news channels, newspapers, magazines etc. The impetus for this development is primarily commercial and industrial, and the result is an increased commodification of both culture and public, political communication. As Schiller (1993) argues:

> I do not believe that globalization of the media industries sector has resulted in the formation of an international civil society as such. Rather, this process has resulted in an international order organized by transnational economic interests that are largely unaccountable to the nation-states in which they operate. (Schiller, 1993: 47).

Seen from the point of view of political economy, the globalization of media industries is of no benefit to civil society or to public deliberation in a public sphere. On the contrary, it represents the empowerment of large commercial interests at the expense of civil society and democracy. Citizens' ability to influence— media public debate and opinion formation diminishes when large media industries are no longer accountable to national political regulation. The political economy tradition holds that globalization is taking place, but it is typically not thought of as a new phenomenon. Rather it is understood as a new stage in a well-known process characteristic of capitalist society: imperialism. Globalization does not entail an opening of public space, on the contrary, it is all about privatization:

> If we need to abandon the term "global public sphere" as manifestly inadequate to designate what we have been analyzing, then a better one is needed.

The one that fits the evidence best is "imperialist, private sphere". If this is unfashionable, so be it. At least it is accurate. (Sparks, 1998: 122)

The criticism emerging from studies of cultural and political aspects of transnational media in Europe tends to stress the conservative nature of local and national culture and political institutions. The attempts to build a European public through European media (e.g., the satellite tv-channel Euronews or the newspaper The European) have either completely failed or only survived as special interest media for a business or political elite. The attempts by the EU to support the creation of such Pan-European media have rested on the untenable political idea that a political community can be built upon a common European culture. As Collins (1996) argues, there is really no evidence that such a common European culture exists or provides a common ground for identification. On the contrary, Europe exhibits a wide and diverse pattern of languages, cultures, political practices etc. Even patterns of media usage in European countries are so divergent that Pan-European media have difficulties surviving. European cooperation may certainly be both desirable and necessary, but a common culture will not play a significant role as a basis for such cooperation. On the contrary, both language and culture are factors working against Europeanization and toward greater localization. A public political agenda of European issues may gradually develop, but this will not result from the formation of a European political public sphere. This agenda will, according to Schlesinger (1999: 21), be domesticated through national and local media: "In reality, any common European public agenda is likely, in the process of media reception, to be diversely "domesticated" within each distinctive national or language context". The process of domestication of foreign news is further enhanced at the level of audience reception. Empirical research demonstrates, for instance, that audiences' interpretation of foreign news is influenced by how they view the position of their own nation in the world (Jensen, 1998).

Both of these skeptical positions question the rise of a global public sphere on the grounds of empirical evidence: the audience for global or regional media is too small and too unevenly distributed among social groups to constitute a public sphere that can in any way be compared to the national public sphere. However, they emphasize different reasons for this phenomenon. The political economy position considers the commodification of public communication by global media companies to be the key factor explaining why a public sphere has not benefited from the rise of global media and has not extended itself into the global realm. According to the other position, this lack of success is due to the continuous strength of national and local political institutions, media, and culture. As such, the two positions entail quite different political perspectives. From the political economy perspective, the possibility of global public communication in the public interest is being eclipsed by global capitalism, and as such a global public sphere is being crushed at birth. The other position holds that the reason for this lack of success is the strength of national politics and culture. From this perspective, the limited extension of the public sphere beyond and above national borders is really nothing to worry about. It rather testifies to the needlessness of a global public sphere and to the viability and necessity of national and local politics and culture.

The Global: Entity or Process?

The argument put forward in this article tries to bridge the gap between some of these opposing viewpoints, while also criticizing the underlying notion of a global public sphere – a notion shared by these viewpoints in spite of their obvious differences. Both hyperglobalizers and sceptics tend to simplify the argument to a choice between a fundamentally new global situation, on the one hand, and a "nothing new under the sun" position, on the other. Instead, it seems reasonable to argue that the advent of global media – particularly news media – has actually brought about some changes in, e.g., the structure of public communication, the formation of public opinion etc. Recognizing this, however, does not necessarily entail a view that the national public sphere is disappearing, nor does it mean that we should ignore the power and influence transnational commercial interests have over how public communication is structured.

The formation of public communicative spaces at a transnational level does not necessarily pose a threat to national public spheres; instead their very precondition might be the existence of national public spheres. In fact, it can be argued that the nation-state itself encourages the development of transnational public fora. As Köhler (1998) suggests, "it is the state itself which, as a result of the need to adapt to processes of globalization and by the increasing involvement in intergovernmental cooperation, provides the impetus for the cosmopolitan enlargement of its own public sphere" (Köhler, 1998: 233-34). The national public sphere may potentially benefit from the growth of public communication across national borders, while it may also be gradually subjected to change itself due to this transnationalization. Thus, if we are to understand current developments, it seems unproductive to address them in an "either-or" manner. The complex of ongoing transformations would better conceptualized as a "both-and" development. A transnational public communicative space may be a sort of supplement or addition to a national public sphere that eventually – during a long evolutionary process – becomes transformed itself.

The most important theoretical problem in current discussions of the public sphere in relation to globalization arises from the fact that the public sphere has been conceptually and historically linked to the nation-state. Thus, the national framework – particularly the national entity – completely informs our perceptions of what a public sphere is – and should be – even when it transcends the national borders. Thus, most discussions of a global public sphere depict it as an extended, geographically expanded version of the national model. It is not different, simply bigger. Thus, a global public sphere is also portrayed as confined to a well-defined geographical territory and located at a specific institutional level. Typically, it is considered as a public forum for deliberation located somewhere between global or regional political institutions like the UN, EU etc., on the one hand, and the global civil society, on the other. Furthermore, it is thought to display the same characteristics as the national public sphere. It is considered to be universal, both in the sense that access to the public sphere is evenly distributed among all citizens, and in the sense that it is open for debate on all matters of public interest; as such it is conceived as a non-specialized and non-professionalized forum for public debate.

Considering the national embeddedness of the social and political sciences in general, this tendency to take the nation as the natural unit of analysis and project the national model of the public sphere to a global level is not at all surprising. Nevertheless, this theoretical heritage poses severe problems for identifying new spaces of publicity and for a discussion of the ways in which these new spaces actually connect to existing national public spheres and how they expand, limit or transform chances for public deliberation. In particular, the limitation lies in the idea that globalization means the creation of a new global *entity* with the same structural features as its national counterpart. Instead of considering the global as a new geographical unit or container of publicity, power and institutions, it may be better to think of it as a *process*: Globalization induces changes in the structure of the public sphere, but it does not necessarily create a new and larger public sphere entity.

An important aspect of this globalization process is an increased *connectedness* across distance. Thus, globalization may not result in an expansion of the public sphere from a national to a global level, but rather in an increased openness and dependency between different national public spheres and between the general public sphere of any national society and different specialized and professionalized public fora that have transnational connections. The boundaries between different public fora become permeable and each forum becomes increasingly influenced by and dependent upon the activities in other fora. As such, the process could be described as a gradual *deterritorialization* (Tomlinson, 1999) of the public sphere: The flow of information, the representation of interests, and the deliberation on arguments may still be primarily concerned with and addressed to a national community and its political institutions, but due to the public sphere's increased openness and connectedness to a world beyond national borders, including other public spheres, a *global reflexivity* gradually gains foothold. Fewer and fewer political topics can be dealt with in the absence of influential information and arguments originating from outside the national realm. Even the most urgent calls for strictly local or national political solutions can be thought of as a reaction to the increased presence of global problems inside the national public sphere. As such, the globalization of the public sphere can be reconceptualized: It should not be understood as the expansion of the national public sphere model to a global level, but as *the process through which the national public sphere gradually becomes deterritorialized*. Through this process it becomes open to and dependent upon other public fora at various geographical and institutional levels and with different degrees of universality and specialization. Thus, globalization of the public sphere is not about the creation of *the* global public sphere, but rather about the increased presence of global connections within the national framework.

This introduces a global reflexivity in the public sphere that, in the long run, will influence and alter the structure of the national public sphere and its relation to both political institutions and civil society.

It is important to avoid a media-centric interpretation of current developments. The globalization of the public sphere is not only a product of increased media flows across borders. The presence and impact of global or regional problems within national political spheres may not even primarily be a media-driven process. In the case of Europe, the development of European political institutions and adjacent bureaucratic machinery and, subsequently, the creation of a general publicity around EU issues in member countries – as well as the rise of specialized and professionalized fora for more or less public debate about EU – have largely been driven by political and economic forces. The EU has tried to use media to foster the Europeanization of the public sphere. The reverse has not been the case: The EU has not been called for by a mediated transnational publicity.

In order to evaluate the influence of media upon the globalization of the public sphere, we must consider that current media developments take place more or less autonomously from the development of political institutions. This is very different from the history of the rise of the national public sphere. Here, the formation of the press, radio and later television was intertwined with the development of political parties, national cultural policies etc. The press, radio and television began as political or cultural institutions within the nation-state, whereas global media such as satellite television or the Internet are not political or cultural institutions in the same sense. Commercial media should rather be considered as media institutions, i.e., their activities are governed qua their status as commercial media enterprises and not by national political or cultural obligations. Global media may certainly influence national public spheres, but they are not from the outset part of political institutions. They may, through their function as mediators of publicity, become political institutions in their own right (Cook, 1998), but the activity and geographical expansion of global media firms are not closely connected to or determined by other political institutions. Thus, in order to understand the impact of news media on globalization of the public sphere, it is particularly important to consider the news media from the perspective of *news as an international industry and business*. The globalizing impact of news media stems from the transformations that are taking place within the international news industry.

Changes in the International News Industry

For most of the 19th and 20th centuries, news media were confined to the nation-state. Newspapers, radio and television addressed a national audience, and only during wars and the Cold War were special news services originating in one country specifically aimed at other countries and regions. Propaganda channels like Radio Free Europe, Radio Liberty etc. were exceptions to the general rule of news media as a national service. News items about international and foreign

affairs were either provided by national media correspondents or by international news agencies. The major news agencies such as Reuters, Associated Press, UPI, AFP and Tass acted on a global scale, but they were not global media in the same sense as some of the big media enterprises are today. They were *international* agencies, each originating in a specific country (The major powers Britain, USA, France, and Soviet Union), and their sole task was to provide news to be disseminated through national news media. Thus, the international agencies were attuned to the needs of national media. They were not news media with an audience of their own.

News media were embedded in a rather stable and simple two-level social geography: wholesale news agencies at an international level and news media at a national level. Due to the deregulation of media industries and the proliferation of new media distribution technologies such as satellite television and the Internet during the 1980s and 1990s, this stable structure gradually altered. Both wholesale news providers and national media began to cross the national borders in new ways, and news services operating at another geographical level began to emerge. Not only did the geographical levels begin to shift, but the types of services and customers also began to diversify and alter through this process. These developments reflected changes in the structure of the international news industry that can be summarized under the headings: The rise of transnational actors, vertical and horizontal integration, commercialization, diversification of output, regionalization, and abundance of supply.

The rise of transnational actors. News media have always operated across national borders in order to distribute news about the world. However, what is new about current developments is the spread of actors that do not operate on the basis of the national unit, but address a region (e.g., Euronews), a language community across several countries (German, Spanish etc.), a religious, ethnic or national community dispersed over a wide territory (e.g., Turks in Europe), or – potentially – the entire globe (BBC World, CNN International etc.).

Vertical integration. The boundaries between the wholesale news providers, the news agencies, the retail level, and the news services have become fuzzy. International news services like CNN and BBC World are aimed at a general audience, but some broadcasters also use them as news agencies. Wholesale news agencies like Reuters can similarly be reached directly by the general audience through the Internet, and some Internet portals use agencies as news services for a general audience almost without any re-editing (Paterson, 2001). Some wholesale news providers also offer complete packages with special news and current affairs that can be used directly by newspapers and broadcasters. Such prepackaged material is frequently used by commercial broadcasters with little money – or few ambitions – to spend on journalism.

Horizontal integration. Transnational media firms merge or develop strategic financial, technical and editorial cooperation with other media firms in order to provide a diverse media platform for whole regions. News and current affairs are important components in a varied media platform; without them a regional media package would appear incomplete. Thus, the broadcast news component

26

CNN is to the Time-Warner-AOL conglomerate, as Sky News is to the Murdoch empire.

Commercialization. In the past, international news services were (apart from the wholesale news agencies) almost entirely an activity of public or government agencies. They served a nation's geopolitical strategies (e.g., keeping the British Empire together, US propaganda against Soviet Union etc.) and were not supposed to be financially viable. The transnational news services of today are predominantly commercial in nature. Some may have public service obligations or serve similar public "duties", but increasingly they must be able to produce a profit in the market place. The same process is taking place at a national level, due to deregulation of national media industries. News is generally being subject to a process of commodification, in which the linkage between news and journalism, on the one hand, and political institutions, on the other, is being weakened.

Diversification of output. In the past, both wholesale news agencies and news services produced and distributed general news for a general audience. There were different journalistic formats such as short news and background stories, and other journalistic genres such as current affairs programs. But across these formats, the journalistic ambition was to present information of general interest to the general public. Today's transnational news services have diversified the output, providing special news themes for special audiences: sports news, entertainment news, business news, crime news, medical/health news, technology news, youth news etc. The wholesale news agencies have adjusted their services accordingly, providing a wide variety of news packages and feeds that make such diversification possible for even small broadcasters. General news is still important, but it has become one news genre among many others.

Regionalization. In the first years of satellite television, many channels tried to reach as broad an audience as possible. CNN tried to be as global as possible, several channels in Europe tried to reach the whole of Europe etc. This globalizing strategy – offering the same menu to more and more people – soon turned out to be a failure. The strategy for the last decade has been to regionalize programming, i.e., adjust it to "local" interests and needs. Often – not least due to financial limitations – what really takes place is a kind of quasi-regionalization, in which some of the content is produced specifically for the region and some of it is recycled from the mother-company's global services. Because of this regionalization of news services, a common outlook and perspective for the region is generated. For instance, the Euronews channel not only distributes news about the different European countries, but a regional – European – perspective is also actively pursued by the editors (Meinhof & Richardson, 1999). Moreover, regionalization is a way to overcome the language problems of global programming; thus, transnational news services try to address specific language communities across borders. Another way to regionalize the news service is to make alliances with local actors; an example is the cooperation between a global actor like CNN and the Danish newspaper Berlingske Tidende. Together they run an on-line news service (CNN.dk/Berlingske Online) that contributes to a

27

change in the social geography of both: CNN becomes domesticated and Berlingske Tidende gets a more global image.

Abundance of supply. During the last two decades, the availability of news about events in the world has increased considerably. Not least the global distribution of pictures and video has grown enormously. Prior to this, foreign news, and particularly foreign news footage, was a scarce resource. Thus, editorial choices were limited to a much narrower scope than today. The Eurovision News Exchange, which has supplied the public service broadcasters in Europe with raw video footage since the late 1950's, only distributed 3-4 news items a day in the first half of the 1960s. Today, there is an almost continuous feed of news video 24 hours a day from both Eurovision and private agencies into the newsrooms of European broadcasters (Hjarvard, 1995). Previously, the editorial problem was to obtain foreign video news. Today, the problem is to choose among thousands of possible stories. Today there is at least the potential for much more diverse, individualized, and extended coverage of foreign news.

The Internet Challenge

Most of the above-mentioned changes in the news industry may be considered as responses to the overall deregulation of media markets during the 1980s and 1990s. However, current changes in the news industry are also spurred by the rise of a new media platform: the Internet. During its short existence the Internet has already had an enormous impact - until now perhaps more on the news industry itself than on the actual consumption of news. The Internet incites a globalization of both news media and public spaces.

Almost all actors in the news industry have developed Internet services. They began by putting more or less the same content on the net as was distributed through their traditional services (press or broadcasting). However, Internet news services have already bypassed this initial stage of development, and Internet news sites are no longer simple reproductions of the newspaper or the television newscast. Increasingly, news sites make use of properties of the Internet and integrate text, audio, and video by combining mass communication (one way distribution from one to many) with interactive, individualized communication (two way distribution: chat, e-mail responses, opinions polls among readers etc.) The Internet medium challenges the traditional news services in many ways, one of which concerns the distinction between geographical entities. The Internet will gradually make the boundaries between national, foreign, and international news media less clear and obvious.

With the advent of the Internet, the problem of global reach is no longer a technical one as seen from the point of view of the news service providers. For television and radio stations, access to satellite distribution platforms has been – and still is – a crucial problem, and in order to have a global reach, tv and radio stations must purchase access to a series of satellites platforms around the world. In case of the Internet, global reach is instantaneous once you have published your news on the net. Global reach is, of course, hampered by uneven (social and geographical) distribution of access to the Internet. From the point of view of the receiver, Internet news media may be inaccessible (due to economic, legal or other restrictions) or only accessible at certain places (work, school etc.). However, once the consumer has access to the Internet as such, *all* news services in the world are potentially available. This is very different from the printed press and broadcasting; they are only available individually or in packages, typically on a subscription basis. The abundance of available material on the Internet makes the question of consumer choice less a matter of technical limitations or distribution costs and more a matter of consumer knowledge about available services. Thus, branding of news and media services has acquired new importance, and we are currently witnessing a veritable "battle of brands" on the Internet, in which transnational media firms try to consolidate themselves as "the places" – places the consumer knows and regularly visits in the new media landscape (Hjarvard, 2000b).

With the Internet, the problem of global reach becomes a question of *language and content.* News broadcasters have had to expand their distribution network in order to technically reach a bigger audience, whereas Internet news providers can enlarge their audience through a differentiation of language (multi-language editions) and content (special editions for different segments of the audience). Differentiation through language has also been a possibility for international news broadcasters, but in practice it has been impeded by practical and financial problems. In Internet news, you can translate text and edit video segments with voice-over in another language, but the television news format is so dominated by the "talking heads" of anchors and journalists that it is difficult to make multi-language editions without considerable extra expenses. Euronews is one of the few examples of such an attempt to produce multi-language broadcast news, but not necessarily a successful one.

The experience of global Internet news services like BBC On-line has been that the audience wants to engage directly with the publisher, i.e., the journalists and editors (Burden, 1999). Practice has already demonstrated that audiences actually respond (through e-mail, chat etc.) to the news. Furthermore, the audience wants their active responses to be taken seriously, responded to, and represented as a part of the news service. In many ways, these responses resemble letters to newspaper editors or phone-ins to radio programs. However, in the case of Internet news, the responses can arrive from any corner of the world. This is not just a hypothetical possibility. Experience from, for instance, the BBC On-line service demonstrates that audiences from many parts of the world respond and become represented on the net. This is in contrast to the older news media. Newspaper readers may write letters to their national newspapers, but extremely few would write letters to the editor of an international newspaper. Similarly, viewers and listeners may write or phone their national broadcaster, but very few would phone international broadcasters like CNN or Euronews. On the Internet – due to the medium's interactive and more spontaneous character – users have fewer reasons to hesitate sending an e-mail to an organization in another part of the world. Internet news services have actively tried to make use of this phenomenon and developed special web-pages with thematic discussions about certain news topics (e.g., BBC On-line's "Talking Point", CNN's "Chat"-section). The contributors to these discussions are not equally distributed throughout the world. On BBC's "Talking Point", a majority of contributors come from Great Britain, former British colonies and English speaking countries, which in part is a reflection of the "British bias" in the editorial selection of themes for discussion. However, contributors are not only from countries with Anglo-American connections, but from many other countries with a different cultural heritage and colonial background. The public discussions on the Internet news sites are, thus, not global in the sense that they encompass all parts of the world to the same extent, but they are globalized fora of discussion because the boundaries between nationalities have become less important for the conduct of political discussion.

The Internet allows for an integration of formerly distinct news media and journalistic genres. Within the same news service, you get both video and audio reports, written news and background stories, on-line discussion etc. Internet news can have both speed and breadth, and as such, it combines qualities of broadcasting and the press. The international news broadcasters have primarily earned their reputation on their speediness. They can provide a news update and overview at short notice to a global audience, but they are rarely of much use for those seeking background information or in-depth analysis. Internet news services have an advantage compared to the tv news broadcasters, because they also provide background, documentation and analysis accessible where and when the user needs it. The Internet stimulates a transnationalization of the newspaper in the same way as broadcast news has been transnationalized via satellite broadcasting. With the Internet, the journalistic content and formats of the newspaper can be transnationalized. The Internet provides an opportunity for newspapers to develop a transnational audience, but it also poses a threat to newspapers because other actors (from broadcasting, publishing industries etc.) may develop transnational news services that in the long run could limit the national newspaper audience. The multimedia character of the new media environment also stimulates a transnationalization of media industries. Increasingly, it becomes necessary for news media to have industrial capacity and expertice within several media. In order to develop diverse news services in television, radio, newspaper and the Internet – and with few possibilities to finance the new services on the Internet directly and fully through advertising or subscription – many media firms are forced to merge or cooperate with other media firms, often forming transnational and regional alliances.

Outward and Inward

Changes in the media sector influence the ways in which public spaces come to be organized and represented, and, subsequently, how social actors may interact with each other in these spaces. Globalization implies a deterritorialization of public spaces, but – as should be clear by now – this gradual de-linkage of social interaction from extant social spaces is not characterized by one singular logic and does not move the public sphere in any single direction. The different logics and directions as well as the tensions between them constitute the topic of the last part of this article.

New media technology has not only allowed transnational media firms to penetrate the national public sphere, but also made it possible for national media institutions to expand their presence on a worldwide scale. Emigrants have long been able to maintain some contact with their country of origin through the short-wave radio services of the national broadcaster or subscription to a newspaper in their mother tongue. With satellite radio and television as well as the Internet, this possibility has expanded both in volume and quality. Through satellite radio and television, they can receive a service that often addresses them as a majority and not as a special enclave living abroad, as has often been the case for short-wave radio. Furthermore, satellite television and Internet provide this long-distance contact with a more sensuous and interactive quality than that of short-wave radio and newspapers. It has become possible not only to hear and read, but also to see people, places, and current events and to some extent interact with them directly on an on-line basis.

The cultural repertoire has also been extended. Satellite television and Internet provide a mixture of music, drama, news, talk shows, information, current affairs etc., whereas the short-wave radio services typically provided a more narrow repertoire of (official) news, current affairs and high culture. It has become possible to maintain or revive a sense of belonging to a culture and society that in geographical terms is far away, but that due to electronic media has achieved a new presence and immediacy in everyday life. This belonging may not necessarily be related to the official national culture or society, but just as likely to a particular linguistic community or culture within a nation, which through transnational media connections is both invigorated and altered.

Current developments not only stimulate an outward distribution of national media, but also an inward orientation in the media content. This is at least the case for broadcasting, including broadcast news. The last decade has not only demonstrated an increase in transnational distribution of television programs but also a growth in nationally produced television programs. Thus, in many EC countries a domestication of prime time television is taking place (Moran, 1998). Due to increased competition and commercial pressures in television news, the proportion of news dealing with foreign or international events has tended to decline. In order to keep high ratings for the news, broadcasters often give priority to coverage of events that audiences can identify with. In story selection, *proximity* to the audience often becomes a more important criteria than societal importance (Hjarvard, 1999 and 2000a). As a result, foreign and international topics, and particularly stories dealing with complex international phenomena, receive less coverage than before. As competition and commercialization increase, this tendency becomes more profound. Thus, commercial broadcasters typically carry less (and shorter) news stories and current affairs programs about

31

international problems than do public service broadcasters (Hjarvard, 1999; Krüger, 1997; Stone, 2000).

Although there is an abundance of stories available about international issues through different transnational media, deregulation of broadcasting has in some areas increased the focus on domestic issues. In terms of news content, national broadcast news media often become more national and domestic than previously. This domestic orientation is, however, somewhat countered by another tendency that potentially alters the notion of "foreign news". Previously, foreign news denoted news about international politics and events in other nations. Today, many other news topics have acquired a foreign or international dimension (e.g., the environment, technology, fashion, culture), making the borders between foreign and domestic news less clear and obvious (Holm et al., 2000).

Adaptation and Synchronization

Due to developments in the international news industry, there is increased transparency and interconnectedness between various socio-geographical levels. Both newsrooms and audiences have access to news services at different levels (local, national, regional, global). For most of the 20th century, knowledge about and access to foreign and international news media were restricted to foreign correspondents and foreign news editors. Today, the same knowledge and access are – at least potentially – becoming available for almost everyone.

These developments have not, however, resulted in major changes in the audience's news media consumption patterns. Consumption of news is – for the majority of the population in most countries – still very much tied to local or national media. The transnational news media are predominantly used by specialized and professionalized fora and by people from the upper social strata. However, the availability of transnational news media may have other – and perhaps more important – consequences than those related to consumption patterns. Developments may influence editorial practices and decisions as well as the presentation formats and narrative techniques of the news. Because transnational news services are present in both newsrooms and living rooms, there is reason to expect that national and local news services will become more influenced by transnational news formats and standards. In an increasingly competitive media environment, the newsrooms will have to consider the alternatives that are available for the consumer, when making their general policies and editorial choices. Thus, one consequence of developments may be an incentive to *increase adaptation* of transnational formats to national contexts.

Adaptation of formats to other contexts is not a new phenomenon in the media or news industry. Thus, the international news agencies have often been considered as an important factor for the spread of Western news values (Boyd-Barrett, 1997; Boyd-Barrett & Rantanen, 1998). However, the increased transparency and interconnectedness mentioned above have both accelerated and geographically extended the process of adaptation, and the impact of adaptation is discernible at more specific levels. In the case of broadcast news, it is interesting to observe that a series of format changes in tv news, such as breakfast news, live-interviews, business news, competitive time-scheduling practices, newsroom set design etc., have spread very rapidly among national broadcasters both in Europe and on other continents. The deregulation of broadcasting and resultant competition can be seen as the main factor explaining why these changes have been adopted. However, the speed and uniformity with which these presentation techniques and narrative formats have spread in Europe and around the globe, may very well be a result of the increased presence of transnational news formats in the newsrooms of national broadcasters.

Similarly, the presence of transnational news services in national newsrooms may not generally influence the editorial choice in terms of concrete stories, but it may provide an inspiration for a gradual change in editorial policies. Local and national commercial broadcasters have very quickly learned to give editorial priority to crime news, health news, soft news etc., and to develop quasi-journalistic formats like "reality tv", "docu-soaps", crime magazines etc. This can arguably be explained by the fact that foreign models are readily available among broadcasters and audiences alike, thus providing both a source of inspiration and an international standard by which to measure one's own practice. In the case of Internet news, the cross-border proliferation of professional standards of both presentation and editorial choice seems to be even faster. In the case of broadcast news, it may still make some sense to talk about national editorial standards or styles of news presentation (e.g., Danish newscasts tend to be less formal or stilted than German newscasts), but in the case of Internet news services, it rarely makes sense to talk about national formats. Internet news services tend to develop on the basis of transnational standards from the outset, and there is one important reason for this: the global availability of all news services on the Internet.

Increased transparency also stimulates a *synchronization* of editorial decision-making between news services in different countries. This is primarily a phenomenon that can be observed during major international events and crises. Because of the availability of breaking news and live-coverage from transnational broadcasters and on-line news services on the Internet, the newsrooms in different countries are simultaneously able to follow how an important story breaks and subsequently develops. This increased knowledge of what other, transnational newsrooms are doing – and, thus, of what one's national competitors also know and presumably may act upon – is in itself an incentive to give editorial priority to the same story. The general audience is also able to receive the same information, making it even more difficult to refrain from covering a story that transnational media have already labeled as major. Because of limited resources, national and local newsrooms may have little time to develop an independent perspective on a story and, thus, they may more readily accept the initial discursive framing of an international event. Thus, synchronization may not only entail coverage of the same story, but also reproduction of a specific discursive pattern. Journalists and editors have always kept a watchful eye on their competitor's choice, but the interlocked nature and the speed of today's global communication system occasionally force actors to copy each other's decisions much more rapidly than before. Just such a synchronization of editorial decision-making across borders has stimulated the production of many of the recent decades' global media events.

Differentiation and Interconnections

In the beginning of this article, a paradox concerning globalization, media and the public sphere was observed: During major international events, the formation of public opinion occasionally expands to a global level, acquiring its own political momentum and influencing both governments and international organizations to act in specific ways. However, most questions concerning day-to-day international and foreign politics are primarily discussed at a national level, through the media and political institutions of the national public sphere. Special and professional public fora have developed at a transnational level, but not a general public sphere. As a result, public discussion in the media about international and foreign affairs is generally framed by national political interests. In this sense, political discussion in the public sphere is less globalized compared to transformations in industry, finance, governance, culture etc.

This apparently contradictory development may be reconsidered in light of the present interpretation of globalization of the public sphere. Globalization of media does not entail the creation of a singular global public sphere, but rather the development of a *multi-layered* structure of publicity, in which new transnational fora for public discussion and information dissemination develop, but also in which national and local public spheres continue to play a very important role. Globalization implies a gradual *differentiation* of the public sphere. This is due both to a general increase in the social complexity of modern societies requiring specialist knowledge even for public deliberation and to transformations in the media industry. News media not only transcend national borders, but are also specialized as regards content, audience, formats, geographical region etc. Differentiation implies a certain degree of separation of public fora, and this, to some extent, challenges the generalist model of the public sphere: general news media for a general public.

Differentiation also means a disembedding of media from other societal institutions. Increasingly, news media create public communicative spaces that do not correspond on a one-to-one basis to the spaces of other social institutions. Media are becoming independent institutions that do not share the social geography of other political or cultural institutions. Media-generated publicity is becoming less tied to the overall purpose or rationale of national or international public institutions, and more attuned to the needs of the media institutions themselves: serving an audience in the market place. Differentiation often favors an inward orientation due to commercial pressures: a domestic orientation (e.g., more domestic and less foreign news), an orientation toward professional interests due to topical specialization (e.g., business and financial news), an orientation toward the private and individual role of the consumer (e.g., entertainment, lifestyle news) etc.

Differentiation is accompanied by another phenomenon that modifies its consequences: an increase in *interconnections*. News media are becoming – potentially – accessible to everyone regardless of geography, content and format. While news media become more differentiated, they acquire the potential of being interconnected globally. Whether these interconnections are activated depends on the specific news event and its social context. During events that have either considerable social importance or great potential for media coverage (or both, e.g., wars), the different media-created fora of publicity may interconnect and create a global resonance chamber. The outcome may be a global media event (Dayan & Katz, 1992) that gets "the whole world watching". Interconnections often favor an outward orientation: a global perspective either geographically (the world as a whole), in terms of mode of address (specialist fora are connected to a general public), or as regards political agency (supra-national agencies like the UN, EU etc.).

As demonstrated above, changes within the news media influence the structure of the public sphere in various and often contradictory ways. Thus, there can be no simple or unambiguous answer to questions like whether the public sphere is getting larger or smaller, more fragmented or unified, more local or global etc. Such questions are tied to the idea that a globalized public sphere should somehow display the same characteristics as the national model of the public sphere.

Although current developments point in many directions, it may be useful - for the sake of conceptual clarity - to try to give a theoretical sketch of the overall dichotomies at work as regards the impact of changes in the news media on the structure of the public sphere. It appears as if two general dichotomies are being played out in the current development of the public sphere. The first is a tension between a *centrifugal and a centripetal* mode of development (McQuail, 1994), and the second a tension between *differentiation and homogeneity*. *Figure 1* provides an illustration of these dichotomies.

Figure 1. News media and the globalization of the public sphere. Dichotomies of tendencies

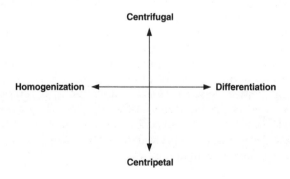

In some respects changes represent a centrifugal force, that enlarges the public sphere: Across countries public spheres become synchronized and interconnected, media practices and norms are adapted from one country to another etc. At the same time - as when centrifugal forces are at work - the public sphere becomes "thinner" and the individual components are stretched across a wider area with less connection to a well-defined center. In other respects, changes constitute a centripetal force, that favors an inward orientation and disconnects national or local public discourse from the world outside. Public discourse thickens around a well-defined center.

At the same time another dichotomy is at work. In some respects the public sphere becomes differentiated, for instance in terms of content or publics, or because of a geographical multilayering of several public spheres (local, national, regional etc.). In another respect, it becomes more homogeneous, because access to almost any kind of news media becomes possible - at least in principle - for everybody at any time and place. The two dichotomies interact, but not in unequivocal ways. Centrifugal tendencies may favor homogenization (as when CNN occasionally succeeds in setting the political agenda on a major issue), but it can also encourage differentiation (as when business news media cater to a cosmopolitan elite audience). Similarly centripetal tendencies may stimulate homogenization (as when nationalistic themes are being actively promoted by media and politicians alike) as well as differentiation (as when transnational media try to localize their news media in different markets).

Mutual Accountability

The globalization of industry, finance and culture has been seen by many as a potential threat to democracy. Because political institutions and the public sphere remain largely tied to a national level, it becomes difficult to exercise governance in global affairs through democratic processes. Neither industrial nor political actors at a transnational level tend to be accountable to the political deliberations of the national public sphere. Potentially, political action could be decoupled from public political deliberation: "Globalization means that those who can be kept accountable have little control over the factors affecting peoples lives, and those who have the decisive power are beyond democratic reach" (Eriksen, 1999: 43). As a political response to globalization, there has been a call for the extension of both political accountability and the public sphere from a national to a global level (Garnham, 1990; Held, 1995). In light of the argument put forward in this article, current developments in (news) media industries do not suggest that a transnational or global public sphere is likely to emerge in the future, if such publicity is understood as a singular entity based on the national public sphere model. The public sphere is not unaffected by globalization, but the impact of globalization is best described as a gradual deterritorialization of the public sphere. However, this objection does not render the question of global publicity and democratic accountability superfluous.

Current developments carry both promises and dangers for democracy in relation to public discussion of governance in global affairs. Differentiation of news media services carries the danger of a fragmentation of the public sphere, in which transnational and specialist news media increasingly serve a well-educated elite, and national and local media increasingly cater to the taste of disempowered social groups for whom globalization only poses a threat. From this point of view, the biggest problem may not necessarily be the unaccountability of transnational media industries to nation-states – as the political economy tradition would suggest – but the tendency of national and local media to develop very domestic, in some cases even aggressive nationalistic perspectives on global affairs.

Globalization of media also provides some opportunities for democratic discussion of global public affairs. The multi-layered structure of publicity is open to a high level of interconnectivity, allowing for the creation of public debate across national borders and the formation of a transnational public opinion that can potentially make international actors (industries, governments etc.) accountable on specific issues. So far, the formation of public opinion on a transnational or global scale has been a very volatile phenomenon, not least because the interconnections between various levels of publicity do not exhibit predictable patterns. When or why an event or problem might develop into a global issue is very hard to foretell.

In order to improve both public debate on questions of a global nature and the accountability of political agency to this publicity, the connectivity between various levels must be strengthened. Globalization of the public sphere is not about creating a world citizenship, but about creating connections of mutual public accountability across various socio-geographical levels. Thus, as regards mediated publicity, the challenge is to make transnational news media more orientated toward and accountable to national and local public spheres, while keeping national and local media orientated toward and responsible to the agenda of the outside world.

Notes

1. Quoted from Taylor (1997: 90).
2. Quoted from Taylor (1997: 92) and Flourney & Stewart (1997: vii), respectively.

References

Boyd-Barrett, Oliver (1997) "Global News Wholesalers as Agents of Globalization", in Sreberny-Mohammadi, Annabelle; Winseck, Dwayne; McKenna, Jim & Boyd-Barrett, Oliver (eds.) *Media in Global Context*. London: Arnold.

Boyd-Barrett, Oliver & Rantanen, Terhi (1998) *The Globalization of News*. London: Sage.

Burden, Peter (1999) Interactivity and Online News at the BBC. Leicester: University of Leicester (unpublished MA thesis).

Collins, Richard (1994) *Broadcasting and Audio-Visual Policy in the European Single Market.* London: John Libbey.

Collins, Richard (1996) "Europæisk Kultur – et Fantasifoster?" [European Culture – a Chimera?], *MedieKultur* no. 25, September 1996.

Collins, Richard (1998) *From Satellite to Single Market.* London: Routledge.

Cook, Timothy E. (1998) *Governing with the News. The News Media as a Political Institution.* Chicago: University of Chicago Press.

Dayan, Daniel & Katz, Elihu (1992) *Media Events. The Live Broadcasting of History.* Cambridge, Mass.: Harvard University Press.

Eriksen, Erik Oddvar (1999) *Is Democracy Possible Today?* Aarhus: Magtudredningen.

Flourney, Don M. (1992) *CNN World Report. Ted Turner's International News Group.* London: John Libbey (Acamedia Research Monograph 9).

Flourney, Don M. & Stewart, Robert K. (1997) *CNN. Making News in the Global Market.* Luton: University of Luton Press.

Garnham, Nicholas (1990) *Capitalism and Communication. Global Culture and the Economics of Information.* London: Sage.

Giddens, Anthony (1999) *Runaway World. How Globalisation is Reshaping Our Lives.* London: Profile Books.

Gutstadt, L.E. (1993) "Taking the Pulse of the CNN Audience: A Case Study of the Gulf War", *Political Communication,* vol.10.

Held, David (1995) *Democracy and the Global Order. From the Modern State to Cosmopolitan Governance,* Cambridge: Polity Press.

Held, David; McGrew, Anthony; Goldblatt, David & Perraton, Jonathan (1999) *Global Transformations. Politics, Economics and Culture.* Cambridge: Polity.

Hjarvard, Stig (1993) "Pan European Television News. Towards a European Political Public Sphere?", in Drummond, Phillip; Paterson, Richard & Willis, Janet: *National Identity and Europe.* London: British Film Institute.

Hjarvard, Stig (1995) *Internationale tv-nyheder.* [International Television News.] København: Akademisk Forlag.

Hjarvard, Stig (1999) *Tv-nyheder in konkurrence.* [Television News in Competition.] København: Samfundslitteratur.

Hjarvard, Stig (2000a) "Proximity. The Name of the Ratings Game", *Nordicom Review,* vol.21, no.2, Special Issue, Göteborg: Nordicom.

Hjarvard, Stig (2000b) *Mediated Encounters.* København: Global Media Cultures/University of Copenhagen, (Working Paper no. 2).

Holm, Hans-Henrik; Kabel, Lars; Kitaj, Torben; Møller, Lars & Ytzen, Flemming (2000) *Verden på Tilbud.* [The World on Offer.] Aarhus: CFJE/Ajour.

Jensen, Klaus Bruhn (1998) (ed.) *News of the World. World Cultures Look at Television News.* London: Routledge.

Krüger, Udo Michael (1997) "Politikberichterstattung in den Fernsehnachrichten", *Media Perspektiven,* no.5.

Köhler, Martin (1998) "From the National to the Cosmopolitan Public Sphere", in Archibugi, Daniele; Held, David & Köhler, Martin (eds.) *Re-imagining Political Community. Studies in Cosmopolitan Democracy.* Cambridge: Polity Press.

McQuail, Denis (1994) *Mass Communication Theory.* London: Sage.

Meinhof, Ulrike H. & Richardson, Kay (1999) *Worlds in Common? Television Discourse in a Changing Europe.* London: Routledge.

Moran, Albert (1998) *Copycat Television. Globalisation, Program Formats and Cultural Identity.* Luton: University of Luton Press.

Paterson, Chris (2001) "Media Imperialism Revisited", in Hjarvard, Stig (ed.) *News in a Globalized Society.* Göteborg: Nordicom.

Schiller, Herbert I. (1993) "Transnational Media: Creating Consumers Worldwide", *International Affairs,* vol.47, no.1.

Schlesinger, Philip (1993) "Wishful Thinking: Cultural Politics, Media, and Collective Identities in Europe", *Journal of Communication,* vol.43, no.2, New York: Oxford University Press.

Schlesinger, Philip (1999) *Media and Belonging: Changing Communicative Spaces and the European Union*. The conference "Reimagining Belonging", Aalborg University, 6-8 May 1999 (paper).

Serra, Sonia (2000) "The Killing of Brazilian Street Children and the Rise of the International Public Sphere", in Curran, James (ed.) *Media Organisations in Society*. London: Arnold.

Sparks, Colin (1998) "Is there a Global Public Sphere?", in Thussu, Daya K. (ed.) *Electronic Empires. Global Media and Local Resistance*. London: Arnold.

Stone, Jennie (2000) *Losing Perspective: Global Affairs on British Terrestrial Television 1989-1999*, Third World and Environment Broadcasting Project (3WE), United Kingdom.

Taylor, Philip M. (1997) *Global Communications, International Affairs and the Media Since 1945*. London: Routledge.

Tomlinson, John (1999) *Globalization and Culture*. Cambridge: Polity Press.

Volkmer, Ingrid (1999) *News in the Global Sphere. A Study of CNN and Its Impact on Global Communication*. Luton: University of Luton Press.

Global News Research and Complex Citizenship

Towards an Agenda for Research on Foreign/International News and Audiences

Daniel Biltereyst

> To begin with a paradox: as the technological capacity and sophistication of the global media expand, news coverage of foreign events on television seems to be shrinking. The situation is perhaps most dramatically illustrated in the case of the United States, the most information-rich nation in the world (...) Although the US case attracts the most frequent charges of parochialism and insularity (linked with accusations of trivialization and 'dumbing down') (...) a similar trend is also evident throughout the developed world. (Tomlinson, 1999: 171)

Introduction

It is a common statement that we can not understand the world, even on a local and domestic level of personal experiences (Morley & Robins, 1995), without taking into account the international and global dimensions in the flow of capital, technology, people, ideas, images, and so on. This powerful "discourse of globalization" (Dahlgren, 1995: 88) may not be fully encountered in the media. Following a broadening stream of critics, the myth of the global information village is confronted with a world-wide shrinking interest for foreign and international news. One notorious criticism came from Claude Moisy (1997: 79), the former chairman and general manager of Agence France-Presse, whose analysis "of the current exchange of foreign news around the world reveals an inescapable paradox":

> The amazing increase in the capacity to produce and distribute news from distant lands has been met by an obvious decrease in consumption. This is

certainly true for the United States, but it appears that the same phenomenon exists, to some degree, in most developed societies.

Moisy's forceful denouncement of the West's indifference, isolationism and inward attitude, had a wide press coverage, at least in some Western European countries[1]. The former AFP chairman referred to several US studies on the decreasing foreign news output, as well as to surveys indicating the public's shrinking interest. Commercial pressure and the reduced demand on the part of the audience are two of the most important reasons for this tendency, but Moisy tries to look further. Although one may heavily criticize Moisy's analysis, it is interesting that he does not only blame the media or the audience. Underneath his analysis we can read that we have to consider the tendency in a broader perspective. He claims that the end of the Cold War, for instance, has turned the world into a space which is increasingly difficult to decipher, while it has made an end at a "user-friendly manicheism" (p. 81-83) in international news. He also touches upon the issue of the convergent tendencies of wider (economic) globalization and localization:

> Without speaking of isolationism, it is obvious that the end of the Cold War has turned Americans inward (...) The globalization of the world economy is reinforcing this tendency to turn inward. An international marketplace where jobs go to the cheapest laborers has replaced nuclear confrontation (...). This fear is especially strong in many developed countries outside the United States where high levels of unemployment threaten national cohesion. In the United States, as in many other countries, the news horizon is tending to draw closer – from the international to the national and from the national to the local (...) There would be a certain irony in seeing our world turn local just as it was about to become global. (p. 83-4)

Recently, this paradox on the *narrowed news agenda with considerably less foreign/international news*, has been signaled by several media scholars (e.g. Hallin, 1996: 255; Franklin, 1997; Krüger, 1997; Utley, 1997; Tomlinson, 1999: 171-2; Hjarvard, 2000: 7, 20). The issue is often treated as a structural case of how a market conception of the media transforms vital "hard news" (the locus of most foreign news items) into softer, more sensationalist formats (e.g. Hallin, 1996: 256). In a competitive media landscape with commercially-driven mass communication, many foreign news items are seen as too complex, while proximity to the audience grows as a news value (Hjarvard, 2000: 20). News media tend to address the audience more than ever as local or national consumers, detached from overall globalizing tendencies.

From this perspective, the paradox fits not only into the debate about barriers to McLuhan's global city and the cosmopolitan idea in general (Tomlinson, 1999), but also into the considerations upon the media's function in organizing and disseminating public knowledge (Curran, 1996). Referring to Habermas's pessimistic public sphere theories (Habermas, 1989)[2], this paradox (possibly) illustrates the declining potential for a free, democratic communication system. It relates to the media's social responsibility and to the civic ideal of making it possible for citizens to really having access to all relevant and diverse forms of information and experiences.

The question, however, which drives this article, is whether these alarming analyses are legitimate. In this piece we argue that many of the arguments on the shrinking foreign news output do not take into consideration many of the technological and other shifts in the world of the news – even up to the point that it becomes quite difficult to define foreign news. Besides this argument on the news ecology (Cottle, 2000), we argue that we do not have sufficient empirical evidence for the paradox, especially not in relation to the audience. Although news research has a long and impressive tradition, also in relation to audiences, relatively few studies have been conducted on audiences in relation to foreign news as such. Only quite recently, Klaus Bruhn Jensen (1998: 10) wrote that "the place of the audience in the international flow of news remains under-researched, especially with regard to the decoding and social uses of the information in context as an aspect of citizenship". In this article we will claim that more qualitatively oriented research on a micro level is needed in order to block ideas about – what Sonia Livingstone (1998) called – the "implied audience" in media and cultural theory. The article ends with suggestions for further research on the role of foreign/international news as a window to the world.

Public Sphere, Complex Citizenship and News

Before evaluating the news paradox, it is necessary to put some recent trends in (foreign) news research into a broader frame. One of the most astonishing trends here is that in recent years there has been a remarkable re-evaluation of media formats which operate *at the boundaries of the traditional news genre*. Since the 1980s a growing number of hybrid formats of news, actuality and reality emerged (various forms of reality television, infotainment, docusoaps, true-life stories, ...), which often explored the private sphere and used dramatized reconstruction (Kilborn, 1994; Corner, 1996). These formats were heavily criticized for subverting traditional news journalism or even threatening a rational functioning of the public sphere. This "new" material was strongly denounced for replacing information by entertainment, while the consumer and "the individual come to occupy the space once filled by the citizen" (Sparks, 1991: 71).

However, some of the most interesting academic reconsiderations of the democratic potential of the media tended to focus upon this material. In-depth studies of infotainment, the tabloid phenomenon (e.g. Bird, 1998, 2000a) or audience discussion programs (e.g. Livingstone & Lunt, 1994) indicated how they operated as an open arena for audience participation and public debate. More than traditional news they allowed citizens to raise their voice and formulate their experiences on concrete social issues.

This move was accompanied by a clear tendency to *de-mythologize the civic ideals of traditional news genres* (Buckingham, 2000: 26). Especially hard news such as foreign and international news, was increasingly considered as a top down and authoritative device with a clear distance towards the audience. Journalists increasingly struggled with how to report on foreign and international issues (see further), given the need for material with a high proximity and relevance to the audience/citizens. This academic move may in part explain why so little empirical work has been done on audiences as citizens in relation to foreign and international news[3]. However it remains a highly relevant question how media report on foreign/international items and how they succeed in widening the citizen's horizon.

This subtle critical move towards the boundaries of the news genre has been strongly related to a vivid reformulation of Habermas's work. In classical public sphere theories, the "ideal citizen" was conceived as a rational public individual. The media helped to found an open communicative space between civil society and the state. From this perspective, news journalism was regarded as a key feature in the constitution of a true democracy. But, although Habermas's account has been central to a broad stream of critical media research, it was heavily attacked too. It was criticized for being historically incorrect, nostalgic and rationalistic, while it did not seem to take into account the possibility of oppositional and plural public spheres (e.g. Dahlgren & Sparks, 1991; Buckingham, 2000).

In the latest decade this all has led to important reformulations of the societal role of news journalism and mediated communication in general, as well as to new concepts of citizenship among social theorists and media researchers in particular (e.g. Golding, 1990; Dahlgren & Sparks, 1991; Van Steenbergen, 1994; Miller, 1998; Calabrese & Burgelman, 1998; Urry, 1999). Especially the "fuller, more multidimensional view" on citizenship (Dahlgren, 1995: 137) has been used as a tool to grasp major societal shifts and the role of the media in them.

The notion of *complex citizenship* responded, for instance, to changing political realities, such as the loss of sovereignty of the traditional nation-state, or the emergence of various levels of political governance and democratic participation. But its emergence was also accompanied by a theoretical rearticulation beyond the political realm. Following T.H. Marshall's work on citizenship (Marshall, 1950), the notion has not only been reserved to political (individual's rights to participate in politics, to vote, to exercise power) or civil rights (legal rights to protect the individual's freedom), but also to various other levels such as social (various rights in relation to welfare, economic and social security) and cultural citizenship (Urry, 1999). The latter refers to the recognition of various cultural rights as part of full citizenship, including, as Graham Murdoch (1999: 11-2) wrote, rights of access to the widest possible range of relevant information, rights to experience, knowledge and participation in the cultural sphere.

The notion of citizenship became to refer to how individuals and social groups belong to and participate within the communities in which they live (Dahlgren, 1995). It is citizenship defined as plural "practices that constitute individuals as competent members of sets of different and sometimes overlapping communities" (Hermes, 1998: 158). From this perspective, citizenship is on many layers to be understood as intrinsically *mediated*, given the centrality of television, radio, Internet and other forms of communication in influencing human experiences (Meyrowitz, 1985). Mediated communication plays a crucial role in identity formation and in the whole process of commitment and belonging to communities (e.g. Hermes, 1998; Murdoch, 1999; Storey, 1999).

Critics claim that these "postmodernist" views on citizenship use it as an interchangeable notion for identity, referring to a never-ending process of production and self-formation, a process of day-to-day becoming rather than being (Storey, 1999). It seems to refer to a quite unstructured concept of the sovereign, atomized individual. It must be seen in today's society in which the individual has various trajectories and choices, given the multiple milieux of action and the existence of alternative life-style options (Giddens, 1991). And, according to Giddens (1991: 84), mediated experience plays an important role in this process of offering a pluralism of choice. Especially "with the increasing globalization of media, a multifarious number of milieux are, in principle, rendered visible to anyone who cares to glean the relevant information".

In this process all types of media output play their role. Traditional forms of information such as foreign news tend to be "degraded", not only on the research agenda, but also in relation to its centrality to public debate and the project of "the making of the citizen". This reformulation of the public sphere and of citizenship might have made traditional (foreign) news into just one of the many possible means to bound citizens, form communities and inform people about what is happening outside their known world (e.g. foreign films and drama as a source of common knowledge).

One may discuss the usefulness of this reformulation and the major revival of interest in this old concept of citizenship (and the role of media in it)[4], but many questions emerge. One of them is whether "almost any approach to citizenship" is acceptable and "whether such a tolerant balancing act is sufficient for any concept of citizenship that includes the ideal of 'empowerment'" (Blumler, 1999: 248). One can ask whether not more research should (again) be done on how media output operates within the classical political realm. Especially because "'the poor state of citizenship' today raises serious questions about the function of the news media" (Harrington, 1998: 472).

Another question deals with how this output addresses the audiences as citizens in their full complexity. A common dichotomy in debates has been the relationship between *consumer versus citizen*. This relates to the debate on the commercialization of media, the use of advertising as a means of financing media, the multiplication of choice, and the market economy rhetoric of the consumer sovereignty (Pauwels, 1998; Corner, 1999). While the consumer is then seen as an individualistic, utilitarian and self-determined notion, citizenship relates to a commitment to a (set of) community(ies). It has often been stated that the neo-liberal and postmodern society has seen a loss or crisis in citizenship in terms of de-politicization and a decreasing participation and interest in the official political arena (Blumler & Gurevitch, 1995; Blumler, 1999). For some critics, these political-societal tendencies have been reinforced or, at least, found strong parallels in the field of mass mediated communication. Others claimed that citizenship is about more than official politics, while media do use various registers or modes of address, including those conveying elements of the civic ideal. Using Peter Dahlgren's phrase (1998: 95), one should look at the topics of course, "but equally to the manner in which viewers are positioned". They may be "addressed as citizens who can potentially do something in the social world beyond their home, not just as spectator-consumers". So, while citizenship is about much more than just political rights, it is equally true that people can be addressed in various ways – to put is simply: both as a consumer and a citizen, often in a mixed way.

A further complication of how media can address people as complex or multiple citizens, relates to the *geographical issue*. And here comes in the paradox referred to above. The question then is whether news is doing justice to the complex (political) identities that people at the beginning of the 21st century do have. Especially in Europe, the issue of the growth of "post-national" citizenship is an urgent one. It relates to a multi-leveled citizenship where, according to Urry (1999: 266):

> national citizenship is losing ground to a more universal model of membership located within an increasingly de-territorialised notion of a person's more universal rights (...). This post-national citizenship is especially connected with the growth of guest-working across many societies, greater global interdependence, increasingly overlapping memberships of different kinds of citizenship, and the emergence of universalistic rules and conceptions regarding human rights formalized by international codes and laws (...) Overall the hybrid and fragmented character of many apparent societies in a post-colonial period is said to result in a disjunctive, contested and inconsistent citizenship, according to Yuval-Davis a 'differential multi-tiered citizenship' order (...)

The paradox then relates to the media's (possible) cultivation of a "singular" imagined community (local, national, domesticated foreign news). Or it might be translated as the (possible) denial of the realities and complexities of post-national citizenship. However, it is important to continue to underline the social construction of identity and citizenship, and the possible existence of dominant identities (which are able to frame others).

Treating the issue of complex identity and the power relations in constructing them, Manuel Castells (1997: 6) acknowledges that "for a given individual, or for a collective actor, there may be a plurality of identities." But, at the same time, it is crucial that "in the network society (...) meaning is organized around a primary identity". This primary identity is strongly related to the issue of power, because, for Castells (p. 7), it is a form of identity "that frames the others". Social scientists should then investigate who is able, and for what, to construct collective identity, determining its meaning for those identifying with it. As news researchers it is important to acknowledge both the process of constructing a multiplicity of identities by the media, as well as the temptations to determine the symbolic content of a primary identity. This paradox might be not so far from the one on the shrinking foreign news output.

Foreign News Output
Decrease, degradation and marginalization?

Returning now empirically to the paradoxical decrease of foreign news in these post-national times, quite alarming figures have been launched. In his controversial "Foreign Policy" article, Moisy (1997: 82) referred to research on the continuing decline of foreign news on US network television. He wrote that "as a percentage of all topics covered between 1970 and 1995, the share of foreign news fell from 35 per cent to 23 per cent, and the average length of those stories dropped from 1.7 minutes to 1.2 minutes". He continued that "worse, while the networks devoted on average more than 40 per cent of total news time to foreign items in the 1970s, that share had been cut to 13.5 per cent of news time by 1995". And these figures only related to the oldest American television networks, which retained "at least traces of their common tradition of international journalism". Among the cable and satellite television stations, "news programs in general – and foreign news in particular – are disappearing in a flood of entertainment and niche-oriented channels" (p. 82).

These tendencies were confirmed by other authors such as Utley (1997), who claimed that foreign news coverage of the leading American networks has halved over the past decade. Hallin (1996: 255) referred to a narrowed news agenda too, writing that in US newspapers international news "has declined from 10.2 per cent of the newshole in 1971 to 2.6 per cent in 1988". Talking about the United States too, Tomlinson (1999: 171) stated that "network coverage of foreign affairs has fallen by two thirds in two decades' (...) and by 42 per cent between 1988 and 1996". And he continued that similar trends could be observed in other developed countries such as the UK, where "documentary output on international topics across all British terrestrial TV channels fell by 40 per cent between 1989 and 1994" (p. 171). And we could go on quoting similar trends in some other European countries (e.g. Krüger, 1997 for Germany).

This quantitative degradation has, in addition, a *qualitative* turn too, more specifically in the way foreign and international items are treated. This can go from scheduling ever shorter bits of foreign news items at the end of the program, putting them into a carrousel format with repetitive muzak beneath it, or using graphic devices and various narrative techniques. Such a dramatizing and marginalizing technique in scheduling foreign items is the announcement of an upbeat story – as a news teaser – before the foreign news carrousel (Zillmann et al., 1994), or the use of irony after it (Glasser & Ettema, 1993). These and other techniques all tend to create formal stability of news as a way of story-telling. Another well-documented technique is "domesticating the foreign", which refers to rendering foreign events comprehensible and relevant to domestic audiences (Gurevitch et al., 1991). Thus, for example, the recent explosion of a fireworks factory in the Netherlands (May 2000) was "domesticated" by many continental news broadcasts into questions of the domestic rules on fireworks, local dramas with fireworks in the past, and so on.

The use of all these techniques show that a great deal of what news makers consider to be relevant foreign news, is considered hard to cover. They all serve the purpose of softening the (often) hard character of foreign/international news, or of making it relevant and comprehensible to the citizens. Many of the techniques, used in domestic news items (Bird, 1998), such as personalization or various forms of bottom-up journalism (e.g. the use of street interviews, showing the "human face", human interest), are often harder to employ in covering foreign news items. These techniques try in a way to mask the top-down communication of traditional news.

Summarizing, it seems that not only the *amount* of foreign news is shrinking. Faced with declining audiences for news and increasing competition for ratings in many Western countries (e.g. in the USA, Moisy, 1997; Bird, 2000b), foreign items tend to be marginalized and, as much as possible, domesticated, personalized and "made relevant". They are presented in a much more fragmented way than local news, often treated without any broader interpretation or comment. In the overall context of changing news genres, many of the foreign news items seem to be treated as ever more disturbing albinos which audiences and journalists have to tolerate.

Following this line of criticism, the shrinking amount and overall degradation of foreign news are only symptoms of a wider trend where parliamentary news, investigative journalism and other types of hard information seem to be disappearing (Franklin, 1997). Commercial pressures and ratings are overall important reasons, which have wide-ranging effects in a competitive environment. Given the highly routinized and standardized form of news production in relation to foreign news as well as the strong dependency on global news services, foreign news items do show big similarities across various media outlets. As such it is hard to get any competitive advantage out of foreign and international news. This is reinforced by the high investment in building a network of foreign news correspondents or improving coverage on international and foreign items (Moisy, 1997: 83). The narrowed news perspectives may thus also be related to the shrinking number of powerful news services, possibly leading to news conformity. Following Hallin (1996) these trends are not only a result of these commercial pressures or audience demand, but also changing technological and regulatory conditions play their role.

Growing complexity in a new news ecology

These alarming analyses on the narrowing news agenda are powerful and convincing, although some weaknesses glimmer through these arguments. First of all, there are some *contradictions and conceptual problems*. It is, for instance, evident that most media outlets still do preserve foreign and international news – even when it is compounded in one page, or, for television, at the end of the news in a terrifyingly fragmented and distracted carrousel system with muzak beneath it. It shows however that, in some way or another, there is a recognition of the centrality of (foreign) news for the civic ideal. Whatever the criticism on the amount and formats of foreign news items, they did not disappear. The same goes for the issue of domestication and other techniques in covering the foreign. Here we may refer to an interesting wider debate on tabloidization and the positive aspects of top-down journalism (e.g. Bird, 1998). As such, these techniques may enhance audiences' engagement with what happens in foreign countries, or they may be excellent ways to show how news can be employed as a resource in day-to-day politics (Jensen, 1998).

Secondly, we have to acknowledge that most examples relate to television. The analysis might be valid for the most important mass medium of our time, which has known an intense flux of transformation since the 1980s. And it may be valid for commercial television in particular (Hjarvard, 2000: 20). But from a somewhat *broader perspective, there are various difficulties in seeing these changes in the direction of less foreign news, as overall trends over a longer course of time.* There is not only a clear lack of longitudinal material, but one should discriminate among different media too (cf. different interests, editorial strategies and audience profiles). As an example we can refer to a longitudinal content analysis on foreign news in Belgian newspapers since the 1940s (Van Gompel & Biltereyst, 1998). What seems to be interesting and maybe somewhat frustrating with this study, was that no real big changes seemed to have occurred in terms of the share of foreign news. Since the Second World War, local Belgian newspapers have seen a tremendous growth in daily news output, especially since the 1990s tendency of providing ever more supplements. There are shifts in the approach to foreign and international news of course, and much depends upon the actual political and economic news situation, but the share of it did not change much. This means that in quantitative terms, there has been a significant growth of foreign/international news. Very important in this all seems to be the profile and the target group, where quality newspapers provide considerably more foreign and international news. They did and they still do. An interesting trend in the last decade is that in various countries, tabloidization has been accompanied by a reverse tendency with substantial new investments in the elite press. Foreign and international news is now often seen as a crucial element in the play of distinction among the quality papers. This process of differentiation, segmentation and targeting in the newspaper market is only one case, and more research is needed, but journalistic parochialism or insularity has been there all the time and it is clearly related to the newspapers' profile.

Thirdly and more generally, we also have to look at the *wider new news ecology.* We already referred to the emergence of various sub-genres at the boundaries of traditional news and information, indicating for instance, contemporary television's obsession with all forms of actuality. But there is much more. Simon Cottle (2000: 20) claims that "(f)or those living in advanced, late-capitalist societies news has become an all-pervasive and an inescapable part of modern existence". Hereby he means that news is embedded in everyday life, using a rich variety of cultural forms, from 24-hours news channels, print media, radio broadcasts to on-line technologies. The case of 24-hour news is interesting in how channels such as CNN International and BBC World Service introduced and cultivated new working practices such as liveness, immediacy and continuity in foreign news coverage (Richardson & Meinhof, 1999). In many countries a growing number of newspapers, agencies and other news providers offer new, interactive services, changing also the very nature of what is foreign news (Hjarvard, 2000: 16-9). In the UK and the USA virtually all newspapers and the vast majority of regional titles are represented on the web, while the major broadcasters (e.g. BBC and Sky) and news agencies (e.g. Reuters) offer comprehensive Internet services too (Williams & Nichols, 1999). When the Internet will grow further into a mass medium, this will influence the way people receive (e.g. the on-line customized newspaper) and use the bulk of their news information, including those on foreign societies. These comprehensive Internet news services will change not only audience's interactive use of foreign news, but it will change the role of the traditional foreign/international news on television and newspapers too (Hjarvard, 2000: 16-7). This process of transformation should be high on the actual news research agenda.

Changing notions of foreign news

Another difficulty with pessimistic voices about the declining amount of foreign and international news on television, is of an overall *conceptual* nature, dealing mainly with *defining* what *foreign and international news* was, is and will be about. We already referred, first of all, to the new news services and the Internet in particular, which "will gradually make the boundaries between national, foreign, and international news media less clear and obvious" (Hjarvard, 2000: 17).

Secondly and more generally, we have to look at a basic element of the news definition. We all know the long tradition of international news values research, especially after Galtung and Ruge (1965), indicating that relevance and especially cultural proximity or affinity are crucial in deciding what's news. Somewhat simplifying, one might claim that foreign news items will only be retained when they are really important, relevant and close to the own cultural values system and history (Westerstahl & Johansson, 1994), and that there is always a process of domesticating the foreign (Gurevitch et al., 1991). As such, foreign news facts will have a high news value only when they are important to the receiving culture, now and in previous times. The idea of *proximity and distance* continuously change, dealing with overall political-economic, geopolitical and military shifts[5]. What seems to be interesting then is to do more historical research in order to look at how these news values on foreign and international items changed.

Thirdly, we should return to *theories on globalization and the recent reconfiguration of the state, the national, and the new geography of power.* Following Saskia Sassen (1998: 17) one can question whether "many global economic and political processes [which are] materialize[d] in national territories and do so to a large extent through national institutional arrangements (...) can be seen as national or foreign". Given the globalizing tendencies and, in Europe, the integration process, it is equally questionable whether, "conversely (...) we cannot simply assume that because a transaction takes place in national territory and in a national institutional setting it is ipso facto national" (p. 17). These overall changes make the very concept of foreign news highly questionable, let alone difficult to operationalize in concrete research.

Now, this all does not mean that foreign and international news coverage is sufficient, good, better or worse than it was, say thirty years ago. It is clear that, notwithstanding the wider news environment, there is a clear problem with the narrowing news agenda on many of the most popular mass media. It is true that, as Bird (1998) claimed, "the human interest story, especially the big, national story, *is* pushing out diversity of information from the news media". It is also true that many foreign and international news items are treated without any interpretation, comment or context. And we would fairly agree with Bird that "journalists must try harder to interpret important national and global issues in personal terms in order to engage audiences". There are huge problems with these approaches of course, such as the threat that only stories with a potential of personalization, emotion and dramatization, will retain news value.

But, as news researchers, we may not become nostalgic or underestimate the emergent possibilities of the wider news culture, while recognizing the complexities and contradictions of the actual news environment. This certainly creates opportunities for journalists and citizens to be better informed about what happens elsewhere. It creates new challenges to the traditional mass media too, while it possibly leads to a further fragmentation and disappearance of the universal audience. It is clear that the times of high modernism in journalism (Hallin, 1994: 179) is over and that a new news ecology is emerging. As such, we clearly need more research in many directions, given the changing news values and news production systems. One of the important questions then is to know whether the new media environment with its interactive media, will put a further pressure on the social bond or hit the commonalty idea (Fuller, 1996: 220; Moisy, 1997: 87). What is also needed is research, which takes into account the different media and industrial strategies, including their audience profile and economic resources. It is necessary also to take into account the changing power structure in the overarching news coverage system where for instance a small number of corporations spread their wings over various media, from print and audiovisual news items to news on the Internet (Paterson, 2001).

Foreign News Audiences
The uninterested and uniformed citizen

In his powerful lament over the declining foreign news output, Moisy (1997: 79) also concentrated on the state of the citizen who "in an open country as the United States is largely unaware of living conditions in many other countries".

He and other critics often quote public opinion research such as the regular surveys of the PEW Research for the People and the Press (e.g. Greenberg & Levy, 1997). Starting in 1963, this American survey reported how viewing of television news has been continuously in decline. The latest reports indicate how channels with a substantial foreign news output (CNN, national networks) are watched on a less regular basis, while the exposure to local channels and to tabloid television programs is substantially higher and remains roughly stable. According to the 1996 report, the "dwindling television news audience is apparent in nearly all demographic groups, but is particularly evident among younger people" (Greenberg & Levy, 1997: 143). According to these studies[6], the American public is most interested in crime, the local community and health, while culture, the arts and international affairs are among the least interesting subjects. Only people over 50 years of age are interested in international affairs (see also Bird, 1998). Another discriminator is the use of personal computers, stimulating on-line news services and diminishing the exposure to television news and the regular use of newspapers.

This powerful discourse was also supplemented by the awareness that the public has the biggest difficulties to grasp or understand foreign news (see further). Together these quite pessimistic accounts on the uninterested and uninformed audience tend to obscure even further the ideal of the news as part of the civic project. News appears to be missing its mission of enlightenment and the production of well-informed citizenry.

These arguments could be challenged by referring to the emergence of transnational media, the Internet and other means which help to create the idea of the global citizenship, community and public sphere (Volkmer, 1999). But global media such as CNN and BBC World are continuously changing their strategies (less global e.g.), while it appears that huge socio-cultural and educational constraints curb the idea of the global audience. On the Internet, new communities are formed, but it is far from clear whether this will strengthen the growth of global networks. Similar to what happens with the consumption of foreign news in the national news media, here too only well-educated citizens and a political and business elite are most willing to engage with a wider new media diet than the national one (Hjarvard, 2000: 8).

The imagined and implied audience

A crucial problem with these powerful arguments on the uninterested and uninformed bulk of the audience, is that so little empirical work has been done. As indicated above, there is an long tradition of research on news audiences (McQuail, 1997), but not on foreign news audiences in particular. A lot of research dealt with news audiences in general, but even an extensive review of the literature has the biggest difficulties in isolating the meaning and function of foreign/international news[7]. This is the more amazing given the impressive stream of studies on foreign and international news flows. Even when foreign news flow studies flourished and nourished wider debates on international communication, global media dependency and policy (Hester, 1973; Masmoudi, 1979; Ravault,

1981; Hur, 1984), practically no work had been done on the audience side (Jensen, 1998). Especially since the 1970s, numerous international flow studies opened opportunities to understand structural issues and reasons for the uneven flow of news.

In recent years, there has been an interest in investigating more intensively public opinion and the audience perception of media representations of distant wars, especially after the Gulf War (Shaw, 1996), but these were often international events with a high domestic involvement and proximity. Research on the bulk of other, low-involvement foreign and international news coverage has been weak, especially in an audience oriented perspective. This is quite amazing if we agree upon the role of mass mediated communication as a means to understand an ever more complicated world, or if we see foreign and international news as crucial in informing people about what happens out of their community.

Notwithstanding these long traditions of studies on news audiences on the one hand, and on foreign/international news flow on the other hand, few specific studies concentrate on the importance of foreign news as a source of information for audiences. In most studies on news flow, the notion of the "implied audience" (Livingstone, 1998) still dominates. This means that, unlike some other fields in international communication[8], the issue of the empirical foreign news audience did not yet seem to be able to refine ideas about the uninformed and uninterested audience.

Though, the audience has never been absent in (foreign) news flow theories, at least in its constructed, imagined or implied sense[9]. Research on news values and factors in relation to foreign news, for instance, had soon included concepts such as proximity (e.g. IPI, 1953; Galtung & Ruge, 1965) or identification (e.g. Östgaard, 1965) as key factors in understanding why some events grow into news. Östgaard (1965) distinguished two kinds of factors influencing the structure and form of foreign news: factors external to the news process, such as political and economic factors including government censorship and media ownership; and factors inherent in the news that enhance the event's news worthiness. Here Östgaard underlined already the importance of simplification, identification and sensationalism as crucial factors implying that news makers actively take into account their (reading, listening or viewing) audiences' abilities and interests in deciding what is news(worthy).

This "implied audience"-perspective has been adopted by much research on news. Especially the growing commercialization and the arrival of more reality-based programming (coupled with the blurring of the line between fact and fiction, public and private sphere, entertainment and information) have stirred up ideas about the importance of the audience (figures) pressures. This means that, at the bottom line, this implied audience conception often nourished analyses on the structural shifts of news production (e.g. Kimball, 1994; Fuller, 1996).

The search for the real audience

All this does not mean that no research has been done on audiences for foreign and international news. In fact, there has been an interest for the audience since the beginning, often related to readership. Here we can refer to "The Flow of News Research", conducted by the International Press Institute in 1953, which tried to integrate different analytical levels, from content analysis, interviews with news makers, to an inquiry with the audience in the USA, UK, France and Italy in relation to foreign news. In all those cases it appeared that the readers were indeed quite uninterested and that they did not know very much about foreign news items.

This can be extended to a wider tradition of research on news comprehension, retention and recall, which has been reinforcing the pessimistic accounts on the democratic value of news. This stream of research continuously underlined the truism that people understand and learn comparatively little from the news. However again, very little work has been done on the 'information processing' of foreign news in particular, while the issue has been mostly treated within a context of overall news processing studies. The news comprehension and recall study by Price and Czilli (1996), for instance, indicated how their respondents were significantly more able to recall news on personalities and domestic items than other types on news, including foreign issues. There were cross-media studies such as Clarke and Fredin (1978), who showed that people learned more about world events through print media than through television. In her more sophisticated study on how people understand the news, Doris A. Graber (1988: 107) confirmed that "a geographic principle is also at work". She concluded that "the farther from the United States and personal concerns the news is, the less attention it receives" (p. 107). But not very much came out of this study in relation to foreign and international news. Although very few studies have been concentrating on foreign and international news as such, one may speculate that the output and format in which it is presented (e.g. low output, fragmentation, lack of context), are the main 'variables' in understanding these (bad) results.

Since the 1980s, a new type of news audience research appeared which did not approach people as rational individuals, but tried to look at news consumption as a process of the active production of meaning. These emerging qualitative audience studies sought to integrate this process into a wider view of news as a ritual or as a forum for the negotiation of (subjective) meanings in context. The news text was regarded as a potential full of meaning which can be actualized by the user. Thus, this range of research was more interested in how news is introduced in the everyday life and contexts of its users.

It would bring us too far to give an overview of this type of qualitative news audiences studies (Jensen, 1986; Buckingham, 2000), but again it appears that the issue of foreign news is not well represented. Only a few exceptional studies dealt with foreign issues, such as the ones in the "News of the World"-project (Jensen, 1998), indicating how audiences interpret foreign news from their own perspective and their countries' very specific, localized position in the world. It seems that audiences use foreign news to construct their own and their countries' identity (Jensen, 1998: 52).

In most studies however, the issue of foreign and international news does still not yet appear or was only slightly mentioned. Among these exceptions, a

Norwegian news reception study underlined the importance of the difference between national and foreign news. Referring to the differences in news preferences among her interviewees, Hagen (1994: 419) noted that "the most apparent difference is that the manual workers are noticeably more interested in *national* news items" and that they "express a wish for more Norwegian news coverage". For this part of the respondents, national and local news was perceived as more relevant, while foreign news coverage was perceived as interesting "in providing a contrast". According to Hagen (1994: 421) news coverage instigates a "process of defining ourselves as 'us' by characterizing 'them'". Foreign news coverage, especially the one on conflicts and disasters, also seems to confirm a sense of Norwegian (read: Western) superiority and safety.

Hagen's interviewees in the higher education category did not indicate this preference for national news. On the contrary, they expressed a desire for more and 'better' foreign news coverage. This more cosmopolitan orientation was linked to the high importance that this group attached to news in general, although they were more critical towards television in general. According to Hagen (1994: 425) they acted as "ideal viewers", although all respondents seemed "to have internalized the duty" to watch television news.

These findings seem to converge with the general perception of the centrality of news as part of civil society in general, contrasting the continuing lament about the decreasing audience attraction for news (e.g. Greenberg & Levy, 1997). It also underlines the importance of education or, more broadly in Bourdieu's terminology, cultural capital in the orientation to news and foreign news in particular. But education is not the only discriminator. As such, more research is needed on the age differences in the attraction of news and foreign news in particular. Recently an increasing number of audience news studies in this qualitative vein seems to be oriented towards the younger generation. These studies started, both in the USA (Bird, 2000a, 2000b) and the UK (Buckingham, 2000), from the perceived drop in newspaper readership and in national TV news consumption. According to an audience news research by Elizabeth Bird (2000b: 31), "it was apparent that younger (under 30) people lacked what might be called a sense of 'obligation to be informed'". Contrary to the older respondents, this "distracted" and skeptical audience characterized traditional news as more irrelevant.

A wider agenda for foreign news audience research

Although these qualitative studies brought some fresh light on how news operates in the lives of the audience, here also a much broader base of research is needed. Much of this type of research is still anecdotal and unclear (Bird, 2000b: 31). What is needed is a more critical form of qualitative audience research, which firmly links news consumption to the idea of the citizen. Following Bird (1998: 33), news researchers should "focus on the audience drive (...) critiquing both the uncritical celebration of the 'active' audience, and the view that audiences are simply mindless recipients of whatever journalists feed them". In his critical account of news research, also Buckingham (2000: 18) recently talked about a wider news audience research agenda:

> this more 'culturalist' approach to television news does help to explain some of the motivations of viewing, and the pleasures it involves (...) it also suggests a rather different approach to questions about the nature of citizenship. Rather than attempting to measure the effectiveness of news in communicating political information, we should be asking how it enables viewers to construct and define their relationship with the public sphere. How do news programmes 'position' viewers in relation to the social order? (...) How do they invite viewers to make sense of the wider national and international arena, and to make connections with their own direct experience?

In general terms, it is essential for news researchers to look at how news is used and given sense in a daily context, especially when the drop of attention for foreign news is taken into consideration. This means that more qualitative audience inquiries are needed with an orientation to the *importance of foreign news as a source of information* about unknown societies in an age of globalization. Thus, we should know how important it is for people to be informed about what happens outside the local and national hemisphere? From where and how do citizens get their information? How do different media and formats operate in this process?

Besides this overall question it is important, secondly, to know how news media *address the audiences* and how they help to *define and represent* them (as citizens) (Urry, 1999). How do they respect the various lines of identity formation within the concept of complex citizenship – in terms of race, gender, class and other differences? A highly important field of research in this respect, which is still underdeveloped, relates to ideas about the *multicultural society*. It deals with how people from various origins make sense of the news in our society. In her study on London based Punjabi families, Marie Gillespie (1995) wrote that "survey figures, to my surprise at first, revealed that TV news is the genre most frequently watched and discussed in families in Southall." Her fieldwork revealed how watching news is part of a domestic ritual in most homes and that it is "seen as the chief source of information about the world, a necessary link to the world outside the local community". Gillespie indicated how, at the same time broadcast news fosters a sense of national identity. Her case study showed how news plays a central part in the constitution of the citizen, although it creates – in this context – complexities and ambivalences of consuming news around the dominant, national modes of identification. So, it is important to investigate how media, even in (or especially through) their foreign news output, organize meaning around Castell's "primary identity" which frames all other forms of identities.

This is, thirdly, closely related to the question *how people do perceive the role of local, foreign and international news as satisfactory for the formation of identity.* Is it open, critical, informative enough to meet the existing forms of complex citizenship? In this effort, also generational and educational differences in the use of traditional news should be included (Bird, 2000b).

Fourth, much more work is also needed on the *everyday understanding of politics through news media*, or how media audiences may engage and employ news as a resource in day-to-day politics.

In all these and other questions it is important to acknowledge the *changing news boundaries*. As such, it would be interesting to look at the *sub-genres of news* and other informative output. It is important here to know how they operate for audiences, how they frame complexity in today's society. In all this, it is clear that television news is definitely not the only window to the world. It is only one part of the material from which the audiences can select their imagery and construct their impressions and knowledge about foreign societies. Viewers are continuously offered images of what goes on beyond the local or the national, especially through fiction and various programs operating at the boundaries of fact and fiction. Reality- or real-life based output most often are exclusively nationally or locally oriented – much more than traditional news output. In this context it might be interesting to investigate how news follows these trends or, eventually, tries to correct the image. And one might speculate about the fact that people learn more about foreign societies through fiction, imported talk shows, than through short bits of foreign news items without any context.

Given the changing *wider news ecology* it will be, finally, crucial to know how central the traditional mass media still are in contrast to other newer information channels. Concentrating on the role of the newer services, one should take into account social and other differences in the use of the Internet and on-line news services (Golding, 1990). Important is to know whether the new media environment will put a further pressure on the social bond (supposedly) constituted by the traditional, modernist news format. The further fragmentation and diversification of news output also calls into question issues on the further process of individualization (Castells, 1997).

Discussion: Issues and Questions

This extensive research agenda on audiences and foreign news was inspired by the apparent paradox of the decreasing output of foreign news in times of growing globalization. The issue has been discussed by several critics in the context of the commercial pressure on media, the audience's waning interest in what happens out of the local or national hemisphere, and the general tendency in the West to turn inward. From this perspective, the paradox was taken as a further indication of the declining and fragmented public sphere.

However, in this article we claim that there is not sufficient empirical evidence for these alarming statements, nor in the direction of the decreasing output, nor in audience research. Referring to the *output issue* (see Table 1), we have to be careful to interpret the low output figures for some countries such as the USA, Britain and other Western countries. This is not only a quite Eurocentric position, but there is clear lack of reliable data for other countries, especially on a longitudinal basis. The paradox must also be seen in relation to a rapidly changing world of news. This goes even up to the point that in today's differentiated ecology of news production, it is quite difficult to define what is news. There are apparent changes not only in the formats or the "blurring of the lines between news and entertainment" or "the melding of public and private" (Schudson, 1995: 171-2). Also the geography of news has changed, partly as a result of wider globalization processes and the Internet, where the local, national, foreign, international or global might easily intertwine. As such, news researchers must not become too nostalgic or, as Simon Cottle recently put it (2000: 21), "become increasingly out of touch with today's production practices, diversified news ecology and wider news culture". In this sense, the paradox might be an inherent part of the changing social geography of today's media. It might relate

Table 1. Key questions and issues in relation to research on (foreign) news output and audiences

		Output	Audience
Quantitative issues	**Key questions**	Amount of (foreign) news output, for different media types and program types, over a longer period of time, etc.	Amount of audience use, viewing, listening, reading, importance of (foreign) news, ...
	Methodologies	Content analyses, data on sales, etc.	Ratings, audience inquiries, survey figures, etc.
	Social differences	-	Differences across gender, social, class, race, educational, age and other lines; growing knowledge gap, etc.
	Conceptual and other issues	What is national/foreign in a globalized world? What is (foreign) news in the wider news landscape? Issues of fragmentation, diversification, globalization, etc. What about the role of traditional news in relation to different media types (e.g. internet) and programme types (e.g. reality-based material)?	Issues of the definition of audience, citizen, identity. Issues of fragmentation, individualization in the use of (foreign) news media. The threat for the loosening forms of commonality, etc.
	Structural issues	Ownership news media, agencies and other sources for foreign news, etc.	Economic and social differences, etc.
Qualitative issues	**Key questions**	Issues of the textual meaning, representation, audience address, formation of identity, etc.	Process of use, meaning, sense making, and reception of (foreign) news in a daily context.
	Methodologies	Discourse and other types of textual analyses.	Reception and ethnographic studies; uses and gratifications-studies; ...
	Conceptual and other issues	Formation of a dominant, 'primary' identity through news. Formation of multiple identities through news. Representation of the citizen, etc.	What kind of knowledge do people get on local and foreign societies? Where do people get their information besides traditional news media? What do people use (foreign) news for? For identity formation, escape, ...?

to the wider, big audience, commercial media, while the interested citizen has a plethora of foreign news outlets.

This lack of sufficient empirical evidence is even stronger in relation to *audience* questions. While quantitative data on the audiences' use and attention for foreign news are only marginally available, qualitative research still is completely underdeveloped. Only a few reception and ethnographically based studies were interested in why and how people make sense or reject foreign news. In general it is clear that, while news research has a long and rich tradition, there is a clear lack of audience research on foreign/international news – especially in a more qualitative vein.

However, this extensive research agenda with a long list of issues, questions and possible methodologies on foreign news media output and meaning (Table 1), may not obscure the overall societal issues. In all of this, we have to acknowledge the importance of mediated communication, which plays an important role in both offering a pluralism of choices and identities, as well as installing a process of intense identity-building around some communal bonds. This might be the heart of the paradox: in these times of huge social change and globalization it seems that "the search for meaning takes place then in the reconstruction of defensive identities around communal principles" (Castells, 1997: 11).

Notes

1. Here we refer to a vivid debate in the French quality press, as well as in Dutch elite newspapers such as 'De Volkskrant' (4/9/1997).
2. For an overview of the critical comments and discussions on public sphere theories in relation to mediated communication, see e.g. Dahlgren & Sparks (1991), Garnham (1992), Dahlgren (1995), Stevenson (1999), Buckingham (2000), Goldsmith Media Group (2000).
3. See also our discussion in the second half of this article.
4. It has been suggested that the concept of citizenship has replaced 'class' "as a magical agent for historical change". Following Toby Miller (1998: 281), citizenship is "more easily mobilized as a justification for state action", while it "has become a site of hope for a Left that has lost its actually existing alternative to international capital". It has also been argued that in media and cultural studies, citizenship has replaced the threadbare concept of the audience and possibly also the one on identity (Barker, 2000).
5. An interesting discussion in relation to the emergence of the global civil society, military conflicts and the media representation, can be found in Shaw (1996) who talks about distance and the process of distancing.
6. See http://www.people-press.org/mediamor.htm.
7. In a recent extensive review of literature on television news and the audience, the authors did not mention foreign news studies or they did not discriminate between local, national, foreign or international news (Schaap et al., 1998).

The author would like to thank Yen Peeren for his assistance and comments on an earlier draft of this manuscript.

8. See for instance the debate on the US dominance in the flow of fiction, where (qualitative and other) audience research has been very useful in redefining theories and in challenging the 'implied audience' views (e.g. Biltereyst, 1995).

9. By "imagined" audience, Simon Cottle (2000: 28-9) refers to the audience constructed by the news producers. It is the "missing link" or the "structural lacuna between the producers and consumers of news" as indicated by Philip Schlesinger (see Cottle, 2000: 28-9). The "implied" audience refers to a level of conceptualizing audiences within cultural and media theories (Livingstone, 1998).

References

Barker, Ch. (2000) *Cultural Studies. Theory and Practice.* London: Sage.

Biltereyst, D. (1995) "Qualitative Audience Research and Transnational Media Effects. A New Paradigm?", *European Journal of Communication*, vol.10, no.2.

Bird, E. (1998) "News We Can Use: An Audience Perspective on the Tabloidisation of News in the United States", *Communication Research*, vol.5, no.3.

Bird, E. (2000a) "Audience Demands in a Murderous Market: Tabloidization in U.S. Television News", in Sparks, C. & Tulloch, J. (eds.) *Tabloid Tales.* New York: Rowan and Littlefield.

Bird, E. (2000b) "Facing the Distracted Audience: Journalism and Cultural Context", *Journalism*, vol.1, no.1.

Blumler, J. (1999) "Political Communication Systems All Change", *European Journal of Communciation*, vol.14, no.2.

Blumler, J. & Gurevitch, M. (1995) *The Crisis of Public Communication.* London: Routledge.

Buckingham, D. (2000) *The Making of Citizens: Young People, News and Politics.* Longman: Routledge.

Calabrese, A. & Burgelman, J.C. (1998) (eds.) *Communication, Citizenship, and Social Policy. Rethinking the Limits of the Welfare State.* Lanham: Rowman & Littlefield Publishers.

Castells, M. (1997) *The Construction of Identity. The Information Age – Volume II.* Oxford: Blackwell.

Clarke, P. & Fredin, E. (1978) "Newspapers, Television and Political Reasoning", *Public Opinion Quarterly*, vol.42.

Corner, J. (1996) "Editorial: Changing Forms of 'Actuality'", *Media, Culture & Society*, vol.18, no.1.

Corner, J. (1999) *Studying Media. Problems of Theory and Method.* Edinburgh: Edinburgh University Press.

Cottle, S. (2000) "New(s) Times: Towards A 'Second Wave' of News Ethnography", *Communications*, vol.25, no.1.

Curran, J. (1996) "Rethinking Mass Communication", in Curran, J.; Morley, D. & Walkerdine, V. (eds.) *Cultural Studies and Communications.* London: Arnold.

Dahlgren, P. & Sparks, C. (eds.) (1991) *Communication and Citizenship. Journalism and the Public Sphere.* London: Routledge.

Dahlgren, P. (1995) *Television and the Public Sphere.* London: Sage.

Dahlgren, P. (1998) "Enhancing the Civic Ideal in Television Journalism", in Brants, K.; Hermes, J. & van Zoonen, J. (eds.) *The Media in Question.* London: Sage.

Franklin, B. (1997) *Newszak and News Media.* London: Arnold.

Fuller, J. (1996) *News Values. Ideals for An Information Age.* Chicago: University of Chicago Press.

Galtung, J. & Ruge, M.H. (1965) "The Structure of Foreign News", *Journal of Peace Research*, no.2.

Gans, H. (1979) *Deciding What's News.* New York: Vintage Books.

Garnham, N. (1992) "The Media and the Public Sphere", in Calhoun, C. (ed.) *Habermas and the Public Sphere.* Cambridge: MIT Press.

Giddens, A. (1991) *The Trajectory of the Self. Modernity and Self-Identity.* Cambridge: Polity Press.

Gillespie, M. (1995) *Television, Ethnicity and Cultural Change.* London: Routledge.

Glasser, L.T. & Ettema, J.S. (1993) "When the Facts don't Speak for Themselves: A Study of the Use of Irony in Daily Journalism", *Critical Studies in Mass Communication*, vol.10.

Golding, P. (1990) "Political Communication and Citizenship: The Media and Democracy in An Egalitarian Social Order", in Ferguson, M. (ed.) *Public Communication. The New Imperatives.* London: Sage.

Goldsmiths Media Group (2000) "Media Organisations in Society: Central Issues", in Curran, J. (ed.) *Media Organisations in Society*. London: Arnold.

Graber, D.A. (1988) *Processing the News. How People Tame the Information Tide*. New York: Longman.

Greenberg, B.S. & Levy, M.R. (1997) "Television in the Changing Communication Environment. Audience and Content Trends in U.S. Television", *Studies of Broadcasting*, no.33.

Gurevitch, M.; Levy, M.R. & Roeh, I. (1991) "The Global Newsroom: Convergences and Diversities in the Globalization of Television News", in Dahlgren, P. & Sparks, C. (eds.) (1991) *Communication and Citizenship: Journalism and the Public Sphere*. London: Routledge.

Habermas, J. (1989) *The Structural Transformation of the Public Sphere*. Cambridge: Polity Press.

Hagen, I. (1994) "Expectations and Consumption Patterns in TV News Viewing", *Media, Culture & Society*, vol.16, no.3.

Hallin, D. (1994) *We Keep America on Top of the World. Television Journalism and the Public Sphere*. London: Routledge.

Hallin, D. (1996) "Commercialism and Professionalism in the American News Media", in Curran, J. & Gurevitch, M. (eds.) *Mass Media and Society*. London: Arnold.

Harrington, C.L. (1998) "Is Anyone Else Out There Sick of the News? TV Viewers' Responses to Non-routine News Coverage", *Media, Culture & Society*, vol.20, no.4.

Hermes, J. (1998) "Cultural Citizenship and Popular Fiction", in Brants, K.; Hermes, J. & van Zoonen J. (eds.) *The Media in Question*. London: Sage.

Hester, A. (1973) "Theoretical Considerations in Predicting Volume and Direction in International Information Flow", *Gazette*, vol.19.

Hjarvard, S. (2000) *News Media and the Globalization of the Public Sphere*. Copenhagen: University of Copenhagen (Working paper No. 3).

Hur, K.K. (1984) A Critical Analysis of International News Flow Research, *Critical Studies in Mass Communication*, no.1, pp. 365-378.

IPI/International Press Institute (1953) *The Flow of News*. Zürich: IPI.

Iyengar, S. & Kinder, D.R. (1987) *News that Matters. Television and American Opinion*. Chicago: The Univiersity of Chicago Press.

Jensen, K.B. (1986) *Making Sense of the News*. Aarhus: Aarhus University Press.

Jensen, K.B. (ed.) (1998) *News of the World. World Cultures Look at Television News*. London: Routledge.

Kilborn, R. (1994) "How Real Can You Get?", *European Journal of Communication*, vol.9, no.4.

Kimball, P. (1994) *Downsizing the News: Network Cutbacks in the Nation's Capital*. Washington: The Woodrow Wilson Center Press.

Krüger, U.M. (1997) "Politikberichterstattung in den Fernsehnachrichten", *Media Perspektiven*, no.5.

Livingstone, S. & Lunt, P. (1994) *Talk on Television: Audience Participation and Public Debate*. London: Routledge.

Livingstone, S. (1998) "Audience Research at the Crossroads. The 'Implied Audience' in Media and Cultural Theory", *European Journal of Cultural Studies*, vol.1, no.2.

Marshall, T.H. (1950) *Citizenship and Social Class*. Cambridge: Cambridge University Press.

Masmoudi, M. (1979) "The New World Information Order", *Journal of Communication*, no.29, pp. 172-85.

McQuail, D. (1997) *Audience Analysis*. London: Routledge.

Meyrowitz, J. (1985) *No Sense of Place*. Oxford: Oxford University Press.

Miller, T. (1998) "Television and Citizenship: A New International Division of Cultural Labor?", in Calabrese, A. & Burgelman, J.C. (eds.) *Communication, Citizenship, and Social Policy. Rethinking the Limits of the Welfare State*. Lanham: Rowman & Littlefield Publishers.

Moisy, C. (1997) "Myths of the Global Information Village", *Foreign Policy*, summer 1997.

Morley, D. & Robins, K. (1995) *Spaces of Identity. Global Media, Electronic Landscapes and Cultural Boundaries*. London: Routledge.

Murdoch, G. (1992) "Citizens, Consumers, and Public Culture", in Skovmand, M. & Schroeder, K. (eds.) *Media Cultures. Reappraising Transnational Media*. London: Routledge.

Murdoch, G. (1999) "Rights and Representations: Public Discourse and Cultural Citizenship", in Gripsrud J. (ed.) *Television and Common Knowledge*. London: Routledge.

Neuman, W.R., Just, M.R. & Crigler, A.N. (1992) *Common Knowledge. News and the Construction of Political Meaning.* Chicago: The Univiersity of Chicago Press.

Paterson, Ch. (2001) "Media Imperialism Revisited: The Global Public Sphere and the News Agency Agenda", in Hjarvard, S. (ed.) *News in a Globalized Society.* Göteborg: Nordicom.

Pauwels, C. (1998) "From Citizenship to Consumer Sovereignty", in Calabrese, A. & Burgelman, J.C. (eds.) *Communication, Citizenship, and Social Policy. Rethinking the Limits of the Welfare State.* Lanham: Rowman & Littlefield Publishers.

Price, V. & Czilli, E.J. (1996) "Modelling Patterns of News Recognition and Recall", *Journal of Communication,* vol.46.

Ravault, R.J. (1981) "Information Flow: Which Way is the Wrong Way?", *Journal of Communication,* vol.31, no.4.

Richardson, K. & Meinhof, U. (1999) *Worlds in Common? Television Discourse in a Changing Europe.* London: Routledge.

Robinson, J.P. & Levy, M.R. (1986) *The Main Source. Learning from Television News.* London: Sage.

Rosengren, K.E. (1977) "International News: Four Types of Tables", *Journal of Communication,* vol.27.

Sassen, S. (1998) "The State and the New Geography of Power", in Calabrese, A. & Burgelman, J.C. (eds.) *Communication, Citizenship, and Social Policy. Rethinking the Limits of the Welfare State.* Lanham: Rowman & Littlefield Publishers.

Schaap, G.; Renckstorf, K. & Wester, F. (1998) "Three Decades of Television News Research: An Action Theoretical Inventory of Issues and Problems", *Communications,* vol.3, no.3.

Schramm, W. (1960) *One Day in the World's Press.* Stanford: Stanford University Press.

Schudson, M. (1995) *The Power of News.* London: Harvard University Press.

Shaw, M. (1996) *Civil Society and Media in Global Crises. Representing Distant Violence.* London: Pinter.

Sparks, C. (1991) "Goodbye, Hildy Johnson: The Vanishing 'Serious Press'", in Dahlgren, P. & Sparks, C. (eds.) *Communication and Citizenship. Journalism and the Public Sphere.* London: Routledge.

Sreberny-Mohammadi, A., Nordenstreng, K. & Stevenson, R.L. (1984) "The World of the News Study", *Journal of Communication,* vol.34, no.1.

Sreberny-Mohammadi, A., Nordenstreng, K., Stevenson, R.L. & Ugboajah, E. (eds.) (1985) *Foreign News in the Media.* Paris: Unesco.

Stevenson, N. (1999) *The Transformation of the Media: Globalisation, Morality and Ethics.* London: Longman.

Storey, J. (1999) *Postmodern Cultural Identities, Cultural Consumption and Everyday Life.* London: Arnold.

Tomlinson, J. (1999) *Globalization and Culture.* London: Polity Press.

Tuchman, G. (1991) "Media Institutions. Qualitative Methods in the Study of News", in Jensen, K.B. & Jankowski, N. (eds.) *A Handbook of Qualitative Methodologies for Mass Communication Research.* London: Routledge.

Urry, J. (1999) "Globalization and Citizenship", *Journal of World-Systems Research,* vol.5, no.2.

Utley, G. (1997) "The Shrinking of Foreign News", *Foreign Affairs,* vol.76, no.2.

Van Dijk, T.A. (1998) *News Analysis. Case Study of International and National News in the Press.* New Jersey: Hillsday.

Van Gompel, R. & Biltereyst, D. (1998) "Crisis en bloei van de vierde macht", in Bulck, J. Van den (ed.) *De Pers en haar vrijheid.* Brussels: Koning Boudewijnstichting.

Van Stenbergen, B. (ed.) (1994) *The Condition of Citizenship.* London: Sage.

Westerståhl, J. & Johansson, F. (1994) "Foreign News: News Values and Ideologies", *European Journal of Communication,* vol.9, no.1.

Williams, P. & Nichols, D. (1999) "The Migration of News to the Web", *ASLIB Proceedings,* vol.51, no.4.

Volkmer, I. (1999) *News in the Global Sphere.* Luton: University of Luton Press.

Zillmann, D., Gibson, R., Ordman, V.L. & Aust, C.F. (1994) "Effects of Upbeat Stories in Broadcast News", *Journal of Broadcasting and Electronic Media,* vol.38.

Östgaard, E. (1965) "Factors Influencing the Flow of News", *Journal of Peace Research,* vol.1, no.1.

New Media, Global News, and Democracy

International Communication Theory in Transition
Parameters of the New Global Sphere of Mediation

Ingrid Volkmer

The terms 'international,' 'transnational' and 'global' communication not only stand for different definitions of an expanding communication space but also reflect the history of worldwide communication – as well as its diversity. When attempting to describe 'ideas' and 'concepts,' 'models' or 'strategies' of international communication, a historical perspective helps to understand the different shades of these terms.

International Communication might be applied to the trans-border information flow in economic circles in mediaeval Europe, where news have already been 'inter-nationalized' to rising European centers of commerce. In the fifteenth century the wheat traders of Venice, the silver traders of Antwerp, the merchants of Nuremberg and their trading partners shared economic newsletters and created "common values and beliefs in the rights of capital" (Stephens, 1988:77). The first postal routes were established in Europe, forming a first 'communication network' and the economic newsletter was invented, which helped to form an already international financial community. With the economic internationalization and growth of major European cities (Venice, Amsterdam, London), news increasingly became internationalized as it was exchanged between these centers of commerce as well as across the Atlantic to the British colonies.

International 'public' communication was invented by the regular print of newspapers as early as the 17th century in Europe and the United States. This process was accompanied by the rise of the 'citizenry', of an informed public, who was interested in international news. The steam engine and Morse's telegraph brought about the professional journalist and the international correspondent, who covered specific international regions. The increasing commercialization and wider circulation subsequenctly called for a new infrastructure in order to provide newspaper editors with the commodity 'news'. The first news 'wholesale' agencies, such as Havas, (the predessor of today's Agence France Presse), as well as Reuter's were founded in the nineteenth century. In the second half of the 19th century, these agencies quickly entered specific continental markets. The German agency Wolff'sche Telegraphenbureau spread through northern Europe, to Denmark, Finland, Sweden and Russia, Havas expanded into Portugal, Spain, Italy, Romania and Serbia; Reuter's expanded into Belgium, the Netherlands, Bulgaria, the British Empire, Egypt, Australia, New Zealand, Japan, China and Malysia (Höhne, 1977: 42pp).

World wire and cable systems were established in the late 19th century and early 20th century by Britain and Germany. Their main purpose was to support military communication networks as well as communication with governments of colonised countries. In 1866, the Anglo-American Telegraph Company laid a cable between England and the United States, the Ostdeutsche Telegraphen-Gesellschaft, established a cable line from Constance to Constantinople to Asia, another one crossed the Pacific Ocean and by 1912 Great Britain already dominated the world cable system. Transnational media organisations such as Intelsat, Eurovision, founded in the middle of the 20th century were the starting point for a now new idea of international communication. International and global commercial media systems characterized the second part of the 20th century. News and program pools of national broadcasters of a specific region have formed models of international cooperation, Eurovison, Asiavision (in Asia) and Intervision (in the former Soviet Union) increased transborder exchange of programs. In 1962, the URTNA (Union of Radio and Television of African nations) was formed, the Arab States Broadcasting Union was establed in 1969, the Caribbean Broadcasting Union in 1970 and the Asia Pacific Broadcasting Union, formed in 1971 supported closer cooperation among 34 Asian nations. International services of BBC and Deutsche Welle entered into the field of television.

It was the establishment of internationally operating media systems, such as CNN and MTV, established not by national broadcasters, but by commercial companies, which have finally inaugurated a new age of global communication by distributing the same program "around the world in thirty minutes" as a CNN slogan impressively stated in those days.

Today, it is the global push-pull medium of the Internet, with around 250 million users worldwide, which not only reshapes the idea of international/global communication and demands new categories of media analysis, communication and content as well as market taxonomies, but which also conveys a myth of a global community. Around ten years ago, with the diversification of satellite technology, with the commercialization of C- and K-band satellite companies in various world regions CNN and MTV became global programming models for entire media industries, which have copied these models on local markets (in many cases as a more successful program than the original, see VIVA and MTV in Germany). In consequence, conventional patterns of international communication had to be refined according to the new global news space – CNN's breaking news and fast paced fact journalism became a successful format for a variety of commercial but also public service broadcasters.

It is not so much the international reach of CNN (and for that matter of BBC and others) but the extension of the public sphere into this global, international arena – which seems to challenge the conventional terminology of international communication theory. Not only global communication, but the concept, architecture and the international effects of the new dynamic 'global public sphere' is the interesting issue. This process became already obvious when CNN inaugurated an international news market-force-oriented process, which has shifted global communication onto a new level, by mixing conventional reference-systems of national news presentation, which replaced the 'home' and 'foreign' news angle with a global juxtaposition of 'internal' and 'external' perspectives. By this development, a substantial new extra-societal sphere has been shaped, which has influenced political and economical processes.

This 'global public sphere' is composed by various societal sphere types: totalitaristic, democratic and other, less clearly defined communication conventions. Whereas ten years ago, CNN as an international news 'authority' mediated these different approaches by including them into a common news frame (such as in the program "World Report"), the global communication platform of the Internet is an open space, where mediating agencies (such as www.yahoo.com), wholesale news agencies, authentic news reports and self proclaimed individual journalists (www.drudge.com), and national news institutions are just small segments in a variety of information categories and sources. Taking a look at the change of the public sphere concept in modern and global viewpoints already reveals a variety of new questions, a demand for new categories: These help to explain this global public sphere, which has become an extrasocietal global sphere of mediation, particularly, enhanced by the internet. Such a global communication platform, which seems to replace the conventional terminology of international communication with a new vocabulary for macro and micro frame analysis and the definition of a new 'dialectic' and 'self reference' discourse mode. Dialectic processes within this de-nationalized global communication territory might become issues of a global communication theory and replace conventional dialectic processes between states/nations, which have been part of modern international communication theory.

Modernity and the National Public Sphere in International Communication Theory

International Communication theory has been developed on the metatheory of modernity – as communication between nations. International communication was considered as a tool for modernization and political reeducation of nations. After World War II when such efforts were geared towards Europe, large-scale economic aid went hand in hand with communication programmes, designed to re-educate citizens about political propaganda also to support economic growth and notions of democracy. These undertakings, which met with considerable success at the time, were then transferred to general efforts to support and sustain economic and democractic developments in developing countries. This idea of the spread of modernization as a development goal inspired economic development projects. A process which was considered as one of "reviving cultures, emerging nations, and new states" in turn increasingly effected a "revolution of rising expectations," such that people throughout the "backward" and "impoverished areas of the world suddenly acquired the sense that a better life was possible for them" (Lerner, 1958:330).

International communication had become a tool for societal development of one nation. The concept of modernization refers narrowly to the implementation of communication infrastructures and societal modernization is strongly related to the two major forces of social dynamics: mobilization and institution building. The role of communication within these societal organizational structures has been analysed from various viewpoints. "Societal change" has to be initiated by mass media in order to enhance "individual change" as well as "social change" (Rogers, 1969:88). Consequently, these ideas defined development communication as a "type of social change in which new ideas are introduced into a social system in order to produce higher per capita incomes and levels of living through more modern methods and improved social organizations" (Rogers, 1969:8). Institution building and transitional theories of (international), so called "development communication" maintained that communication was a tool of modernization process in the sense of distributing Western lifestyles and ideas of nation-ness of roles of citizens to traditional societies in order to inaugurate a process of transition.

Since the mid-seventies the concepts of development communication have been critically reviewed not only by Western but also by communication experts from developing countries. This criticism cumulated in a profound criticism of the whole modernization concept, since development is an "integral, multi-dimensional, and dialectical process which can differ from one society to another" (Servaes, 1983: 63). The belief that Western ideas of modernization can and should be transferred into diverse economic environments implies the unquestioned universalism of the modernization project, while dependency theories bring in the concept of particularism of 'peripheral' countries. Media Imperialism is concerned with exports of commercial and political strategies, with corporate superstructures, with media products, "flowing from the centre to the periphery", which are "the most prominent means by which weaker societies are absorbed culturally into the modern world system" (Schiller, 1979:25).

One of the first concepts, which focuses on cultural impacts of international communication and less on the ouvert influence of societal processes through the means of modern communicaton processes, was Gerbner's approach of international cultivation (Gerbner and Gross, 1976, Morgan, 1990). This approach reveals the effects of American programmes in various societies, on public consciousness of gender roles and "Western lifestyle" stereotypes and can be conceptually located on the borderline between media imperialism and pop cultural consumerism, in "which mainstreaming middle-class values are presented on the screen, regardless of the type of programme; the actors are surrounded by durable commodities, material conveniences, and many aspects of the 'affluent society' (Kato, 1976:255). Theoretical models of a relativistic approach of modernity and communication have more recently entered the debate. This approach rejects stereotypes of 'developing' and 'developed' economies and proposes a cultural approach instead. Mowlana's communication approach attempts so supersede the concept of modernity by looking at international communication and its national impact from a cultural point of view (Mowlana, 1993).

Globalization and the Global Sphere of Mediation: Dialectic in the Global Discourse

Despite debates about modern and postmodern globalization processes, debates about democratic achievements, economic market expansion and political risks, the – in view of communication theory – interesting paradigm change was the assumed dualism of globalism/localism, which has enterered the sociological discussion of globalization in the late eighties. The sociological debate of globalization has influenced the discourse in communication theory.

The tremendeously influencial debate about this new idea of globalization was based on the assumption – as Roland Robertson phrased it – that the world 'moved' from being merely 'in itself' to the problem of its possibly being 'for itself' (Robertson, 1990: 23). This means, in Robertson's view, a need for 'systematic comprehension of the macro-structuralisation of world order', which is 'essential to the viability of any form of contemporary theory and that such comprehension must involve analytical separation of the factors which have facilitated the shift towards a single world' (Robertson, 1990:22). While modernization is constructed along state/nation lines, globalization involves the new structures of nation-state in a globalization process and also extra-societal worldwide communities in the format of a globalized public sphere. It was the issue of a relativistic modern (see Mowlana, 1993), postmodern or late modern globalization process, in which world citizenry exist in parallel with strong 'tribal' collectivities. It is in Barber's (1994) terms the parallelism of "McWorld" and "Jihad." This parallelism has implications on nation-state communication spheres (i.e. cultural protectionism) and for extra-societal worldwide communities, on issues of cultural intertextuality (Wilson and Dissanayake, 1996), on the redefinition of the nation as a 'local' entity in the empire of cultural universalism (Ferguson, 1993) and a relocation of languages and cultures. It can be argued that the public (and its opinion) is no longer a substantial element of the political system of one society but has entered into a more or less autonomous global public sphere, a global sphere of mediation, which can be considered not as a space between the 'public' and the state but between the state and an extra-societal global 'imagined' community. It is a new global dialectic not in Hegel's terms between private and public spheres, which gave shape to democracy concepts of the emerging middle classes in Europe in the 19th century, but between the societal and extrasocietal communication sphere, giving shape to the concept of 'Being in the World' of a world citizenship or – in its totality of a 'global civil society'.

It was the advancement and diversification of satellite technology, from the 'Early Bird' to DBS and unlimited bandwidth capacities, which provided the architecture for new programming strategies, targeting not *inter*-national but a diffuse *trans*-national audience – along special interest channels. This development had a tremendous influence in a variety of world regions on the national/statist public sphere by extending political news and information beyond national borders. The influence of CNN, which had internationally the role of a global authority throughout the nineties of the 20th century, has been widely underestimated! The Internet, as an icon of a globalized media world, with around 250 million people (of which 130 Million live in the USA, 49 Million in Europe) globally 'being online' seems to finally unfold the totality of the global sphere of mediation. It is the push-pull (Internet) technology – the paradigm change from (mass- or narrow-) distribution to network technology, which finally shifts the global/local dualism to the one of universalism/particularism, without reference to local authenticity and has formatted a new global communication. These global processes, in which knowledge, values and ethics, aesthetics, lifestyles are exchanged, are becoming autonomous, a 'third culture', a "generative frame of unity within which diversity can take place" (Featherstone, 1990:2).

Whereas the modern public sphere spaces (see Habermas, 1992) required citizens, forming 'rational' political opinions, today's global sphere of mediation is a multi-discursive political space. It is a sphere of mediation without center nor periphery, the agenda setting, contexts are shaped – mediated – by autonomous operations, not only by big news authorities, such as CNN, but also by drudge.com, yahoo, chatrooms and 'authentic' reports.

It can be argued, that fantasies and 'ideas' of 'the world' as a somehow common place have existed since Plato described in his Timaeus the history of the world by the affiliation of the four elements to each other, since Aristotle defined the 'world state', since Francis Bacon distinguished between different world concepts 'globus terrestris,' and 'globus intellectualis'. It was the idea of a 'world society' as a universe of nature and reasoning, a global arena for public debate during the Enlightenment which has inaugurated modernity. Postmodern thinkers replaced 'reasoning' by 'simulation' and Hegel's term of 'World Spirit' (Weltgeist) by an idea of 'instant' truth, created by the media and conveying the image of a shrinking world (Virilio, 1989) in a permanent presence (Virilio, 1999). The moon landing, broadcast 'live' worldwide, was indeed a large step for mankind: simply because for the first time Planet Earth was seen as a common habitat, without borders, a blue planet of landmasses and oceans. The idea of the 'world' seemed to have switched from a metaphysical concept into a material reality, a new relativity within a global whole and triggered, in conjunction with new international political and economical alliances, a debate about the macro-structuralisation of "Globalization".

In such a global environment, 'the international information order' conventional patterns of international communication – of North/South, developing and developed, central and peripheral nations – are becoming obsolete. International communication theory, modeled in the age of modernization (mainly around push technologies) reveals the imbalance in global media images and portray-als, analyses media imperialism of global conglomerates, investigates cultural effects of 'main-streaming' through internationally transmitted media produc-tions in terms of cultivation, analyses the varying role played by news media in times of international crisis. Only a few, very recent approaches in cultural studies and sociology, interpret global news flow by a new globalized perspec-tive (Boyd-Barrett and Rantanen, 1998 and Ginnecken, 1997). It is not the glo-balization of news flow, of converging media and the reformatting of programs to 'content,' which transforms the global communication infrastructure: content itself becomes the independent variable in a (global) "Cybersociety" (Jones, 1998), subsequently replacing the 'local' material community. However, what seems widely unexplored and neglected in communication theory is a new terminology, which interprets arising new communication segments within the global context of inter-relating communication structures and options.

International communication theory should discuss a methodology for the understanding of 'particular' interpretations, meanings, relevances of the global public sphere, to detect the specifics of the dialectic in the widening communi-cation sphere between the societal and extra-societal communication space. I would like to give two examples, which might serve as illustrations for such a discussion. These examples represent two models for dialectic processes in the context of universal and particular issues in the global sphere of mediation.

CNN World Report
– Particular/Universal Issues in the Global Discourse

CNN's World Report was launched in 1987 and is a globally unique news pro-gram. It is made up of reports produced from broadcasting companies around the world. CNN broadcasts all sent-in programs unedited and 'uncensored.' The initial idea was to develop a news program, in which many voices from around the world could be heard. "World Report" is therefore an interesting open global platform, a microcosm of the global 'public' sphere, initated by the push me-dium TV. For developing nations, the programme offers the chance to present their points of view on international political and social issues or present topics which are not on the gate keeped agenda of the big news agencies. Many critics argue, that CNN as a U.S. based commercial company use common news for-mats in which contributions have to be submitted and the idea of a global diversity is just illusionary. However, I claim that this program model is a unique and interesting news strategy, which bears the chance to open the otherwise nationally dominated political discourse internationally.

In my content analysis of 397 reports (Volkmer, 1999), I found that this program is used in crisis regions (Cyprus) not only as a global newscast but also as a communication platform in order to communicate bilaterally with the op-posing party (such as Antenna TV Greece and TRT Turkey). "World Report" is also used as a propaganda forum for totalitaristic nations, bringing press confer-

71

ences of national affairs to a global audience (Cuba, China). It is used as a marketing medium, to delete stereotypes and a communication tool between expatriates and their home countries. My study also revealed, that national, regional, international, public, state-owned, commercial and private broadcasters use CNNWR as a carrier program to deliver their reports to 'the world' from all world regions. The majority of topics cover political, economic or military issues, followed by International Aid, Human Rights, liberation, agriculture/environment, culture and education.

"World Report" also reveals new international journalism: interactive journalism, a type which reacts to another news report on the same issue, clearly biased, not objective, reciprocal journalism, reports are transmitted back into countries of origin and avoid censorship by airing a topic via CNNWR than via own broadcasting station, showcase journalism, presentation and marketing of regional cultures. Players in this microcosm are: news organizations of global political organizations (UN; UNESCO TV), of regional and continental political organizations, of partisan political organizations (then PLO TV, Afghan Media Center, South Africa Now), publicly funded national broadcasters, political and private broadcasters, such as TGRT, a Turkish television channel that is owned by Türkye, a Turkish right-wing fundamentalist newspaper, news organizations that operate on the agency level, local broadcasters.

Internet: Particular Issues in a Universally Accessible Public Sphere

Whereas CNN's "World Report" model might serve as an illustration for one example of the global sphere of mediation in the selfreferenced medium of satellite television of the late eigthies, the Internet opens the view for new developments. A closer analysis of the different world regions in their Internet use (and their idea of a global public sphere) is important. A global analysis of the global diversity of the relevance of the Internet in different media cultures is another example of attempting to understand the specific use of the global public sphere in various world regions. The determination of a specific profile helps to understand different attitudes and perceptions of this global sphere and the medium of the Internet. I propose to characterize these environments in light of overall media structures in order to determine specific Internet profiles within the overall media setting. Based on this model, at least four basic environments can be identified, which reveal a different approach to this technology as well as to its 'globality'.

Spillover environment

This environment can be identified by a low level of technical infrastructure. It is located within or on the border of relay satellite footprints of major media environments. The term "spillover" relates to this relay function of major satellites, to 'footprint' a center and a spillover zone. Spillover zones are many African regions (spillover from European footprints), Asian and South American territories, also Yukon Territory in Alaska. Internationalization in Africa is tied to overspill communication with Europe and the US.

The profile of Internet use in spillover environments can be defined as community and professional communication. The Internet can be used in remote regions to facilitate community-wide communication that would be impossible otherwise. Of the 54 African countries, 53 have Internet access at least in the capital cities and of these only a minority has full Internet connectivity (at the end of 1996, only 11 countries had Internet access). It is estimated that each computer serves around three users. Although Internet penetration is low on the African continent, with around 2 Million users (around 3 per 1000 inhabitants), the Internet has the potential to bridge gaps within shortcomings of communication systems (telecommunication: long distance calls).

There are various levels of community-wide communication via the Internet in Africa, where – in many regions – email is the major segment of Internet service. Africa Online, a major commercially operating ISP (besides public telecom providers) founded by former African MIT students, which provides Internet access in the southern part of the continent, has a strong regional emphasis. This approach is evident in topics such as "news and information", "Health," "kids", "Women" and "business and education," which list a variety of African and regional headlines, and links to information related to Africa, located in other parts of the world (such as African Studies Site of University of Pennsylvania). Database oriented sites provide information about the region for tourists and entrepreneurs.

The Internet also improves the communication infrastructure for journalists, MISANET, an Internet project for journalists improves the flow of information among newspapers in the region, where international news used to come almost exclusively from Reuters, the South African Press Agency and Associated Press. Due to bandwidth problems a variety of African sites are hosted on computers, located in the US and Europe. Low-cost satellites are used, particularly in the southern part of Africa, to overcome these problems and carry content across vast distances. African based search engines have been established to increase local content, such as af.orientation.com and www.woyaa!.com, which seems to copy yahoo's service.

State-regulated, limited international communication environment

This model includes media environments, where governments practice censorship over domestic news media, but minimal control over international (commercial) programming. China is an example for this environment model. Given the fact that there are only around 9 Million Internet users in a population of 1,2 billion, the rate of growth of the Internet is the highest in Asia (Frankfurter Allgemeine Zeitung, May, 2, 2000).The Chinese government carefully monitors websites in Chinese and less so English language sites. This political strategy is already reflected in the topography of Chines websites: Of 9114 sites, dealing with China, the majority of 6156 represent "provinces and regions" and 1869 cover the topical section "business and economy." Only 73 are related to "news and media", critical political issues, however, are covered by international organizations (ngo's), such as www.actionworkds.org.

For this reason, an important issue in this environment is 'reciprocal' communication. In such a restricted context, where access to communication infrastructure is extremely limited and closely monitored, web sites that allow true interactivity and information exchange have been set up outside the region, for instance in the USA and Hong Kong, where the Information Center for Democracy and Human Rights is located. Because the Internet's program flow is global, websites dealing with domestic Chinese issues (in Tibet) are located anywhere. One of these sites, the Digital Freedom Network, publishes the writings of Chinese political prisoners and monitors human rights abuse not only in China but also in Burma and Bangladesh. Another type of reciprocal communication is the use of the Internet by political minorities or opposition groups within a restricted media environment (Singapore, Malaysia).

Post communist transition environment

This environment can be characterized by the fact that the "push"-mass media, such as Television are undergoing the transition from communism towards democracy, which requires a transformation of journalistic approaches. Ideas of the 'public sphere' are not clearly defined and the role of media in a democratic society seems to be ambiguous. Furthermore, this environment can be characterized by an ill-defined legal situation, a still vivid history of socialist media policy and a commercial market in which international and domestic broadcasters exist alongside various unlicensed local and regional stations (Russia and former USSR states). The Internet seems to be used on the side of traditional media as an additional outlet (TASS, Interfax) as well as a new approach to reach a world community (see for example, www.Allnews.ru and www.RussiaToday.ru almost an equivalent of USA Today). New, more critical approaches, such as Argumenty i Facty, a glasnost product, exercise new, more critical journalistic styles in the tradtion of a democratic public sphere.

Pluralist environment

This environment can be characterized by only basic media regulation. Media are less regarded as cultural goods, but commercial enterprises. Due to this approach, the Internet (and related technologies) are commercially exploited and – by the same token – offer a high degree of freedom of information flow. The USA is one example for this environment. The technologically available "superhighway" has initiated a new space for interaction and information as well as commerce. This environment also provides information space for 'reciprocal' political communication as described above.

Conclusion

Whereas CNN's "World Report" represents a self referential sphere of mediation, where the global dialectic discourse is included into the strategies of a television program model, the Internet reveals, even on the level of the infrastructure of different Internet environments, the dialectic of a variety of different societal public spheres which 'mediate' in this new global communication platform.

The meaning of globalization and of global communication is not homogenous, but different in various world regions. As system theorists assert, growing density and complexity of communication are the sign of a growing 'world community.' To understand the new global sphere, its autonomy, independency and ist 'mediation' will support the transition into a world community in the 21st century.

References

Barber, Benjamin R. (1994) "Zwischen Dschihad und McWorld", *Die Zeit*, no.42, p. 64.

Boyd-Barrett, Oliver & Rantanen, Terhi (1998) *The Globalization of News*. London, Newbury Park, New Delhi: Sage.

Featherstone, Mike (1990) "Global Culture: An Introduction", in: Featherstone, Mike (ed.) *Global Culture. Nationalism, Globalization and Modernity*. London, Newbury Park, New Delhi: Sage.

Ferguson, Marjorie (1993) "Media, Markets, and Identities: Reflections on the Global-Local Dialectic", *Canadian Journal of Communication*.

Gerbner, George & Gross, Larry (1976) "Living With Television: The Violence Profile", *Journal of Communication*, vol.26, no.2, pp. 178-201.

Ginnecken, Jaap van (1997) *Understanding Global News*. London, Newbury Park, New Delhi: Sage.

Habermas, Jürgen (1992) *The Structural Transformation of the Public Sphere*. Cambridge, Ma, London: MIT Press.

Höhne, Hansjoachim (1977) *Die Geschichte der Nachricht und ihrer Verbreiter*. Baden-Baden (Germany): Nomos Verlagsgesellschaft.

Jones, Steve (1998) *Cybersociety 2.0*. London, Newbury Park, New Delhi: Sage.

Kato, Hidetoshi (1976) "Global Instantaneousness and Instant Globalism – the Significance of Popular Culture in Developing Countries", in: Schramm, Wilbur & Lerner, Daniel (eds.) *Communication and Change. The Last Ten Years – and the Next*. Honolulu, Hawaii, East-West Centre, pp. 253-258.

Morgan, Michael (1990) "International Cultivation Analysis", in Morgan, Michael et al. (eds.) *Cultivation Analysis*. London, New Delhi: Sage, pp. 225-247.

Mowlana, Hamid (1993) "The New Global Order and Cultural Ecology", *Media, Culture and Society*, no.15, pp. 9-27.

Lerner, Daniel (1958) *The Passing of Traditional Society. Modernizing the Middle East*. Glencoe, Ill: The Free Press.

Robertson, Roland (1990) "Mapping the Global Condition: Globalization as the Central Concept", in Featherstone, Mike (ed.) *Global Culture. Nationalism, Globalization and Modernity*. London, Newbury Park, New Delhi: Sage, pp. 15-30.

Rogers, Everett M. (1969) *Modernizing Among Peasants: The Impact of Communication*. New York: Holt, Rinehart and Winston.

Schiller, Herbert I. (1979) "Transnational Media and National Development", in Nordenstreng, Kaarle & Schiller, Herbert I. (eds.) *National Sovereignty and International Communication*, Norwood, N.J: Ablex Publishing Corporation, pp. 21-32.

Servaes, Jan (1983) *Communication and Development: Some Theoretical Remarks*. Leuven: Ablex Publishing Corporation.

Stephens, Mitchell (1988) *History of News. From the Drum to the Satellite*. New York: Viking.

Virilio, Paul (1989) *Der negative Horizont: Bewegung-Geschwindigkeit-Beschleunigung*. München.

Virilio, Paul (1999) *Polar Inertia*. London, Newbury Park, New Delhi: Sage.

Volkmer, Ingrid (1999) *News in the Global Sphere. A Study of CNN and Its Impact on Global Communication*. Luton: University of Luton Press.

Wilson, Rob & Dissanayake (eds.) (1996) *Global/Local. Cultural Production and The Transnational Imaginary*. Durham/London: Duke University Press.

Media Imperialism Revisited
The Global Public Sphere and the News Agency Agenda

Chris A. Paterson

Introduction

This article describes the dominant role of international news agencies in the provision of news in cyberspace. I begin with an examination of the relationships between institutional actors in the cyberspace political economy, and then attempt to demonstrate an extreme concentration of control over international news on the Internet and how such concentration contradicts many common assumptions about Internet journalism and the democratic potential of new media.

To start from an economic perspective, here I treat Internet based journalism as a transactional relationship between news producers and news consumers which takes place through electronic networks. In aggregate, such relationships of information exchange form a subset of the broad field of electronic commerce (e-commerce). For this discussion, I term this subset "e-journalism". E-journalism depends upon many of the same processes and channels of networked communication as do other sectors of e-commerce, but given the unique role of journalism in social relations and the formation of public consciousness (i.e. Berger and Luckman, 1966), it must be addressed as a special case.

It is argued here that manifestations of convergence have resulted in an e-journalism sector in which the production of public affairs information is more highly concentrated than it already was, and in which information delivery is becoming increasingly concentrated. Such trends indicate a Global Information Infrastructure (GII), which contrary to popular dogma, is profoundly undemocratic and incapable of challenging existing macro-level inequalities in human relations. Such an hypothesis is clearly at odds with popular perceptions of the Internet as a pluralist and democratizing environment, a mythology reviewed thoroughly by Aufderheide (1998).

In their analysis of Internet commerce, Sarkar, et al. (1999) propose that contrary to predictions that reduced transactional costs afforded by electronic networks will lead to direct consumer-producer links which bypass intermediary information processors (termed "disintermeditation"), Internet growth is reinforcing the strength of traditional intermediaries and resulting in the development of new intermediaries (which they label "Cybermediaries"). These authors argue that since many intermediary functions in e-commerce cannot be easily assumed by producers, and that the economies of scale afforded by GII often favor the intermediary over the producer, the rumors of the death of the intermediary are greatly exaggerated.

Economic analysis of network structures, as these authors undertake in regard to Internet commerce broadly, has not commonly been applied specifically to the provision of journalism on the Internet. This article does so, with specific attention to the structures of international news provision currently dominating the world of cyber-journalism.

Sarkar, et al, employ transactional cost theory (TCT) to articulate the decision process whereby firms either "make or buy" an intermediary function. In this case, this is the choice of vertically integrated production and distribution processes internal to the organisation, or "the use of external market agents for carrying out activities that constitute its value system". Here in the case of e-journalism, the transactions are between news producers, intermediary distributors (who are adders of content value), and news consumers.

I submit that through monopolistic control of international news production, effective brand marketing, efficient use of economies of scale in news production, and useful alliances in both news gathering and on-line distribution, news agencies play a dominant and generally unacknowledged role in determining the vast majority of international news in cyberspace.

Analysis of journalistic systems in cyberspace remains fairly rare, and the effects of convergence on journalism still poorly explained. Newhagen and Levy (1998) write, "of such moments of convergence, the meaning of basic concepts, which might have seemed obvious to an earlier generation, demand re-examination and explication". In so doing, these authors deem news to be "survival enhancing information", to be compressed into data by news providers, and transmitted via communications networks to the mass audience. But the systems of transmission, which favor certain actors over others, are not well described in this model.

Using the categories of network-based intermediaries in electronic commerce as defined by Sarker, et al (1995), and others, we can delineate the various forms of e-journalism which are currently common. Most of the major (that is, most popular) e-journalism sites can be grouped into the four basic categories shown below.

In *table 1*, the major type of on-line news provider is the gateway or portal site, which usually offers a range of navigation and search services, and a link to a news section under their control. Here, more general, all purpose portals like *Yahoo* are distinguished from those more fully dedicated to searching, like *Infoseek*. For both types, international news content is typically from a single secondary producer like Reuters news agency. That is, news content is not originally created for the site.

Table 1.

Type	Main Service Provided	Examples	Typical News Content
gateways/portals	(general directories)	Yahoo	a single secondary producer
	(search services)	Infoseek	
malls	group producers	Cybereditions	variety of secondary producers
publishers	offer content	CNN	mixture of original and secondary
push services	continuous delivery	BBC	secondary producers

Malls group producers together. As an on-line shopping mall might group clothing producers, an on-line journalism mall groups a variety of news content producers, usually according to some particular notion of quality or in conjunction with some ancillary service, such as searching of selected news content (www.newstrawler.com or cybereditions.com are examples). These offer users a variety of secondary content.

Internet content publishers produce their own content, but as demonstrated below, usually mix it with a great deal of content from secondary producers. Push services – normally provided by major e-journalism portals or publishers – deliver a continuous stream of tailored news content, usually from major news producers, directly to computer screens throughout the day. The information provided, however, rarely comes from news providers other than the Associated Press or Reuters, with the exception of major broadcast and newspaper run services, which mix original with agency content. The *BBC Online's* "News Ticker" is one such service. (Sarker, et al, define a variety of other forms of cybermediary, such as those providing consulting services to e-commerce firms, which are less relevant to this analysis of e-journalism.)

As put in a recent analysis by the BBC, the "World Wide Web, widely thought of as an endless myriad of choice, appears to be shrinking" (BBC On-line, 1999). That is, *fewer* major news providers are informing *more* people and (the BBC fails to note) doing so from *fewer* sources. Global multi-media information conglomerates Associated Press and Reuters dominate Internet news in mostly inconspicuous ways. To demonstrate this phenomenon, I narrow the focus now to the intersection of news agency political economy and cyberspace information exchange.

News in Cyberspace

Industry research continues to show that news consumers are making less use of television and more use of the Internet. One recent survey reports that 76% of US news consumers still "turn to broadcast or cable TV for information on breaking news", but that 12% go to the Internet, 9% to the radio, and 2% wait for the next edition of their newspaper (NUA Internet Surveys, 1998).

Some industry research contradicts the hypothesis of this article: that e-journalism is largely unoriginal and minimally relevant. A US survey recently found major newspaper and magazine sites provided substantially more original content in 1998 than they had in previous years, and reported that more than half of US newspapers have merged their print and on-line newsrooms (Ross and Middleberg, 1999). Newspapers are reported to be increasingly breaking new stories on-line rather than waiting for the next edition, as has been the tradition from the outset of Internet journalism (Hanson, 1997). Based upon their survey, Ross and Middleberg declare "1998 marks a historic moment – news organizations have now clearly broken away from their tendency to use on-line technology (Web sites usually, but not always) as a distribution device more than as a new medium".

There is little evidence of such a trend amongst broadcaster run sites, however, and Burden (1999) finds in a recent study of the BBC On-Line newsroom that content remains closely tied to broadcast output and that only minimal use is made of the interactive capabilities of the Internet medium. Tremayne (1997) found indications of interactivity in many major sites, but does not indicate any are substantial. Despite recent evidence that only the major sites do well, more and more forms of e-journalism constantly come on line. Major news sites continue to experience astronomical growth. According to the European Journalism Centre (1998), CNN now reaches more people over the Internet than through broadcasting. A CNN Interactive news producer explained her view of the site's popularity, observing that unlike print or television media, "we don't have space problems with Interactive ... we can keep going deeper and deeper and deeper" (Yancey, 1997).

Popular Internet news sites typically become immensely more so when a single news event is receiving saturation coverage from all media. Such was the case in the US in April, 1999, when following the Colorado High School shootings Internet news sites saw as much as a 70% increase in traffic (in the case of the AP.org) (Media Metrix,1999).

Among Internet news consumers, national and international news is preferred over local content. An industry study reports that 61% of Internet users read national and international news on-line, while just 26% do so for local news (NUA, 1998). Indeed, a July, 1999, industry survey in the US indicated that news consumers are unsatisfied with the quality of local news available on the Internet, and that users prefer to get their national and international news from major news sites rather than their local newspaper (Strupp, 1999).

And in what may be an even more telling trend, an industry research group, MediaMetrix, has recently reported that although the number of published websites continues to rise astronomically, web users are actually spending more of their time with fewer sites. Most of these are the major news/gateway sites. The company reports that US web users "now spend almost 20% of their time on the Web visiting only the top 10 sites", down from 16% one year earlier. Further, "the amount of time spent at the top 50 and 100 sites has risen even more since 1998" (BBC On-line, 1999). The top nine web sites identified were:

1) Yahoo
2) AOL
3) MSN
4) Geocities
5) Netscape
6) GO
7) Microsoft
8) Lycos
9) Excite

While this line-up of major sites is likely to have changed by the time you read this, closer examination of these top cybermediaries begins to evidence the news source concentration alluded to at the outset of this article. When inspected for this research, the *AOL* (America On-Line) site provided only unedited Associated Press stories for international news, and only unedited Reuters stories for US domestic news. *Geocities* is geared to supporting home web page developers, but after being taken over by *Yahoo*, it provides only the Reuters news which *Yahoo* offers. The popular *GO* Network portal site offers mostly unedited international news from Reuters, with some stories by ABC news mixed in. However, as noted below, ABC's on-line stories appear to be mostly minimally edited AP and Reuters stories. Such curious alliances as this, by which *GO* offers ABC, which offers barely reworked news wires, evidences the complex layers of mediation in e-journalism, especially in regard to international news provision. The processes of information concentration resulting from structural convergence are evidenced by the links between Microsoft products and General Electric (NBC) produced news, as well as other cases.

Both the *Lycos* and the *Excite* portal websites appear to offer only Reuters international stories, provided in essentially the same format and order as the Reuters stories provided by *Yahoo*. In the UK, the BBC offers one of the most popular news sites with BBC On-line, but as shown below, despite its extensive resources, much of its international content is news agency provided. It is therefore evident that unlike the fading – but still kicking phenomena of public service broadcasting – public service web-casting, especially in the arena of international news – has almost *no* popular foothold, and where it does exist, its content remains substantially commercially determined.

Web users are fed the limited agency diet of international news in other ways as well. One way is the "push" technology described earlier. Additionally, Yahoo and other services offer an email alert service, which will send subscribers – at no cost – email with news stories (presumably by the main Yahoo provider, Reuters) on selected topics of interest. Such services are increasingly migrating to wireless communications services, with a number of new alliances between news content providers and cellular telephone companies. These are the latest manifestations of "create your own newspaper" technologies which encourage the news audience to consume only the type of news stories which most gratify them.

Your computer may also direct you to news agency content with little encouragement on your part. Netscape.com, which is the portal site directly linked to the most popular browser software, offers a news menu of mostly Reuters international stories, with some Associated Press stories. Microsoft's portal site, of course, links news junkies directly to MSNBC, which Microsoft co-owns with General Electric. Microsoft faces legal action in the US and Europe for integrating its Explorer browser and various direct links to Microsoft websites into its Windows operating systems. Their news service is *MSNBC*, which provides international stories, which – unless they happen near one of the few international NBC bureaus – will be written almost entirely by Reuters and the Associated Press (demonstrated below). The popular web sites operated directly by Reuters and by Associated Press, of course, provide exclusively the content generated by each company.

News Agencies and Cyberspace

Through still poorly understood layers of mediation, the news product and news perspectives of major wire services are reproduced directly and indirectly in the web content of cyber-news providers, often despite claims of editorial independence by the major cyber-intermediaries of e-journalism. The process of on-line news production has received little close examination through comprehensive ethnographic research in newsrooms. It is known that journalists specializing in the on-line distribution of their news product have had to develop numerous strategies to adapt to this new form of journalism.

Some researchers have argued that new forms of highly interactive journalism are emerging (i.e. Fedlin, 1997), but the evidence offered here suggests that the dominant Internet news sites do little more than redistribute the work of other – mostly news agency – journalists, with a minimum of editing or re-interpretation. To date, only a few small studies have actually detailed the news production environment of on-line journalists, and in these cases, they have depended more on survey and interview questions than newsroom observation (see, for example, Brill, 1997; Burden, 1999). The extensive dialogue about on-line journalism and the information content of cyberspace cannot be fully informed until substantial ethnographic analyses of on-line news production have been undertaken (also see Christopher, 1998) .

There is some indication that journalism as a whole is coming to depend more and more on e-journalism for ideas and source material, and that the Internet sources preferred by journalists are the same major ones dependent on news agency content. For example, Ross and Middleberg (1999) found that journalists heavily use the major web portal sites both to navigate the web and to read news, and the majority of these prefer the Reuters-dependent Yahoo news site.

Dependence on news agency content is not always the result of a desire for perceived high content quality at little cost, but is also a function of brand association. Websites seek to draw users through association with well-known brands, especially those with strong positive associations for the user. Dependence on AP or Reuters provides these, for each is (at the time of this writing) a vaguely known brand name with no negative associations in the public mind, for the mass audience has little direct experience with them which could create such associations. Professional journalists, on the other hand, are quick to recite the many pros and cons of each. It is also important for populist web sites to be seen by their users as reliable providers of what is widely regarded as the important news of the day, and the only way to demonstrate that to the mass audience is to provide the same news other major media are providing. As put by Dillinger (1995), here in reference to US commercial television,

> ... competition is the driving force behind the structuring of news frameworks. If one commercial news program or network devises a commercially or politically successful frame for a story, competitors are obliged to pick up the frame and continue with the story. To reinterpret an existing frame would be running the risk of contradicting media-established "truth," while frames tend to filter back to re-establish and re-define reality.

Industry consultants are pressuring news providers to reduce the depth of news analysis they provide on-line, and instead to use editorial resources to "develop stories around headline stories" (presumably, those selected by wire services) (NUA, 1998). This advice is based on usage data indicating that, on average, just ten minutes is spent by consumers in each on-line news consuming session (ibid).

Analysis of news agencies remains sparse, and the news agency production process poorly understood. To date, this author's research remains the only larger ethnographic study of news agencies, although its focus is only the television side of these institutions. There have been several smaller ethnographic projects and important works on agencies employing other methodologies (Hjarvard, 1995; Read, 1992; Boyd-Barrett and Thussu, 1992; Fenby, 1986; Boyd-Barrett, 1980). I have described elsewhere, as have Boyd-Barrett and others, how increasing concentration of control over the global wholesale news system have made the major news agencies more influential than they have ever been (Paterson 1998, 1996; Boyd-Barrett 1998).

Golding and Elliott (1979, 210), argue that through what they term its "invariable neglect" of the power relationships between people, nations, and cultures, that news does provides a distinctive kind of world view. In so doing news will "reinforce scepticism about ... divergent, dissident or deviant beliefs." (op cit. 211). Similar arguments have been advanced regarding U.S. media by Tuchman (1978), Gans (1980), Altschull (1984), and Schudson (1992). News agencies, in their desire to please all of their clients, all of the time, must work even harder than their client journalists to create the appearance of objectivity and neutrality. In so doing, they manufacture an ideologically distinctive and homogeneous view of the world. News agency stories are inherently, and especially, ideological products, which, through their pervasiveness, are all the more influential than the standard news product of a newspaper or broad-caster.

But the news agency role is crucial for additional reasons. News agencies set the agenda for what international stories other media choose to carry. This is done through the choice of stories they distribute to clients, the amount of visuals provided (moving for TV, still for newspapers and magazines, and both for webcasters), and in the case of agency provided TV pictures, the nature and amount of accompanying audio and textual information provided with the video. In television, broadcasters write their stories around the video these organisations offer, and if they are not offered video images, they generally do not report, or at least, will minimize, an international story. Various studies of television newsrooms have reported that the availability of visual images is an important factor in determining whether a foreign news story is included in a newscast (Cohen et al., 1996; Helland, 1995; Rodriguez, 1996; Molina, 1990; Schlesinger, 1987; Golding and Elliott, 1979).

Global and regional news agencies are crucial due to the potentially substantial agenda-setting influence on other media, but now even more crucial since they so effectively bypass or control the intermediary processors of news in cyberspace enabling them to directly reach – for the first time – a large portion of the mass news audience (and potentially cultivate a new audience uninterested in traditional media).

News agencies have historically sought to minimize their public exposure, for their success had previously rested largely with their ability to make news audiences believe that their local media outlet – not an international agency – has brought them the news of the world. But now agencies depend on the popular appeal of their brand names for audience loyalty in cyberspace, and so market their names aggressively. The major wire services were ideally positioned to capitalise on both the technological and structural aspects of convergence. Each had a 150 year history – more or less – of continuously generating a great deal of textual content for delivery over wired networks. Digital and structural convergence now permits them to provide their product to a mass audience.

It is a presumption of this chapter that a diversity of information is a necessary prerequisite of democracy and a desirable goal, so it is not necessary to specifically indicate fault with the news content provided by the wire services. This is to argue, in effect, that the central weakness of the international wire services is their success – their ubiquity is the problem.

Former APTN chief executive Stephen Claypoole told me (in Paterson, 1996) that the, "Associated Press believes that its future in the next century depends on the ability to provide all the components of multi-media..." With Reuters, AP has been tremendously successful in doing so, and has skillfully exploited every new production and delivery option afforded by digital convergence. The importance of the Internet to Reuters is evidenced by its recent announcement that it would be creating a position of web strategist at the corporate board level, and putting the head of their highly profitable Trading Systems Division in that post (Reuters, 1999).

But such success permits news agencies to monopolize a sector of the economy in a manner causing not only economic harm, as monopolies normally do, but social harm, for a limited public diet of international news affects the ability of societies to function democratically and to understand one another. It is important to note, however, that the public diet of international news is not only limited by such concentration quantitatively, but qualitatively in many ways.

The limited diet of international news provided mostly by a few organizations suggests that e-journalism follows a distribution model more closely akin to broadcasting than other aspects of cyberspace. That is, in the provision of international news on-line, a few large organizations generate and broadcast – with essentially no feedback loop – most of the content for most of the audience. Further, it is a very limited and homogenous content dictated by the ideological, structural, and cultural nature of these organizations.

It is a view of the world as seen mostly through London, where international news providers are centered (Clarke, 1995). London is the home of Reuters, and despite on again, off again attempts to decentralize, their London headquarters continues to closely control news selection and provides much content and most editorial control for most of the world. For Associated Press, content is mostly shaped from New York, with considerable influence from the London bureau of the wire service and the London headquarters of the corporation's television arm, APTN.

It makes good economic sense that the two leading news agencies should dominate international news delivery in cyberspace, for as in any open and unregulated market, the strongest producers with the lowest unit costs will succeed, and usually, crush competition. Such is the case for the major wire services, which each have a century and a half of experience in developing production processes which generate massive amounts of news. Digital technologies have made all aspects on news agency production more efficient, and their convergence has permitted easy access into new markets through the creation of news products tailored to new media, but built from the same agency words and pictures upon which traditional media have long depended.

News agencies take advantage of structural convergence within the information industries primarily through the formation of strategic alliances that increase their news gathering reach and their news distribution reach. Such alliances could allow a picture of a remote plane crash to be moved in a matter of minutes through the equipment of a local, allied news organisation to some minimal processing in London (or another agency centre) and on to the web pages of an allied Internet portal site and into the news junkies' gaze.

A news agency can digitize and compress textual descriptions, still pictures, video, and sound at the scene of a news event and transmit these to their headquarters potentially simultaneously via the same laptop computer and satellite telephone. But such rapid processing of images or words is also dependent upon technical convergence, which permits simple digital processing and transmission of words and images.

Here, through processes of digital convergence and industrial alliances, news is gathered in various forms but its various textual, visual, and aural components may typically be transmitted digitally to a central newsroom (normally in London) for processing and distribution. There, different news agency departments confer on the construction of the news and share each of these elements in the construction of stories for various audiences. Finally, the news consumer in cyberspace is reached through any of several processes of mediation, simplified by the convergence of digital distribution mechanisms.

At the level of news distribution, the primary Cybermediaries in e-journalism take two forms: on-line media which consist of popular sites relaying agency content to audiences, and content producing on-line media, which tends to combine original content with agency content. The latter category includes mostly traditional media like the BBC or the New York Times or news companies which began on the web (*Nando Times* is the best known example). Since much of the web content of these organizations is barely reconstructed agency material (mostly in the case of the former), the agencies reach a large *secondary* audience as part of the "original" content of these services.

Since agencies also serve their traditional clients like newspapers and television broadcasters, and much of the content designed for those media is simply transferred to the WWW, the agencies reach an additional *secondary* on-line audience through these traditional media, serving in a cyber intermediary role.

Analysis of Content

The nature of news agency content has received relatively little scrutiny. Hjarvard (1995), Malik (1992), and Paterson (1996) have described television news agency and television news exchange content in some detail, while a few studies have examined the textual output of the wire services at the international (Schiff, 1996) and regional (Hagen, 1996) levels, and have looked at wire service coverage of specific events (Paterson, 1996; Giffard and Rivenburgh, 1998). Reuters and AP output has typically been found to address a quite limited range of news frames and deal with a highly proscribed range of news actors (Schiff, 1996). In a study for Fairness and Accuracy in Reporting (FAIR), Amster-Burton and Amster-Burton (1997) found "consistent official and male bias" in Reuters stories provided by Yahoo. They quote Yahoo as claiming that their Reuters content was then the "by far the most popular on-line news service".

Of 69 Reuters stories analyzed in a late 1996, week-long, sample, only 6% of news sources were women. Few other studies of gender bias in agency output are apparent, but in a study of television news agency output Paterson (1996) determined that where a main actor could be coded in internationally distributed television news agency stories, only 13% were female. And that statistic was intriguingly generated from stories appearing during the week of the 1995 United Nations Women's Conference. Mainstream news services, and agencies are the most mainstream, also privilege official sources, as Tuchman (1978) and many others have chronicled. Amster-Burton and Amster-Burton found that the Reuters content they analyzed was comprised of 91% official governmental and corporate sources. Such data is similar to that of numerous other content studies of major international news services.

To date social critics have taken note of news agency dominance in e-journalism, but detailed quantification is sparse. For instance, in a 1997 essay, Magid wrote, "Surf the Web long enough and you begin to notice some patterns. Wire services, like Reuters and Associated Press, sell the same stories to the Web sites of multiple publications. So do the major newspaper syndicates. Surf long enough and you're bound to find the same articles again and again... You can change the channel, but its a lot harder to change the story or even the perspective."

As Magid notes correctly, web sites buy agency content directly from the agencies, even if their parent company – like CNN Interactive's parent Turner Broadcasting – are also agency clients. So while there is some indication that broadcast and newspaper web sites do recycle a great deal of traditional media content from their sister organisation in cyberspace, they also draw directly and extensively from a full range of news agency material. The EJC (1998) reports that "at MSNBC ... the editors select the news, but do not write it", but adds somewhat questionably – at least according to the data offered here – that "the 400 MSNBC journalist repackage what 1200 NBC journalists produce".

Content analysis of on-line media remains rare, and there is to date little empirical evidence to test the hypothesis of news agency dependency offered here – apart from the very limited original analysis of content provided below and the other small studies reviewed. Evans (1998) thoroughly reviews the challenges of content analysis of cyber media. However, the mostly technology-based solutions proposed may not completely address the interpretive challenges to such research. Tremayne (1997) has analyzed the content of major news sites in some depth, but for the purposes of assessing interactivity and the extent of non-linear story telling.

News agency dependency in international stories is demonstrated in a pilot study I have conducted which might be tentatively titled "a day in the life of a news story"[1]. I have encountered no other studies such as this, although Magid (1997) does briefly analyze agency use across several major news web sites for a given story, finding, for example, that "ABC and CNN primarily used the same article from the Associated Press".

For this analysis, a single, relatively fast breaking, and relatively major (in the sense of gaining worldwide coverage) news story was selected. The story was the escalation of violent student rioting in Tehran on the morning of July 12, 1999. The available news covered the late hours of July 11 and preceding days. Over a period of just a few hours, the text of stories being published on-line by each of the following were copied and electronically stored: Reuters, Associated Press, Agence France Presse, Yahoo, MSNBC, ABC On-line, CNN Interactive, and BBC On-line. Other sources, which might typically be used by journalists on such a story, were also stored, including US State Department statements, the relevant output of the Iran News Agency, and the statements of a London-based Iranian dissident group.

Since there is normally a small amount of rewriting of news agency copy, we cannot precisely quantify news agency use. It was very easy to demonstrate, however, that these major services produced almost no original journalistic writing in this case, and published stories that were almost entirely barely-edited wire service material.[2] Of course, in the case of Yahoo and other major sites that just relay wire services stories, the material is identical to the wire service output.

For the purposes of this pilot study, results have been compressed just to the review of how CNN Interactive, MSNBC, and BBC On-line handled this news story. These data indicate nearly total news agency dependence, since for almost every paragraph of each sample of e-journalism service, there is an identical or nearly identical paragraph provided a few hours earlier by a wire service. In this sample (which omitted the end of longer stories) less than five paragraphs from the three services combined were *not* close duplications or exact duplications of wire service paragraphs. Of 38 nearly duplicated[3] wire paragraphs in this small sample, 37% (n=14) of such paragraphs are by Reuters, 58% (n=22) by Associated Press, and 5% (n=2) by AFP. The large dependency on AP in this sample is likely due to the fact that two of the three on-line services are US based, and US media typically make heavier use of AP than Reuters.[4] This case analysis is limited and does not benefit from random selection of news events, comparison of multiple stories, or longitudinal analysis of story coverage over an extended period, any of which would yield richer and more reliable data. However, there is also little reason to suppose this data to be atypical, and other small studies of on-line content (Amster-Burton and Amster-Burton, 1997; Magid, 1997) and studies of agency dependence by other media (Paterson, 2000) suggest such high levels of agency usage are not uncommon. Far more in-depth empirical research of this kind is clearly necessary, however.

Some other interesting news production procedures by on-line journalists can be seen in these examples. The choice of specific story frames by the on-line journalists is evident, as when MSNBC opens their story with mostly AP copy, but prefers the Reuters framing (main focus) of the story (in this case, marches in Tehran in defiance of government bans). Limited attempts to localize wire copy for an American audience can be seen, especially in the opening paragraphs of the CNN and MSNBC stories. MSNBC, for example, turns the news agency provided phrase "marched" into "took to the streets"; "hard-liners who have thwarted efforts to institute reforms" become "hard line clerics". CNN Inter-active editors can be seen making numerous attempts to sensationalize wire copy, but not paying great attention to the process. In their on-line story, they insert a sub-headline reading "Women reportedly assaulted", when none of the agency coverage, or any of the CNN story, make such a reference, and change the AP's reference "leading newspapers" to "leading medias" (sic).

Conclusion

From this research and the other research reviewed in this article, a number of misconceptions about e-journalism are suggested. Most crucially, while the multitude of on-line information providers evidence increasing "cybermediation" (Sarker, et al, 1995) of news, it is a fairly *limited* diet of news. But other trends are apparent. I submit that the limited evidence reviewed here suggests that E-journalism is generally *not*:

> *interactive* (Burden, 1999; Niekamp, 1997)
>> and by extension, not *more accountable* to audiences than traditional media (EJC, 1998)

> *diverse* or *pluralist* (BBC On-line, 1999)
>> and by extension, not *ideologically alternative* media

> *original* in content

> more *localized* or more *relevant* than traditional media

> and from examples studied for this research, seems rarely more *in-depth* or *non-linear*,
>> although researchers are finding it increasingly so (Ross and Middleberg, 1999; Tremayne, 1997)

Where is the threat in news agency dependency? Heavy public dependence on the limited news diet of the (essentially two) major agencies not only results in limiting and homogenizing public discourse on agency covered topics, but also limits the range of topics available for public consideration. CNN correspondent Ralph Begleiter suggested in a Freedom Forum seminar that the problem with Internet news is that "you can find what you want to know on it, but you miss the seeding of stories on subjects about which you may not know anything" (Hoge, 1997).

The apparent concentration of international news in the on-line environment is mirrored by similar, and closely related, tendencies in other, traditional media. Thus through a lack of any international regulatory controls, market forces of convergence have resulted in a comfortable situation for media conglomerates Reuters and Associated Press, but an uncomfortable one for the public at large.

If further empirical analyses support the hypothesis of agency dependency and high concentration of information provision, provided here, it begins to seem that the *diversity* of information offered by the Internet is a mythical aspect of information globalisation and convergence. Discourse on international events of consequence within the global public sphere – to the extent one exists – is substantially determined by the production practices and institutional priorities of two information services.

In the case of e-journalism, the political economy of convergence is distinctly undemocratic and anti-pluralist. If we accept that the public has a right to diverse information, we should accept that existing political economic structures violate those rights. Given preliminary evidence of such distinctly undemocratic trends, the concentration of influence over international news in the nominally *democratic* environment of cyberspace merits further investigation.

Notes

1. More comprehensive research by this author of wire content in Internet sites is now underway with hope of publication in 2001.
2. Texts were compared visually in a simple side-by-side comparison, where text from each of three major e-journalism sites was placed next to identical (or nearly identical) sentences in wire service copy. The author can furnish further detail of the study.
3. Nearly duplicated means a news agency sentence or paragraph is not reproduced verbatim, but is reproduced with only a few words altered.
4. Further research of this example will compare on-line stories to broadcast stories for news organisations which provide both, and will attempt to ascertain news agency content in additional major on-line sources, such as the web sites of major newspapers.

References

Altschull, J.H. (1984) *Agents of Power: The Role of News Media in Human Affairs*. New York: Longman.

Amster-Burton, L. & Amster-Burton, M. (1997) "New Media, Old Bias: Reuters On-line Provides Instant Access to Views of Establishment Men", *FAIR Extra!*, no. 25, January/February.

Aufderheide, P. (1998) "Niche-Market Culture, Off and On Line" in *The Electronic Grapevine: Rumor, Reputation, and Reporting in the New On-Line Environment,* in Borden, D. & Harvey, K. (eds.) Mahwah, N.J: Lawrence Erlbaum Associates.

BBC On-line (1999) "Web Is *Shrinking" BBC On-line* available at http://news2.thls.bbc.co.uk/hi/english/sci/tech/newsid%5F428000/428999.stm

Berger, P.L. & Luckman, T. (1966) *The Social Construction of Reality: A Treatise in the Sociology of Knowledge*. Garden City, New York: Anchor Books.

Borden, D. & Harvey, K. (1998) *The Electronic Grapevine: Rumor, Reputation, and Reporting in the New On-Line Environment*. Mahwah, N.J: Lawrence Erlbaum Associates.

Boyd-Barrett, O. (1980) *The International News Agencies*. London: Constable.

Boyd-Barrett, O. (1998) "*Global News Agencies*", in Boyd-Barrett, O. & Rantanen, T. (eds.) *The Globalization of News*. London: Sage.

Boyd-Barrett, O. & Rantanen T. (eds.) (1998) *The Globalization of News*. London: Sage.

Boyd-Barrett, O. & Thussu, K. (1992) *Contra-Flow In Global News*. London: John Libbey.

Brill, A. (1997) "Way New Journalism: How the Pioneers Are Doing", *Electronic Journal of Communication* vol.7, no.2.

Burden, P. (1999) *Interactivity and On-line News at the BBC*. Unpublished Masters dissertation, University of Leicester – CMCR.

Christopher, C. (1998) "Technology and Journalism in the on-line newsroom", in Borden, D. & Harvey, K. (eds.) *The Electronic Grapevine: Rumor, Reputation, and Reporting in the New On-Line Environment*. Mahwah, N.J: Lawrence Erlbaum Associates.

Clarke, S. (1995) "London: International News Capital", *Variety*, no.18, December.

Cohen, A.; Levy, M.; Roeh, I. & Gurevitch, M. (1996) *Global Newsrooms, Local Audiences: A Study of the Eurovision News Exchange*. London: John Libbey.

Cottle, S. (1999) From BBC Newsroom to BBC News Centre: On Changing Technology and Journalist Practices (Unpublished paper).

Dillinger, B. (1995) *Finnish Views of CNN Television News: A Critical Cross-Cultural Analysis of the American Commercial Discourse Style*. University of Vaasa (Doctoral Dissertation).

European Journalism Centre (1998) *The Future of the Printed Press: Challenges in a Digital World* (summary) Available at www.ejc.nl/hp/fpp/execsum.html

Evans, W. (1998) "Content Analysis in an Era of Interactive News: Assessing 21st Century Symbolic Environments", in Borden, D. & Harvey, K. (eds.) *The Electronic Grapevine: Rumor, Reputation, and Reporting in the New On-Line Environment.* Mahwah, N.J: Lawrence Erlbaum Associates.

Fedlin, E. (1997) "Rethinking the News Story for the Internet: Hyperstory Prototypes and a Model of the User", *Journalism Monographs,* no.163.

Fenby, J. (1986) *The International News Services* A Twentieth Century Fund Report, New York: Schocken Books.

Gans, H. (1980) *Deciding What's News.* New York: Vintage Books.

Giffard A. & Rivenburgh, N. (1998) *News Agencies, National Images, and Global Media Events.* The IAMCR annual conference, Glasgow (paper).

Golding, P. & Elliott, P. (1979) *Making the News.* New York: Longman.

Hagen, L. (1996) *Foreign News in German Media in 1979 and in 1995.* The IAMCR annual conference, Sydney (paper).

Hanson, C. (1997) "The Dark Side of On-line Scoops", *Columbia Journalism Review,* May/June.

Helland, K. (1995) *Public Service and Commercial News.* University of Bergen (Doctoral Dissertation).

Hjarvard, S. (1995) *Internationale TV-nyheder. En historisk analyse af det europæiske system for udveksling af internationale TV-nyheder.* København: Akademisk Forlag.

Hoge, J. (1997) "Foreign News: Who Gives a Damn" *Columbia Journalism Review* available at http://www.cjr.org/year/97/6/foreign.asp

Magid, L. (1997) "All Roads Lead to Reuters", *Currents.net* on-line. Available at www.currents.net/magazine/national/1513/uout1513.html

Malik, R. (1992) "The Global News Agenda" *Intermedia,* vol.20, no. 1.

Massey, B. & Levy, M. (1999) "Interactivity, On-line Journalism, and English-Language Web Newspapers in Asia", *Journalism and Mass Communication Quarterly,* vol.76, no.1.

Media Metrix (1999) "Heavy News Week Drives Traffic at Web Sites", via *NUA Internet Surveys,* available at www.nua.ie/surveys

Molina, G.G. (1990) The Production of Mexican Television News: The Supremacy of Corporate Rationale. University of Leicester (Doctoral Diss., unpublished).

Newhagen, J. & Levy, M. (1998) "The Future of Journalism in a Distributed Communication Architecture" in Borden, D. & Harvey, K. (eds.) *The Electronic Grapevine: Rumor, Reputation, and Reporting in the New On-Line Environment.* Mahwah, N.J: Lawrence Erlbaum Associates.

Niekamp, Ray (1997) "Television Station Web Sites: Interactivity in News Stories", Paper for the Association for Education in Journalism and Mass Communications annual meeting in Chicago.

NUA Internet Surveys (1998) *Jupiter Communications: Internet a Growing News Provider,* December 9, available at www.nua.ie/surveys

Paterson, C. (1996) *News Production at Worldwide Television News (WTN): An Analysis of Television News Agency Coverage of Developing Countries.* University of Texas (Doctoral Dissertation).

Paterson, C. (1998) "Global Battlefields", in Boyd-Barrett, O. & Rantanen, T. (eds.) *The Globalization of News.* London: Sage.

Paterson, C. (2000) "An Exploratory Analysis of the Transference of Frames in Global Television", in Reese, S.; Grant, A. & Gandy, O. (eds.) *Framing in the New Media Landscape.* Erlbaum, in press.

Read, D. (1992) *The Power of News: The History of Reuters 1849-1989* Oxford: Oxford University Press.

Reuters (1999) "Reuters Creates New Division to Exploit Web", 6 July via *Media Central News Wire,* on-line.

Rodriguez, A. (1996) "Made in the USA: The Production of the Noticiero Univision", *Critical Studies in Mass Communication,* vol.13, no.1, pp. 59-82.

Ross, S. & Middleberg, D. (1999) *1998 Media in Cyberspace Study* available at www.middleberg.com/toolsforsuccess/cyberstudy.cfm

Sarker, M.; Butler B. & Steinfield, C. (1995) "Intermediaries and Cybermediaries: A Continuing Role for Mediating Players in the Electronic Marketplace", *Journal of Computer-Mediated Communication* on-line at http://www.ascusc.org/jcmc/vol1/issue3/sarker.html

Schiff, F. (1996) "The Associated Press: Its Worldwide Bureaus and American Interests" *International Communication Bulletin* 31(1-2), Spring, 7-13.

Schlesinger, P. (1987) *Putting 'Reality' Together: BBC News*. London: Routledge, (2nd ed.).

Schudson, M. (1992) "The Sociology of News Production revisited", in Curran & Gurevitch, M. (eds.) *Mass Media and Society*. New York: Routledge, pp. 141-160.

Strupp, J. (1999) "Local News Wins Popularity Contest on Newspaper Web Sites", *Editor and Publisher,* June 30.

Tremayne, M. (1997) The Internet: Is the Medium the Message? University of Texas, Dept. of Journalism. (Unpublished paper).

Tuchman, G. (1978) *Making News: A Study in the Construction of Reality*. New York: Free Press.

Yancey, K. CNN (1997) Lecture, Georgia State University, Atlanta.

Why Virtuality Can Be Good for Democracy

Klaus Bruhn Jensen

Introduction

It is a rare occasion when a single publication is considered sufficiently signifi-cant, or provocative, to produce an entire conference session where its merits and implications can be addressed, particularly if the debate is not a retrospec-tive celebration, but takes place before the ideas have had a chance to harden into orthodoxy. At the 1999 meeting of the International Communication Asso-ciation, that mixed blessing fell upon an article by Michael Schudson, entitled "Why Conversation Is Not the Soul of Democracy" (Schudson 1997). The session addressing his article featured several key contributors to, and agenda-setters within, the field of media and communication research, including the 'grand old man' of the American substream of cultural studies, James Carey (Carey 1989), who had been taken to task by Schudson for an idealization of a conversational public as the essence of democracy. Following a number of interventions by Carey, Elihu Katz, and others, Schudson had the opportunity to reply and, in fact, reassert what might seem an untenable, even selfcontradictory assertion. How could conversation *not* be the soul of democracy?

In summary, Schudson's (1997) point is that what he calls a "romance of conversation" (p. 307) has produced a confusion regarding the relationship be-tween politics and communication, especially on the issue of how communica-tion on a societywide scale may be conducted in practice and subsequently translated into a form of unified action that has institutional consequences. Two distinct notions of conversation – what Schudson calls sociable conversation and problem-solving conversation – have apparently been mixed up in one meta-phor. On the one hand, sociable conversation is of an informal and often private nature, with spontaneity and egalitarianism as its most important features. On the other hand, problem-solving conversation is of a formal, or at least rule-governed, and essentially public nature. Democracy depends on an ongoing problem-solving conversation, which recognizes both disagreements and the need for rules and procedures of resolving such disagreements, so that decisions can be taken and collective action proceed. As Schudson puts it, "democratic conversation is conversation not among intimates nor among strangers but among citizens who are acquainted by virtue of their citizenship" (p. 306). It might be counterproductive, to the point of undermining political democracy itself under conditions of industrial capitalism, to think of it as a conversation that ought to simply run its own informal, unregulated course. As far as democracy is concerned, the response to the familiar rhetorical question, 'Can't we just talk about it?', should be: No.

In this article, I build on Schudson's insightful point, but take further steps in the direction of theorizing the relations between media and various associated political as well as other social processes, without appealing to a conversational ideal. My point will be that the field is well-advised to push in the direction of deromanticizing its object of study, not only in the area of political communication. Dialogue can occur at a distance, even if it does not take the form of a classic, embodied conversation. The various technological forms of communication have proven difficult to theorize, however, as part of an inclusive explanatory framework of modern culture. The first section of the article, accordingly, proposes to distinguish different varieties of communicative interaction, drawing on the sociological concept of 'roles.' The second section revisits the interdisciplinary concept of 'contexts' in order to explore in more detail the nature of the linkages between, on the one hand, conversation and other communicative genres and, on the other hand, the institutions and practices of the wider social setting which are informed by these genres. The third and final section returns to the question of how mediated communication, specifically its latest variant of virtual interaction via the Internet, can serve the goals traditionally associated with the notion of democracy. Far from undermining democracy, virtuality can be good for democracy, because it extends and accentuates an important aspect of modernization in which the media have been instrumental. The point is not to carry on one's conversation with unvirtual, real intimates or strangers for as long as possible. Instead, it is by *ending* communication, and by translating interventions and representations, whether from the media or other sources, into actions which address and affect social contexts far beyond the participants' immediate surroundings, that they could be said to contribute to democracy in practice. The end of communication serves the ends of democracy.

Hollow Men: Roles

An important ingredient in the process of modernization, as far as the structure of society is concerned, has been a redefinition of human beings in terms not of essences, but of functions, relations, and roles, as studied by the comparatively recent discipline of sociology. As suggested by Turner (1999),

> The emergence of sociology in the late nineteenth century can therefore be seen as part of a larger reorientation of European social thought, which was brought about by the secularization of consciousness, the erosion of traditional

values, the growing dominance of instrumental rationalism and the diversification of cultures through global trade and imperialism. (pp. 38-39)

In the longer perspective of the history of ideas, the development of key sociological concepts can be understood as an aspect of a much more inclusive
process of secularization (Finnemann 1999: chap. 10). If the Renaissance had
begun a process of placing the human subject at the center of universe, *vis-à-vis*
an objectifiable reality, the socalled 'natural' sciences, from the seventeenth century onwards, proposed to study the world as a separate empirical reality, that is,
as an external form with no inherent meaning or value. What was ultimately put
at stake, was the assumption of any predefined order of the universe, especially
the understanding of perceived reality as providing evidence of a higher and
deeper metaphysical reality. In social and cultural domains, hierarchies of privilege
and taste would be challenged in the longer term.

The religious interpretation of this predefined order has been referred to by
Arthur Lovejoy as 'the great chain of being,' in which everything has its rightful
place (Tillyard 1972). Not only could the natural order of the earth be seen to
map onto a primary, heavenly order. Also social arrangements within the church
as well as in state administrations arguably served to articulate a hidden, but
superior order with divine origins and sanctions. Within such an order, each
constituent is endowed with a particular quality, value, or essence, not so much
because of its position within the chain of being, but because of the transcendental nature of the chain as such: Whatever is, is good, true, and beautiful in
itself. Further, the essence of the order escapes, even prohibits, human reflexivity
beyond a certain point, as determined historically by religious authorities.

The scientific approach to objective reality as an extended form – *res extensa*
– which was codified most famously by Descartes, can be taken as the first step
in a long process of secularization which, in turn, came to include the human
subject and its means of communication. While Descartes had reserved a privileged
domain for the human subject – *res cogitans* – the nineteenth century in particular came to question the perspicacity of this thinking entity. In philosophy as
well as politics, humans were increasingly suspected of being subject to forces
beyond their control. This current in the history of ideas was pinpointed by Paul
Ricoeur in his reference to a 'hermeneutics of suspicion' that was shared by
philosophers as different in other respects as Marx, Nietzsche, and Freud (Ricoeur
1981). Like texts, humans do not always say what they really mean. Worse, they
themselves may not even know what they mean, because their subjectivity is not
unified. The forces beyond human control came to be conceived, most notably,
in a psychodynamic form, simultaneously biological and psychological. The human
subject is divided, sometimes against itself, by physical drives whose mental
expression bears witness to contradictory or unresolved interests. The
secularization of the human subject, thus, entailed a questioning, not only of the
order of both the natural and social universe, but of the very means of gaining
insight into that order. The transcendental status of the subject in sciences as
well as arts had fallen victim to the widening process of secularization.

It can be argued that the development of information and communication technologies has contributed to a third phase of secularization, which, for example, supplants unique works of art with flexible reproductions; I return to the implications of this argument in the third section. With respect to the category of roles, the dual secularization of social structures and subjects paved the way for a new understanding of humans as autonomous agents across a whole variety of contexts. Given the fundamental nature of the shift in the history of ideas, it is not surprising that its impact was felt in the emerging social sciences as well as in practical politics. In the media field, Jürgen Habermas (1989) has traced the fall of a social order of communication that was premised on the essential attributes and positions of individuals, and the rise of a different order which, at least in principle, conceives of speaking positions in society as blanks to be filled according to reason and merit. The passing of the European feudal order in politics and communication amounts to a variation on the disintegration of 'the great chain of being.' What emerged was an at least partially secularized social order, to be informed by, and debated according to, the principles of the bourgeois public sphere. Despite structural blindnesses and silences, the public sphere held out the promise of a form of communication that would question and reflect upon itself without end, being a self-correcting forum of rationality. Within a public sphere, all positions are created equal and accessible to all citizens – again despite historically exclusive definitions of citizenship.

The notion of formally empty positions in a system of communication recalls the more general concept of roles as employed across the social sciences. In fact, a 'communicative turn' might help to move social theory beyond the common understanding of societies and communities as systems of communication, to a further conceptual specification of how social agents ascribe meaning to different roles as part of their ongoing interaction. Habermas, in his later works, has made an influential contribution to such a turn. As a background to his own contribution in *The Theory of Communicative Action* (Habermas 1984; 1987), he has traced a line from Max Weber, through Talcott Parsons, to his own examination of communicative and other social action. As the point of departure for this line, Habermas identifies Weber's analysis of secularization, of "the *process of disenchantment in the history of religion*, which is said to have fulfilled the necessary internal conditions for the appearance of Occidental rationalism" (Habermas 1984: 143). Habermas, like other recent work (see Schroeder 1992; Turner 1999), takes Weber to be a theorist of modernity, rather than the liberalist, individualist flip side of Marx. According to Habermas (1984),

> among the classical figures of sociology, Max Weber is the only one who broke with both the premises of the history of philosophy and the basic assumptions of evolutionism and who nonetheless wanted to conceive of modernization of old-European society as the result of a universal-historical process of rationalization. (p. 143)

Again in contrast to much other critical social theory, Habermas similarly credits Parsons' elaboration of Weber's analysis of the processes of modernization, although he quarrels with Parsons' specific systemic approach to society (e.g., Parsons 1951).

Habermas' theoretical-political agenda involves a commitment to a primordial lifeworld which is said to have been subordinated to systems of rationalization under contemporary social arrangements. This commitment leads him, among other things, to insist on a distinction between 'communicative' action, defined as "the *original mode* of language use [...] with an orientation to reaching understanding" (Habermas 1984: 288), and instrumental or 'strategic' forms of communication and other action. Despite the tendency of Habermas' later work to thus ontologize the historical public sphere examined in his earlier work (Jensen 1995: chap. 11), his approach to communication can nevertheless be read as an attempt to explore the relations between everyday meanings and institutionalized actions. His general question appears to be how individuals come to serve as carriers of social structures larger than themselves and, importantly, how these relations are established, negotiated, and sometimes contested in communication. These relations amount to roles, also in Habermas' terminology (Habermas 1987: 395). Roles furnish meanings that enable social agents to act together in a coordinated fashion. Since Max Weber, social theorists have been attempting "an interpretive understanding of social action in order thereby to arrive at a causal explanation of its course and effects" (Weber 1964: 88), a definition in which the concept of roles seems suspended between the interpretive and causal poles of social action. On the one hand, roles constitute forces in an already configured field of action, with predictive value for what an agent is going to do next. On the other hand, roles are subject to interpretation and redefinition, both by their present occupants and by their partners in social interaction. Through role-taking, society is reproduced, reinterpreted, and, to a degree, reformed.

A preliminary conclusion regarding social roles would be that an important legacy of sociology for related fields of research is the conception of societies as systems of positions which are taken up by shifting participants in social action, and which are endowed by these agents with meaning. A parallel set of concepts is found in modern linguistics, which, following Saussure (1959), came to assume a model of deep structures, particularly in grammar, that would manifest themselves in different surface structures depending on the context. The 'linguistic turn' which is most commonly associated with philosophy (Rorty 1967), has been a distinctive feature of twentieth-century scholarship in a range of scientific disciplines. These expressions in science of a secularized worldview have themselves contributed to the general process of secularization, just as scientific fields have taken part of their inspiration from a social context under secularization. The efficacy of the notion of social roles, then, is an outcome of a longterm double hermeneutic which has taken place between scientific and other social practices, and across disciplinary boundaries (Giddens 1984).

It remains to note that this relativization of social identities from around 1900 gave rise to elaborate and sometimes vehement reactions. These responses took the form, for example, of a renewed research interest in cultural tradition within the emerging field of anthropology, but also of a backlash in public debate against new forms of culture, such as cinema and advertising, which could be identified as symptoms and sources of a new and unstable social character. Particularly in literature but also in other arts around the time of early social theory, the apparent emptying of values and traditions fueled a cultural pessimism, which, further, seemed to be confirmed by social upheavals and international disasters, as epitomized in World War I. While contingent roles could be taken as evidence of potential social progress, they might also result in a dangerous flux, a void, where once firm identities used to be. One memorable formulation of this concern was T.S. Eliot's poem about "The Hollow Men" (1925):

> We are the hollow men
> We are the stuffed men
> Leaning together
> Headpiece filled with straw. Alas!
> Our dried voices, when
> We whisper together
> Are quiet and meaningless
> [...]
> Remember us – if at all – not as lost
> Violent souls, but only
> As the hollow men
> The stuffed men. (Eliot 1950: 162)

The metaphor of hollow men whispering their meaningless communication to each other echoes more recent positions in theories and debates about the decline also of political dialogue in the public sphere. By implicit contrast, it recalls the ideal of essential human beings coming together to deliberate on, and act in, contexts that they share as full persons, body and mind. The civilizing potential of hollow roles, however, may be greater than has been allowed for in either poetry, social theory, or public debate on the endangered future of democracy. Like social roles, the contexts of political interaction can be filled in more ways than one. The next section considers 'contexts' of interaction and communication, their restructuration during modernization, as well as some of their enduring constitutive features. The concept of contexts holds one key to understanding both the differences and the similarities between virtual and other political interaction.

Imagined Communities: Contexts

'Contexts' joins 'roles,' along with 'culture' and 'communication,' as a candidate for the social-scientific concept with the most, and the most varied, definitions. My working definition, following Giddens (1984), takes a context to be a configuration of time, space, and social relations which enables certain forms of action, while ruling out others. At this general level, contexts serve as the specific arenas in which social agents accomplish society together on a daily basis, relying on available material resources and rules of social interaction. Contexts, then, can be examined as concrete instantiations of the interplay of structure and agency. To exemplify, the process of socialization, which, in a sense, structures agency, is an instance of how social roles are offered, negotiated, and performed in particular settings and institutions – families, workplaces, schools, and peer groups. At the same time, each context implies a wider frame of reference that incorporates economic conditions, legal traditions, political rights, and cultural heritage, all of which are virtually present in the context in the form of discourses that can be mobilized to make sense of past events as well as future plans.

The widespread acceptance of the term, 'contexts,' also outside hermeneutic, phenomenological, and critical varieties of social theory, may suggest a growing appeal of a textual or discursive notion of the social setting, perhaps as an aspect of the linguistic turn. Certainly, the understanding of communication as a facilitator of other social action seems consensual to the point of being almost selfevident to current social science. Increasingly, most media and communiction researchers would presumably endorse Carey's (1989) elaboration of John Dewey's point that societies exist not only *by* communication, by transmission, but also *in* communication, in the ritual sharing of meaning. Communication implies community, at least the possibility of community. With the coming of new means of communication, new forms of communities – and societies – become possible. A central issue in the debate between Carey and Schudson over the soul of democracy, is how communication could and should be translated into community, and whether certain forms of communication are royal roads to community.

The concept of contexts offers a point of contact, then, between communication and community. Not only is communication carried on and received in multiple everyday contexts that feed into the life of communities, but these contexts are themselves constituted through communication. Contexts exist not only by, but also in communication. It is communication which serves to maintain contact and to coordinate the attention of social agents towards joint action, and the acts of communication include intervention into the stream of events, perhaps to repair contact, perhaps to redirect the attention of coagents. One characteristic competence of knowledgeable social agents is that they are able to account for the context of which they are a part and their own place in it – to contextualize what they are up to – although most of the time they will not be challenged to do so, but can merely go about their business, relying on practical consciousness (Giddens 1984). Another competence of social agents is that they are able to recontextualize events by introducing new elements or interpretive frames into the situation, not least to modify what others are doing. For instance, by describing that I see you with your hand in my bag, I can indicate that I know what you may be up to, by accident, in practice, or unconsciously. In doing so, social agents cumulatively construct a setting for their actions out the available material as well as discursive resources. Contexts, in short, have material as well as discursive existence.

The duality of contexts links up with the paradigm debate in the field of media and communication research. Whereas the humanistic tradition would tend to take the textual conception of the social field as a context quite literally, at least in a methodological sense, treating everyday interaction on a par, for example, with (other) narrative genres, the social-scientific tradition would rather take the term as a synonym for theoretical constructs such as situation, structure, or system, to be operationalized with reference to behavioral and cognitive categories. The difficulty of convergence between the traditions has been due, in part, to the fact that a common denominator for 'contexts' and similar key concepts has not been arrived at. Contexts, like communication itself, would have to be accounted for simultaneously as material and discursive phenomena. I import real people, time, and space into my understanding through any number of mental representations and communications, and I reexport that context, as interpreted, in my practical engagements with the social field. Both aspects of contexts are real; both have consequences for my agency.

A partial solution to the ambiguity of the notion of contexts can be derived from earlier work by Benedict Anderson on the status of communities, specifically in the case of the nation-state (Anderson 1991). He gained fame within cultural studies during the 1980s for coining the phrase 'imagined communities.' The central point in the book of that title was that nations are imagined political communities; they are imagined "because the members of even the smallest nation will never know most of their fellow-members" (p. 6). As a result, nations must rely on a wealth of symbolic resources, including mass media, to ensure cohesion and stability. The point is valid, but limited. On the one hand, communities do exist 'in communication,' joining virtual partners in interaction. On the other hand, the relationship between communication and community is not really clarified by Anderson beyond the elegant formulation provided previously by Carey. More important, the imagined status of the nation is not due exclusively, or even primarily, to the limited reach of face-to-face interaction. Although Benedict Anderson is not arguing that 'imagined' equals 'imaginary,' he does implicitly privilege interaction in copresence and implies that the communities arising from such interaction are somehow not imagined. In fact, there is a theoretical bonus to asserting the opposite. Also communities which are maintained predominantly face to face are imagined, because that is the nature of community. For one thing, community within a family or a peer group is presumably imagined when its members are not physically present in the same location. For another thing, copresence is no guarantee of community: Spouses have been known to cheat on each other sexually and financially; friends have been known to manipulate each other for the most unfriendly, selfish reasons.

The implication is that Anderson's (1991) notion of imagined communities is rather too specific, but also that the notion may be opened up for further explanatory value. All communities are imagined. This does not make communities, whether large or small, any less real, nor does it deny the fact that, for example, nations, diasporas, or subcultures are also material phenomena. An alternative formulation, then, would insist that communities rely for their maintenance on communication; that such communication is conducted in a range of fora and media; and that the outcome of communication across sites and times is communities of different types, not of inherently primary or secondary status.

This line of argument may clarify the definition of contexts, communities, and other concepts which commonly accompany theorizing about media and communication. The argument may also facilitate historical and other comparative studies, avoiding the suggestion that, for instance, oral cultures throughout history have not imagined themselves as communities. Comparative research remains one of the most fertile, but underdeveloped approaches to theory development in the media field (see Blumler et al. 1992; Jensen 1998). Most important for the present argument, it becomes possible to specify the dual status of contexts as material as well as discursive factors in communication. On the one hand, contexts can be defined as a particular set of material means and associated procedures – resources and rules in Giddens' (1984) terms – which are historically and culturally available, and which prestructure the communicative event, from the global flow of capital, to national legislation, to subcultural practices of media use. On the other hand, the context of a communicative event is whatever the participants imagine to be relevant to that event and hence include in their discursive interaction. The participants in communication, have an understanding prefiguring what they might expect from the interaction, and what would be appropriate acts and moves by themselves and their partners. Indeed, their expectations make up an entire virtual configuration of the time, space, and social relations to which the communicative event applies, also beyond the immediate event of the interchange. In this perspective, the context of a communicative interaction is what might be called its domain of relevance, what it is 'about,' as far as the participants are concerned. That relevance is to be measured by the actions that the participants, such as media audiences, engage in with reference to the communication – its content, form, or process – actions which subsequently can be seen to fan out from the moment of communicative contact. Communication is a resource for social action; the limits of the context of communication coincide with the limits of conceivable action.

The redevelopment of the concept of contexts, further, helps to identify one fundamental and concrete difficulty of how to study the place of media in relation to other social institutions and cultural processes. How wide should the methodological net be thrown, and what specifically should it be designed to catch? This section has suggested that the participants' perspective on the context – its discursive or virtual conception – is of equal interest, compared to its technological, economic, and legislative frameworks, for empirical studies of the nexus between communication and society. Agency is always informed by a conception of structure, of how the frameworks may be engaged and negotiated, for example, in the area of political life, and it is a conception which cannot simply be read off from either surveys of political-communicative ideals or indicators of the technological or economic potential at any particular point in history. Therefore, the situated uses of media in political practices also need to be studied as ongoing engagements and negotiations. These considerations return the media field to the classic distinction between the native's perspective and the analyst's perspective, what has been referred to in anthropology as the emic versus the etic aspects of a given context (Pike 1967). One of the contributions of anthropology to other social and cultural research is an insistence that the two analytical perspectives are interdependent (see Headland et al. 1990). The emic, internal perspective is necessarily grasped from some analyst's etic, external perspective (and, the analyst's position, in turn, is itself an instance of the emic perspective of a particular academic culture). Accordingly, parallel to studies of various economic, technological, and other institutional indicators of the material conditions of communication, which, to a degree, take effect behind the backs of the participants, more detailed studies are required of how audiences for different media conceive of political action, perhaps in equally implicit and unrecognized ways. The task will be to move beyond the participants' discursively articulated ideals of communication, to research on their various practical conceptions of how communication links up with agency and structure. For this purpose, the redeveloped concept of contexts provides one element in an interdisciplinary theoretical framework of media and communication research.

A special current challenge for research is the growing variety of mediated forms of social interaction that involve remote partners. The process of economic as well as cultural globalization which is made possible, in part, by the digitalization of the communications infrastructure, is an opportunity to reconsider the nature of the contexts – both real or virtual – of communication.

We Have Always Been Virtual

One of the most commonly noted features of communication which occurs across great physical or phenomenological distances is that it may contribute to the emergence of a virtual reality, not merely in the case of VR technology in a strict sense. Perhaps this secondary form of reality is different in kind from the direct experience of the individual social actor, and perhaps, on a pessimistic note, this virtual reality is increasingly competing with, and taking the place of, what used to be a primary reality of the human senses. As is the case with most previous media, computer media, notably the Internet, have thus stirred the public as well as the scientific imagination, partly reiterating fears about an impending cultural decline, but partly also reasserting romantic ideals regarding a democratization of politics through universal access to these new media.

By contrast, it seems worthwhile to explore the possibility that the virtualization of social relations may carry a more general, modernizing, civilizing potential. In the long perspective of modernization, the rise of a network society might represent more of the same, perhaps for the better. To anticipate the conclusion, I refer to the title of a much debated volume in the history of science and ideas, *We Have Never Been Modern* (Latour 1993). One of Latour's points is that 'the moderns' have tended to assume and promote separate domains of reality, such as "Nature,

Discourse, Society and Being" (p. 89), and that, since these domains prove to be inseparable in scientific as well as other social practices, we have never been modern, if we accept the premises of the moderns. Latour's strategy is to reject several of their premises, along with premises of the postmoderns, the premoderns, and the antimoderns, in order to redevelop what he calls a 'nonmodern' worldview, which does away with absolute distinctions between the natural and the social, and between the discursive and non-discursive aspects of reality. Scientific, political, and other social institutions are neither perfect vehicles of *res cogitans* nor victims of the natural forces of *res extensa*. While Latour's inclusive and ambitious polemic against the vision of modernity as a utopia outside of history and biology is illuminating, I want to reemphasize here an element from the moderns which also Latour would want to recuperate, namely, their inclination to imagine alternatives, including alternative social arrangements for themselves and their others.

A positive alternative to Latour's negative formulation could be, 'We have always been virtual.' In premodern as well as modern settings, communities have been established and maintained through communication for the purpose of imagining other people, projects, and solutions – for getting jobs done. In modern societies, both the jobs and the media have changed, but the virtual solutions and their coordination at the level of both individuals and communities have been constants. Certainly, virtuality can and should be examined as a matter of degree, at least in phenomenological terms, since different information technologies and forms of human interaction give rise to different experiences of sociality, with implications for social action. However, in response to the common dichotomy of virtual as opposed to real social relations, it is important to insist on a point of departure for further research which recognizes the discursive component of any social interaction.

The consensus of much research on modernization and globalization is that information technologies – from the printing press to the Internet – have fundamentally changed the possible forms of communication and, as a result, the forms of social interaction across time and space (Castells 1996; Harvey 1989; Thompson 1995). It has been less common for research to examine in detail the place of media in such interaction, approaching it literally as contextualized action which involves numerous concrete individuals and organizations, and which relies on diverse mediated representations. A classic example is the telegraph, which, among other things, transformed the conditions for exchanging economic news, with implications for the organization of production and trade on down to the localized exchange of goods (Carey 1989). What distinguishes recent forms of computer-mediated communication in this regard, perhaps most of all, is the increased differentiation of the constituent communicative acts, not only because of a multiplication of the available applications and genres on the same platform, but also because of the adaptability and programmability, broadly speaking, of each act. This characteristic feature of computer-mediated communication promotes the integration of communicative and other social practices. While that feature is made possible by the often cited convergence of technologies, it also facilitates a *divergence* in the social practices which the technologies will support.

The differentiation, diffusion, and distanciation of communicative events throughout the social field do not make either the communicative interaction or the social field any less real, more imaginary. By imagining other people, in face-to-face as well as in mediated communication, we become virtual partners in real social activity. Communication prefigures the kinds of action that we might undertake with others. In fact, the increasingly manifest presence of media technologies in everyday life can serve as a reminder that social life has always been facilitated by communication. Furthermore, modern media technologies are heirs to the technology of writing, also in the sense that they offer an externalized, discursive coin of exchange in social interaction. Havelock (1963), among others, has suggested with reference to classical Greece that alphabetic writing helped to introduce a new understanding of knowledge not as memory, but as a public record of statements that could be verified and disputed. In this respect, the development of hypertext as a principle of much computer-mediated communication, including the World Wide Web, can be understood as another phase in the long history of writing (Bolter 1991).

In order to assess the specific potential of the Internet for political democracy, it remains necessary to take into account the perspective of the social agents who enact politics and society on a daily basis. Partly in reaction to Schudson's (1997) anti-conversationalist argument, Wyatt, Katz, and Kim (2000) have suggested not only that ordinary political conversation is widespread in everyday life and not particularly controversial, but also that such conversation is an important ingredient of actual democratic practice. The basis of their conclusion was a survey with Americans about their approach to political topics in various conversational contexts. Accordingly, one might argue, recalling W.I. Thomas' dictum that, "If men define situations as real, they are real in their consequences" (in Rochberg-Halton 1986: 44), that conversation is the soul of democracy because people define this to be the case. One difficulty with the argument is methodological, because a survey of this nature can be expected to reproduce common ideals of political democracy, rather than specifying how political conversation relates in practice to political action. More importantly, the argument seems to miss Schudson's (1997) main conceptual as well as normative point, which I take to be that democracy is guaranteed by explicit and debatable procedures of how to *end* communication and transform it into collective action, not by a relatively informal consensus concerning how the individual may participate in the flow of communication. It is mainly for this reason that the metaphor of conversation, as applied to mass media and now increasingly to the Internet, is questionable and should be challenged by alternative conceptualizations that emphasize political communication as a specific form of social action with institutional consequences. Especially in view of the recency of the Internet, it is incumbent on research to begin to ask what social difference it could make in the long term, given its embedding in long-standing political and other social institutions and its many forerunners in virtual interaction.

As a minimum, computer media offer additional channels of social interaction, including means of political deliberation and debate which point beyond the prototypes of conversation and mass communication. One early account of the computer as a medium emphasized its potential for organizing social interaction around common interests, rather than common geographical locations (Licklider and Taylor 1999: 108). Compared to broadcast communication, which has traditionally been focused at the national level, computer media facilitate narrowcasting as well as transnational political organization (see Rheingold 1994). Compared to conversation, computer media enable sustained interaction across time and space with natural, but perhaps unrecognized allies – and enemies.

It is, however, the adaptation of the networked computer to a wider range of social genres of communication and interaction which must be examined in order to assess its democratic potential. A familiar use of the computer in leisure is the kind of role playing which is associated with gaming or multi-user dungeons (MUDs). In a wider sense, Internet Relay Chat (IRC) and other forms of online interaction allow participants not only to encounter the positions and identities of others, but simultaneously to explore their own positions and identities, in part by relying on multiple and fictional *personae*. Whereas such new technological forms of playful interaction might contribute to an identity crisis (Turkle 1995: 255), and certainly merit serious research attention, it is important to recall that the formal and anonymous definition of communicative roles is a general feature of modern social systems, with or without a mediating computer, within or without genres of play. A case in point is communication in political democracy. The roles of sender and receiver, information provider and partisan, advocate and opponent, are available, in principle, for the asking, just as elections and offices are held and filled only to be vacated at the end of term. On the Internet, news groups as well as other political fora constitute social systems of roles which can be taken on by different participants at different times. Such virtual interaction does not displace embodied interaction, since no quantity of face-to-face communication could replace news groups. Print, broadcasting, and computer-mediated communication are neither add-ons nor plug-ins, but constitutive elements of modern social systems.

As in the case of previous media, computer media may carry a specific message (McLuhan 1964), depending on their technological and institutional implementation. By participating in political democracy, in part with reference to media, citizens are socialized not only to know particular things about the world of politics or to perform appropriate interventions, but, over time, to understand the nature of the system, particularly the relations between their rights, roles, and possible courses of action. One cumulative effect of broadcasting, arguably, has been the imagined political communities of the nation-state (Anderson 1991). Another long-term socializing effect of computer media may arise from their emphatic relativization of roles in social interaction. To some degree, this feature could counteract what has been referred to in social psychology as 'the fundamental attribution error' (Ross 1977), that is, assigning responsibility for events and actions to individuals, conceived as essences, rather than considering, as well, the conditions and roles under which they must act. On the one hand, an understanding of actions as the result of both structural contingencies and personal intentions can promote tolerance as a first prerequisite of dialogue about political ends and means. On the other hand, this same understanding can create a healthy skepticism regarding the strategy and tactics underlying the explicit statements of (other) political agents. Computer-mediated political communication is yet another contestable resource in the process of modernization and democratization.

Like roles, contexts may be reconceived through the social uses of computer media. Whereas previous media have most often been studied and debated with reference to their representation of some reality, the computer is more evidently also a resource for action which coconstructs reality, as evidenced by applications ranging from computer-aided design and manufacture (CAD/CAM) to accounting and conference systems. Through computers as general media, people share representations of the world, but in doing so, they shape and reshape contexts, simultaneously as material and discursive phenomena. At least in this respect, computer-mediated communication resembles political communication as such. By definition, political communication has a purpose, being embedded in highly regulated and contested institutions which are reproduced in the acts of communication. In the long term, computer-mediated political communication may introduce a new configuration of the contexts in which influence is exerted, resources allocated, and power exercised, but this does not make those contexts any less real or important.

The action-representation nexus of communication is key to Michael Schudson's (1997) point that democracy is characterized by problem-solving rather than sociable conversation. Political speech is a particular kind of speech act (Austin 1962). Notwithstanding Habermas, there can be no such thing as innocent or ideal speech in politics (Jensen 1995: chap. 11). Therefore, more attention could be given in the politics of communication to the *end* of communication and to the procedures by which ideas, positions, and arguments are translated into practice in a variety of contexts. One of the apparent motivations behind Schudson's intervention was to promote a less romantic, more pragmatic assessment of democratic communication by clearing up some of the theoretical confusion that may get in the way also of practical politics. In response to Michael Schudson's argument that references to democracy as conversation tend to depict a golden past, James Carey, at the 1999 ICA panel, expressed concern that Schudson would instead end up painting a golden present. The future of political communication, like its past and present, is unlikely to be golden, not because of its virtual components, but because that is the unromantic nature of both communication and politics.

Conclusion

In research on media, globalization, and everyday life, a distinction is often made between 'space' and 'place,' to make the point that social spaces are never merely geographical or material, but are engaged in discourse as concrete places that are filled with cultural significance (e.g., Morley and Robins 1995). While recognizing that point, this article has suggested that the roles and contexts which are articulated in discourse also need to be considered as blanks. Such a formalist as well as functionalist model of society and communication is one of the legacies of modernity for research on media, a legacy that remains to be cashed in by developing theories of communication which, finally, do not defer to traditional inspirations from other disciplines, such as the study of conversation or, alternatively, engineering. The emergence of the Internet and other computer-mediated communication as major factors of social life is a historical opportunity to reconsider some foundational concepts in the field of media and communication research.

The challenge is perhaps most evident in the case of news and other genres of political communication, since they specifically address the relations of power in modern societies. This fact helps to explain some of the high hopes regarding the democratizing potential of Internet media. The link between news media and political democracy also helps to explain the vehemence of the debate at the conference session addressing Michael Schudson's (1997) article. The title of the article was a negative sentence, asserting what is not the soul of democracy, but leaving ambiguous the question of what, then, *is* the soul of democracy. The rhetorical premise would have to be that democracy has a soul, a sacred essence, and perhaps also that its rituals must be implemented in certain primordial forms of discourse. My proposal is to give up on the soul altogether, also in the political domain. It is one of the paradoxes of modern societies that they return, time and again, to quasi-religious interpretations of their most secular institutions. Democracy is a human, social, modern fact – a fact that needs to be continuously reasserted and reenacted. There is neither eternal bliss nor damnation to be had in political communication, only a lot of hard organizational and discursive work.

The spread of digital networks and of socalled virtual interaction has introduced new conditions for the conduct of political democracy, fueling romantic ideals as well as cultural fears, but it is doubtful whether virtuality, at least in its presently conceivable forms, represents a dramatically different condition, for better or for worse. My conclusion has been that virtuality can be good for democracy, not because of any revolutionary qualities, but because it contributes to an ongoing process of secularization. Virtuality might signal yet another phase in the process of secularization (Finnemann 1999: chap. 10). The first phase of secularization claimed external, extended reality as an object of human understanding and enterprise; the second phase reclaimed the human subject as part of the natural and animal world, and as less than a perfect mirror of nature and society (Rorty 1979). A third phase of secularization may be said to involve the very means of articulating the relation between subjects and objects. These means are media in a broad sense, that is, flexible physical systems that generate variable forms representation, consciousness, and action – in a word, computers. One of the most ambitious visions in this respect was found in traditional artificial intelligence research beginning in the 1940-50s, hoping to invent machines that think. A more modest and realistic vision would take the Internet as one example of a flexible physical system of representation and interaction in which the status of subjects and objects, representations and actions, is programmable and variable. Subjects can take on a variety of identities – roles. Objects can both represent and perform as subjects in the form of avatars and intelligent agents. And, the Internet can serve to establish new domains of social life – contexts – in which actions online are the only manifestation of major sectors of economic or political activity, from e-commerce to computerized political campaigns and, in time, elections. How such conditions of communication will affect either the social agent's awareness of self, roles, and contexts, or the institutions of modern politics and economy, is a question that merits much more theoretical as well as empirical research, and less normative speculation.

Like democracy, the computer does not have soul. Like other media, it can be a virtual forum of democracy.

References

Anderson, B. (1991) *Imagined Communities: Reflections on the Origin and Spread of Nationalism*. London: Verso.

Austin, J.L. (1962) *How to Do Things with Words*. Oxford: Oxford University Press.

Blumler, J., McLeod, J. & Rosengren, K.E. (1992) *Comparatively Speaking: Communication and Culture across Space and Time*. Newbury Park, CA: Sage.

Bolter, J.D. (1991) *Writing Space: The Computer, Hypertext, and the History of Writing*. Hillsdale, NJ: Lawrence Erlbaum.

Carey, J. (1989) *Communication as Culture*. Boston, MA: Unwin Hyman.

Castells, M. (1996) *The Rise of the Network Society*. Oxford: Blackwell.

Eliot, T.S. (1950) "The Hollow Men", in Mack, M.; Dean, L. & Frost, W. (eds.) *Modern Poetry*. Englewood, Cliffs, N J: Prentice-Hall.

Finnemann, N.O. (1999) *Thought, Sign, and Machine: The Computer Reconsidered*. http://www.hum.au.dk/ckulturf/DOCS/PUB/nof/TSM/contents.html (December 2, 1999).

Giddens, A. (1984) *The Constitution of Society*. Berkeley, CA: University of California Press.

Habermas, J. (1984) *The Theory of Communicative Action*. vol I. Boston: Beacon Press.

Habermas, J. (1987) *The Theory of Communicative Action*. vol II. Cambridge: Polity Press.

Habermas, J. (1989) *The Structural Transformation of the Public Sphere*. Cambridge, MA: MIT Press.

Harvey, D. (1989) *The Condition of Postmodernity*. Oxford: Blackwell.

Havelock, E.A. (1963) *Preface to Plato*. Oxford: Blackwell.

Headland, T.; Pike, K. & Harris, M. (1990) *Emics and Etics: The Insider/Outsider Debate*. Newbury Park, CA: Sage.

Jensen, K.B. (1995) *The Social Semiotics of Mass Communication*. London: Sage.

Jensen, K.B. (ed.) (1998) *News of the World: World Cultures Look at Television News*. London: Routledge.

Latour, B. (1993) *We Have Never Been Modern*. Hemel Hempstead: Harvester Wheatsheaf.

Licklider, J.C.R. & Taylor, R.W. (1999) "The Computer as a Communication Device," in Mayer, P.A. (ed.) *Computer Media and Communication: A Reader*. Oxford: Oxford University Press.

McLuhan, M. (1964) *Understanding Media*. New York: McGraw-Hill.

Morley, D. & Robins, K. (1995) *Spaces of Identity: Global Media, Electronic Landscapes, and Cultural Boundaries*. London: Routledge.

Parsons, T. (1951) *The Social System*. Glencoe, IL: The Free Press.

Pike, K.L. (1967) *Language in Relation to a Unified Theory of the Structure of Human Behavior*. The Hague: Mouton.

Rheingold, H. (1994) *The Virtual Community*. London: Minerva.

Ricoeur, P. (1981) *Hermeneutics and the Human Sciences: Essays on Language, Action and Interpretation*. Cambridge: Cambridge University Press.

Rochberg-Halton, E. (1986) *Meaning and Modernity: Social Theory in the Pragmatic Attitude*. Chicago: Chicago University Press.

Rorty, R. (ed.) (1967) *The Linguistic Turn*. Chicago: University of Chicago Press.

Rorty, R. (1979) *Philosophy and the Mirror of Nature*. Princeton: Princeton University Press.

Ross, L. (1977) "The Intuitive Psychologist and His Shortcomings: Distortions in the Attribution Process". *Advances in Experimental Social Psychology*, no. 10, pp. 57-96.

Saussure, F. de (1959) *Course in General Linguistics*. London: Peter Owen.

Schroeder, R. (1992) *Max Weber and the Sociology of Culture*. London: Sage.

Schudson, M. (1997) "Why Conversation Is Not the Soul of Democracy". *Critical Studies in Mass Communication*, vol.#14, no. 4, pp. 297-309.

Thompson, J.B. (1995) *The Media and Modernity*. Cambridge: Polity Press.

Tillyard, E.M.W. (1972) *The Elizabethan World Picture*. Harmondsworth: Penguin.

Turkle, S. (1995) *Life on the Screen: Identity in the Age of the Internet*. New York: Simon & Schuster.

Turner, B.S. (1999) *Classical Sociology*. London: Sage.

Weber, M. (1964) *The Theory of Social and Economic Organization*. New York: The Free Press.

Wyatt, R.O., Katz, E. & Kim, J. (2000) "Bridging the Spheres: Political and Personal Conversation in Public and Private Spaces". *Journal of Communication*, vol. 50, no. 1, pp. 71-92.

Regionalization and Domestication
of Global News

The Effect of Globalization on Media Structures and Norms

Globalization and the Choice of Foreign News

Hans-Henrik Holm

Globalization is hardly understudied. Indeed, most media studies today seem to relate to aspects of the process and effects of globalization. The reasons are simple. Following the end of the Cold War and the collapse of the Soviet Union, globalization has become a highly visible process. Triggered by these two factors, but not created by them, many domestic, societal phenomena now seem to have global import. Political ideas, economic events and communication spread much more easily now than before. We all seem to be affected by changes in other economies, political systems and cultures. The effects of globalization appear to be visible for all.

In fact, globalization is seemingly so ever present that it has become difficult to arrive at a common definition, and consequently to understand or even study its effects. Here three central problems are highlighted. First, globalization both causes other phenomena, e.g., homogenization or differentiation, and it is itself an effect of, e.g., economic interdependencies. Second, globalization is such a pervasive and shifting phenomenon, that it is difficult to identify the conjunction of events, processes and conditions of which it is composed. Finally, there has been a tendency to see globalization as all pervasive, and thereby to overestimate its effects.

In the study of globalization and the media, there has been almost exclusive attention to the effects of globalization on media structures. The process is seen as a result of integration of the media industries. "The process of globalization is very much a function of increasing corporate integration" (Morley and Robins, 1995:32). Through this process of integration, content is changed and some countries are able to define the world while others have their "history stolen". Globalization, thus, has direct consequences for the identity of peoples. The media and news agencies become unwilling partners in this process (Boyd-Barrett and Rantanen, 1998:11). Globalization is part of a news revolution, claims

Mark Alleyne (1997:137). A global news system has been created because of democratic and economic necessities.

Surprisingly, very little attention has been paid to date to the links between globalization and journalistic practices. This study aims to redress this imbalance. This article offers three conclusions:[1]

1. Globalization has had a profound impact at the level of media structure and media policy, and resultant changes in media content are visible.

2. Globalization has made an impact on the internal editorial structure of media organizations in terms of foreign news. This impact is less than that at the level of media structure and policy, but clearly observable.

3. To date, globalization has made little impact at the level of journalistic practices and news criteria as employed in the Danish editorial process when foreign news is selected.

Thus, in sum, globalization is influencing the foreign news process from the top down. The effects are most clearly seen at the structural levels. At the level of journalistic practices and norms, there is still little evidence of globalization effects.

Globalization: A Definition

This article starts from the assumption that globalization may be defined as "the intensification of economic, political, social and cultural relations across borders" (Holm and Sørensen, 1995). In a subsequent contribution, Ougaard argued that despite the academic debate over the nature of this phenomenon, its core is the clear and well-documented changes in economic integration between states (Ougaard, 1999:22).

Economic globalization is viewed as the center of the process. Globalization signifies a qualitative change, because the global economy dominates the various national economies (Jackson and Sørensen, 1999). Globalization skeptics argue that little is new even in economic terms. Globalization is a myth, and at most reflects quantitative change (Hirst and Thompson, 1992). In a comprehensive review of this debate, Held and McGrew argue that globalization is best understood as a process of transformation. Economics is at its core, with wide ranging transformative effects on social and political processes (Held and McGrew, 1999). Others have pointed out that communication has become globalized, with resulting changes in conceptions of social space (Giddens, 1996). Nations must respond to challenges stemming from the resultant restructuring of social relationships (Fukuyama, 1999).

Furthermore, values and institutions of primarily Western origin are spreading across the globe and presenting different nations with universalistic agendas of human rights, democracy and economic efficiency.

Finally, some observers point out new common global problems, such as ecological constraints, as yet another set of challenges that globalization presents the nation state (Bornschier and Chase-Dunn, 1999:293). Globalization is seen as a transformation of social relations and transactions "generating transcontinental or interregional flows and networks of activity, interaction and the exercise of power" (Held and McGrew, 1999:16).

Volkmer attempted to add meaning to the term globalization in terms of communication theory (Volkmer, 1999). Globalization is part of a post-modern world, whereas internationalization was a modern "project". Thus, globalization in the world of TV communication implies programs that are globally distributed from various countries. It reflects intercultural content and identification with a global community. Globalization refers to communities "of an extra-societal kind". Distinctions between foreign and domestic are no longer useful.

Transformations take place in political communication such that "a mediation sphere" replaces the public sphere (Volkmer, 1999:24). Robertson's theory of globalization proposes a kind of global consciousness under development. The role of global media becomes one of mediating between governments and between people. By continuously broadcasting ongoing live events such as the war in Kosovo, the global media create open global communication. State leaders and audiences are now being informed at the same time and in the same way. We see, thus, the slow birth of a global public.

The Kosovo war in 1999 demonstrated that global broadcasting and mainstreaming of events can not be assumed to have the same effects on different audiences. In Russia, audience interpretation of given events was totally different from that of the same events in Western Europe. As a consequence of the globalization process, there is at least as much differentiation as homogenization (Geoff 1999). Globalization should be seen as a transformative process, the outcome of which is not predetermined. The role of the media is not a mere reflection of a cosmopolitan dream of global consciousness, nor is it a simple function of market structures and market concentrations. Globalization should be understood in terms of the choices made, the definitions chosen, and the journalistic practices employed.

The debate over how to define globalization (Bislev, 1999; Alleyne, 1997:27) highlights the inappropriateness of the term itself. Globalization is not global, but instead a very uneven process (Holm and Sørensen, 1995).

From the perspective of journalistic practices, the globalization debate is about political, social and media choices. At the political level, these choices are being made. At G7 meetings, globalization is now on the agenda. Politicians and governments in many countries are commissioning studies of globalization and its impact. Globalization is presented as an almost extraterrestrial force that everybody must adapt to. The question is how. Globalization has been presented as one of the driving forces behind the Third Way debate on how to renew the left-of-center philosophy of the European labor parties (Giddens, 1998). In the media world, globalization is evidenced as a push towards consolidation and change.

115

In order to study such a complex phenomenon, we need a limiting definition of globalization that will allow us to see the wider context, without getting
bogged down in teleological or normative debates on cosmopolitanism versus
realism or a methodological debate on cause and effect interaction.

In this study, I will focus on globalization as consisting of two elements –
structural and technological:

1. Globalization is at its core a process of economic integration and
   interdependencies.

2. As discussed, it is also a process of technological change, particularly in the
   field of communication technology where the technological means for instant
   global communication are created and utilized.

A Model for the Study of Editorial Choice

The choice of what news to publish is the result of a process of decision making
whereby thousands of possible stories, events and units of information are culled
down to the few stories that are actually published. The scope of choice in this
process is very different depending upon your perspective.

When viewing the selection process from the outside, it is stressed that the
media, as independent units, have the freedom to select whatever stories they
want. They may choose many or few stories from the US; they may choose more
or less reporting about the latest hurricane. Critics of choices made by the media
have often stressed the media's ability to choose. Many studies of media content
employ this perspective. Studies on the coverage of Africa lament that more
news dealing with Africa is not published (Eldrige, 1993).

Seen from the inside, most journalists and editors perceive the selection
process as much more restricted. "The selection is self-evident today" was a
common phrase we encountered when discussing the selection process with
various editors. Their point is that when applying traditional news criteria to
agency reports, there is little doubt about what to choose. The classical news
criteria determine the choices:

Is it new? Is it prominent? Is it significant? Is it controversial? (Moeller, 1999:17).
The more criteria that are satisfied, the more obvious it is that the story should be
chosen.

Is there a large scope of selection in the editorial process or not? Are the
journalists right when they claim that news selection is almost automatic, or are
the outside analysts correct in stressing news desks' opportunities to choose
differently? The answer lies in understanding the entire process of news production.
The final choice that journalists and editors make in the editorial process is the
end point of a long process, where most of the "choices" have already been
made. Tuchman's studies showed how the production of meaning in society is
itself a factor in the choice of news (Tuchman, 1978:215). Studies of international
news agencies have shown how concentration and homogeneity of perspective

confines news agencies' coverage to a narrow and similar selection of news items (Paterson, 1998:95). *Figure 1* highlights how daily choice is predetermined and affected by crucial external factors.

There is a vast body of literature on these news processes, and here the focus is primarily on the effect of globalization (Ginneken, 1998; Willis, 1990).

Second, we have chosen to focus on three important aspects of the news process, with respect to which editorial choice is affected:

1. Media structure and policy: The degree of government regulation of print and electronic media strongly affects both the utilization of technology and the degree of competition and concentration in the industry (Williams, 1998). It has been clearly documented that story choice is affected by degree of commercialization of the media (Hjarvard, 1999).

2. Editorial Structure: How are domestic and foreign news production organized? Is foreign news a separate unit or integrated into other departments? How many correspondents and staff members are available? What sources are made available to the reporter etc.?

3. Journalistic standards and professional values: Particular norms for what is good and bad reporting have been developed within the journalistic professions and within foreign news. Criteria for what constitutes news determine which stories are important and essential. These criteria have become part of the professional norms of people in the business.

Figure 1. A model of factors influencing the process of daily news choice in foreign news

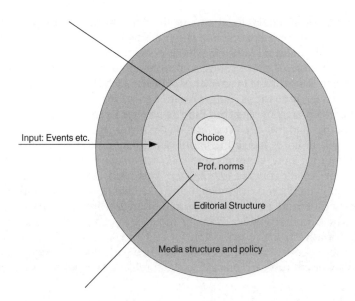

The focus in this article is on the question of how globalization has affected the scope of editorial choice in terms of our three main parameters: Media policy, Editorial structure and Journalistic self-conception.

Media structure and policy

That technological changes and economic integration has affected media policy is well documented and need not be elaborated here.[2] Technology has profoundly affected the regulatory possibilities of governments. In the 1980s, the Danish government tried in vain to maintain a ban on satellite reception. In some instances, the police were sent out to cut wires from illegal satellite dishes. This was a policy that could obviously not be maintained, but illustrated the political desire to keep electronic media under control. Other governments have struggled with unwanted television being beamed in from other countries, as was the case with the "Red Hot Dutch" porno channel. Technology has, however, also opened up new venues for governments. The Internet allows governments to bypass the media by offering the public direct access to news and documentation (Hutchinson, 1999). Due to regulation difficulties and with a view to the opportunities offered by new technologies, governments have deregulated the electronic media and introduced market mechanisms into the halls of public service stations (Stephenson and Bromley, 1999).

Economic integration has had various independent effects on media policy. Internationalization has pushed the media business towards larger and larger units. In countries like Denmark, where legislation makes foreign ownership difficult, local TV and radio has become the target of media multinationals. SBS (Scandinavian Broadcasting System), a US based media company, now owns or services local TV and radio stations in Denmark and a number of smaller European countries.

In the world of print media, local papers all over Europe are disappearing and national papers are consolidating into larger media houses locked in intense battles over readership and advertising. Media policy during the last ten years has largely served to referee these changes. In some countries, press support is still a factor in maintaining the life of smaller papers, but such cases are exceptions. At the European level, discussions on European regulation of concentration and transmedia ownership are ongoing, but little action has been taken so far.

Globalization has had two distinct effects on the media structure in Denmark.[3] In terms of TV and radio, it has led to rapid deregulation of state control and created a multitude of new channels and alternative news programs for the audience. In terms of the printed media, the increased costs of newspaper production have triggered a wave of mergers and consolidations. The newspapers are, however, larger and more professional than before the process of consolidation. The overall result is a dramatic increase in competition among all types of media for advertising revenue and for audiences.

Evidently, the process of editorial choice has been affected. Considerations of reader and viewer interests are pushed to the forefront. Foreign news editors must demonstrate that more than a small elite is interested in foreign news. How the story is told becomes, thus, an even more important consideration. Foreign news must be dramatic and easily accessible. Moreover, each medium's need to differentiate itself from others becomes an important concern in selecting and presenting the news. One Danish paper has defined a foreign news profile with special emphasis on human rights coverage, others stress financial news (Holm, 2000: 104).

Globalization and editorial structure

Within most news organizations, the foreign news desk has traditionally been a very separate unit. First, the technology created a need for separation. Expensive and cumbersome telex machines or expensive international phone lines were necessary. Just ten years ago, most editorial offices still relied on a row of constantly ticking machines producing endless streams of white paper. Today, everyone in a news organization has computer access to international news feeds by the mere touch of a button. Communication costs both in terms of phone or satellite transmissions have decreased markedly.

Second, foreign news departments were previously staffed by people with special qualifications and interests. They were required to speak foreign languages. Travel was a necessity, and significant journalistic experience a must. Today, the majority of news is available in English, and many journalists today have some ability in English. Travel has become relatively easy and inexpensive. A special group of people in a newsroom dedicated to foreign news would no longer seem to be necessary.

Finally, foreign news used to be a sharply defined field in terms of content. Foreign news was about political and economic events in foreign countries. Particularly events related to these countries' foreign policies and the consequences of such policies for one's own country. International news was largely diplomatic news. Although we only have data for 1998, our conclusions are based on existing research on how foreign news was structured and defined in the past (Taylor, 1997:58-75). Today foreign news has become global news. Economic events now play as much a role in foreign reporting as does politics. In addition, descriptions of culture, sports or general living conditions are now gaining prominence. Here globalization is clearly visible. In many news organizations, the name "foreign department" has been dropped and changed to "global" or "international department". Correspondents must report on many different aspects of life in their assigned countries. They write for many different sections of the newspaper.

In our study of foreign news content, these changes were quite prominent. In *Table 1*, subjects have been divided into "traditional" and "non-traditional" foreign news.

Table 1. Subjects of International Coverage (Nov. 1998) in Danish Media (percent)

Subject	Newspapers	Electronic media
Traditional	58	76.7
National eco+pol.	26	43
Internat. politics	11	20
European union	7	6
Internat. economics	4	0.2
Danish foreign policy	2	1
War	2	0.5
Aid	4	3
Disasters	2	3
Non traditional	42	23.3
Culture+lifestyle	10	1
Person stories	6	4
Human rights	6	5
Environment	4	3
Business	4	3
Social subjects	4	5
Historical	4	1
Adventure	2	1
Curiosities	2	0.3
Total	100	100

In the electronic media (radio in particular), "traditional" subjects still dominate foreign news. This is partly because radio produces fewer stories, and must therefore go through a more rigorous selection process. In newspapers, almost half of the stories are now "non-traditional".

Globalization is changing the editorial structure of foreign news desks, but it is worth noting that this is a recent and ongoing process. Our study of the structure of Danish newsrooms today showed that changes were being discussed, but few were in fact implemented.

Within DR, the traditional public service radio and TV broadcaster, management has drawn up a plan to demand "bi-medial" production of foreign correspondents and to merge radio and TV news departments. So far, this has created a great deal of controversy. It remains to be seen, however, whether this will lead to the creation of a larger and more separate foreign news department or to the kind of general newsroom integration envisioned by management.

In the print media, several of the newspapers have been experimenting with news editorial structures. The separate foreign news department is less separate today. At one Danish newspaper (Politiken), the Brussels office now has a rotating domestic reporter. Political reporters get a feel for foreign reporting, and domestic concerns are present on the foreign desk. In other papers, the business section and the foreign desk share offices and editors (Jyllands-Posten). Integration is made easier by the fact that foreign reporters are younger and less experienced today. The young journalist is cheaper, and more willing to cover the multitude of subjects required of today's foreign reporter.

Globalization and journalistic norms and self-conceptions

The importance of professional norms for news production has been amply documented in the literature. The standardization of international news is in fact explained by the "globally defined implicit journalistic codes for the production of news" (van Dijk, 1988:131).

The market-driven nature of modern media and the intense pressure on journalists to deliver sellable products are affecting overall news content and foreign news production. Journalists and editors lament that stories on TV are becoming shorter and shorter. Print journalists feel that they are asked to cover such a wide range of subjects that it is difficult to be thorough, hard hitting and critical.

Surveys demonstrate that trust in journalists is continuously low and among the lowest of all professions surveyed.[4] Data from the US show that journalists themselves share this lack of trust in their colleagues. Forty to fifty-five percent agree with the criticism that news reporting is full of factual errors and sloppiness. This has increased 10 percentage points over a ten-year period. Almost two-thirds of journalists and reporters say that the distinction between reporting and commentary has seriously eroded (Pew, 1999).

When asked, journalists and editors explain this erosion of trust in terms of the increased use of sensationalism and emotionality as criteria for news selection. It is no surprise, then, that journalists tend to adhere to traditional norms of news gathering and reporting when asked to describe what they do in the news selection process. The traditional news criteria are still the dominant arguments used in selection of foreign news.

But the editorial selection process is changing. More non-traditional subjects must be covered, and it is becoming harder to choose the boring, but important, story (Graham & Holm, 1999:42). Many journalists express a reluctant awareness of the fact that the journalist's role is changing rapidly as a consequence of globalization. No longer is he/she the only purveyor of foreign news. There is now a large number of sources to select from, ranging from the Internet to international 24-hour news channels. Consequently, it is difficult to be first, and it is even harder to have an "exclusive". The journalist becomes a news organizer who must tell the story in a better or more relevant way to her/his audience. Journalists, however, feel acutely pressured to choose the more sensational and person-oriented stories (Holm, 2000: 195).

In our survey, 6 percent of the foreign news stories in the print media were categorized as "person" stories. In the electronic media, the corresponding figure was 3.3 percent. The figures for stories categorized as odd or curious were 1.3 and 1.4 percent, respectively. These are not large figures, but in the coverage of stories about celebrities, journalists feel trapped by the need to tell stories attracting large audiences instead of reporting on subjects they themselves define as important.

Editorial Choice

Will we be able to detect the effects of these different limitations on editorial choice when studying the arguments used for selecting or not selecting stories as part of the daily editorial choice process? Does globalization reach down and affect daily choice?

In the following, an analysis is presented of the arguments used for story selection. Specifically, we will look at how much these arguments reflect considerations related to editorial structure ("We want this story because at this paper we place priority on transnational stories"; "the correspondent was too busy, so we cannot include that story"). How important are arguments reflecting journalistic norms and self-conceptions ("It is a well-told story"; "It is an important story")? Finally, arguments reflecting increased media competition are examined ("we need to "tease" a program later on tonight". "TV2 had that story, so we won't").

The empirical sample consists of participant observations at 5 newspapers, two TV stations and the main Danish radio station. For each organization, we closely followed the work from early morning to late evening, and systematically recorded arguments used during the selection process. While making choices, journalists and editors were asked why they made the selection they did. All of the arguments were then recorded and categorized (Holm, 2000: 8). The interviews were conducted during a "normal news period" including several international stories, but no single major story dominated. We feel confident that our data provide a valid reflection of the types of arguments used across different media, but obviously the sample is relatively small. Consequently, care should be taken in generalizing the results.

Table 2.   Editorial arguments for selection or rejection of stories

	Arguments N =223	Percent of total=100
Media structure/ competition	16	7
Editorial structure	62	28
Journalistic self-conception/ news criteria	145	65
Timeliness	44	20
Importance	45	20
Conflict	9	4
Sensation	24	11
Identification	23	10

Two things stand out very clearly in *table 2*:

1. The classical news criteria are still by far the most influential arguments used in the selection of foreign news.

2. More than one-third of the arguments used reflect considerations other than news content.

We have no data on how this may have changed over time, but it is interesting to compare these findings with those from some previous gate-keeping studies. A study of criteria used by American newspaper editors in selecting foreign news revealed that "most editors appear to focus more on factors having significant impact or consequences, especially when American security and national interest are involved." This study also pointed out that individual differences (political orientation) and organizational constraints in the newsroom where important in shaping editors' perceptions of foreign news factors (Chang and Lee, 1992:554-561).

Previous studies of the gatekeeper function have demonstrated that gate-keepers' approaches to choosing news agency stories have changed surprisingly little from the first study done in 1949 to the second in 1989.[5]

> Newspaper gatekeepers read and asses about 1000 stories a week. They are usually experienced journalists who have spent many years reading news sto-ries sent by the wire services, which in turn have gatekeepers with similar experiences. Gatekeepers tend to select news by being gatekeepers. As a group gatekeepers – to do and keep their job- share high exposure, acceptance, and comprehension of the same media messages every day. (Bleske, 1991:92)

News is, thus, selected in very predictable ways that have changed very little. Our study indicated that as many as one-third of arguments related to considera-tions other than the news. In a study on community and regional newspaper gatekeepers, the questions of the impact of editorial structure and organizational constraints were specifically examined. The data are from the US and from 1989, and comparisons should, therefore, be made with great care. The data showed that – both at small and large daily newspapers – the dominant "concerns for decisions you make on your paper" were *editorial concerns. Concern over ad-vertising* was more prominent at the smaller papers, whereas *production and circulation* were greater concerns for the large regional papers. These data tend to corroborate our results. For example, in the American study, 19 percent of editors mentioned "organizational problems" as the "major concerns" at their paper (Donohue et al., 1989:807-812).

It seems reasonable to conclude that, despite the changes introduced through the process of globalization so far, the actual approach to news selection has changed relatively little. However our interviews show that we are in the midst of a process of change and that the figures obscure the fact that the conditions for change are prime. To look closer at this, we need to examine in more detail the nature of the arguments used in the news selection process.

As evident from *table 2*, only 7 percent of the arguments were directly related to media structure/competition. For example, in our study of the TV editorial process, we found that stories were rejected because the other channel already had that story. (The story was about an international environmental conference and the issue was whether to cover it. Since the other channel al-ready had a planned segment on the Danish angle, the first channels declined to select the story. The importance of the story was not in question).

A large number of the arguments in this category relate to the question of getting the right mix of news every day. The media strive to highlight their own stories in order to achieve higher reader/viewer identification. Thus, stories planned at the news desk are given priority. In this case, the journalists are more visible and the story might even be presented directly as "one of our own".

In the selection of stories the right mix is also important. There should be a more humorous or soft story included every day. "We want this because it enlivens the page and has the humor that is necessary for the mix". "This story is a curious one and it contributes to creating a good mix". Arguments like these reflect the fact that editorial choice is influenced by competitive pressures. It is important to "lure" people into the foreign news. During the coverage of hurricane Mitch, the TV news editor wanted something lighter to spice up the broadcast and got a story about alligators that had escaped from a crocodile farm and were now swimming in the rivers of Honduras. This was used as the last story in the news broadcast, with a short intro and as background for the credit roll.

Twenty-nine percent of all arguments referred to organizational structure, staffing issues, etc. (editorial structure): "The correspondents are very tired and have been working hard". "Moscow doesn't want to produce more stories because he already has three stories that haven't been used." "We can't get the people in the graphics department to do it today and the story needs graphics". Some arguments reflected considerations of picture coverage. A good picture can get even an unimportant story included. No pictures can kill a good story. How the story is told is also an important consideration in its own right.

Journalistic goals of covering the world and limitations of editorial structure often clash. The production of foreign news is a time-consuming and difficult process despite technological changes. Many things can and do go wrong. So how do you cover all the essential stories when you can not produce your own? You use the short newsflash. Both in print and electronic media, the number of shorter stories has been increased in order to "cover the world". Even if there is no staff to write about the recent election it Pakistan, it must be covered in the news. Shorter items and telegrams are a means to this end. Another common argument is to publish smaller news items "to keep the story alive until our own stories come through".

Table 3. Short as compared with longer stories

	Newspapers	Radio and TV
Number of larger/longer stories	1 828	361
Number of notes/short stories	1 568	194
Notes as % of total in mm or sec.	10 %	4 %

As seen in *table 3*, notes/small stories cover a large number of subjects and thereby cover the "rest of the world", even though they only occupy a small percentage of news space and time.

The predominant arguments for story editing come from the category of journalistic self-conception/news criteria. *Table 2* shows that 65 percent of arguments are related to this category. Of these arguments, the most important are "Timeliness" and "Importance". Forty percent of all arguments related to the statements: "This is an important story". "This just came in". "We have to go with this story, it may affect a lot of people." These are journalistic standard arguments, and reflect a core understanding of what journalism is all about: The reporting of important events. They may in part also be standard arguments used for any story that the gatekeeper finds relevant, but nevertheless, there seems to be agreement on what these stories are. When we looked at the stories selected as the top foreign news stories at the different editorial offices, about 80 percent were the same. The classical hard-nosed news criteria are strongly internalized and mutually reinforced by looking at the selection of others. The mainstreaming of news is the inevitable result.

As many as 20 percent of the arguments refer to receiver identification or sensationalism. "It is very exotic and so far away that it is interesting". "Because it is a story of the type man bites dog" (in reference to a story about a South African priest who turned out to be a crook). The coverage of both Princess Diana's death and the Lewinsky affair were clear reflections of such arguments. One editor argued " Everything about Lewinsky is good stuff just like the Diana stories". Identification is also the reason stated for using a Danish angle in stories. This was an often-used argument particularly among radio editors and reporters. "There is a Danish angle". "It is important for Denmark". "There is a demonstration about this issue in Copenhagen".

However, the majority of the arguments come from the conviction that what is essential news must have priority. "This is an important story". "This has regional significance". "This fuels further nationalism". "This will be one of the main problems for the future", etc., etc.

Examination of the arguments leads to two conclusions. Classical news criteria are still the best predictors of what news will be chosen and used. The range of arguments used today reflects the fact that other concerns are becoming accepted into the newsroom. Whether one interprets these results as indications of professional consistency over time or of impending change is, in the absence of clear longitudinal data, more a matter of conviction than of science.

Conclusion

Globalization affects media structures and has totally restructured the environment in which foreign news is selected. Today, foreign news must leave the old ivory tower of intellectual and elite journalism and confront the diverse needs of the modern media market.

> The traditional media will lose even more of their role as mediators between events and the public. In short, the force that was instrumental in bringing

down the Berlin Wall is likely to bring down many walls in our own country (Grunwald, 1993:16).

Rapid technological changes create a global market for foreign news and information. Today there is no monopoly on "reporting from Tokyo". Future developments of "news on demand" will place foreign news on a par with all other types of news that may be selected or ignored at will. Globalization *per se* is transforming politics and creating new transnational audiences and means of communication. The political reality is in place, and the media must and will follow.

Our study of the process of editorial choice shows how these transformations have been clearly visible at the level of media structure and competition. They have had and are having clear influences on the present restructuring of newsrooms. Foreign departments are changing and merging with other departments in the editorial offices. The status of foreign news as a special sanctuary is eroding. As Garric Utley points out, "Today everyone is a reporter". Equipped with simple camcorders and computers everyone can send video and stories everywhere (Utley, 1997:9).

In the actual selection of news, however, traditional news criteria still stand. Seen in a longer time perspective, the selection of foreign news is still largely dominated by classical journalistic norms and traditional news criteria. At the same time, however, we see that the number of non-traditional foreign stories is as high as four out of ten. This is the result of an expansion of the total number of international stories.

Globalization is changing how foreign news production is structured. It has also had a strong impact on media policy. But the fundamental norms that editors and journalists express still reflect traditional news values. Will these norms remain unchanged, or will structural change gradually globalize news criteria as well? The answer will be largely determined by how well journalists and editors are able to make important news reflect a broader agenda for what is of global relevance.

Notes

1. The following is based on work by a research group at the Centre for Journalism and Further Education, where a detailed survey of foreign news coverage in the Danish media was undertaken. Spanning a two-week period (Nov. 11- 24, 1998), all foreign news (in a broad sense) in 9 newspapers, and on two TV stations and the national radio network was collected. In addition, a study of the organizational structure of each of the news organizations was conducted. Finally, observation of the editorial process at seven of the major media took place, with a specific focus on the process of editorial choice (Holm, 2000).

2. The Danish Government created a Media Committee in 1994 to review media policy in terms of access, quality and freedom of information. The result of the work was a series of reports (Medieudvalget, 1996).

3. This discussion excludes the interesting and essential debate on the effects of globalization in a wider framework, i.e., cultural dependency and homogeneity (Hjarvard, 1996).
4. The latest figures from Denmark show that only 1 percent of the population think that journalists have high credibility. It received the lowest ranking of all the evaluated professions (October 1999).
5. David Manning White wrote, in 1950, the classical study "The "Gate Keeper". A Case Study in the Selection of News" (White, 1950:383-396). The study was replicated and updated in a study called "Ms. Gates takes over. An Updated Version of a 1949 Case Study" (Bleske, 1991:88-97).

References

Alleyne, Mark D. (1997) *News Revolution. Political and Economic Decisions about Global Information*. London: Macmillan.

Berkowitz, Dan (1997) *Social Meanings of News*. London: Sage.

Bislev, Sven (1999) *En ny og større verden? Globaliseringens ansigter*. København: Fremad.

Bleske, Glen L. (1991) "Ms. Gates Takes Over", *Newspaper Research Journal*, vol.12, pp. 88-97.

Bornscheier, Volker & Chase-Dunn, Christopher (1999) *The Future of Global Conflict*. London: Sage.

Boyd-Barrett, Oliver & Rantanen, Terhi (eds.) (1998) "The Globalization of News", in Boyd-Barret, Oliver & Rantanen, Terhi (eds.) *The Globalization of News*, London: Sage.

Chang, Tsan-Kuo & Lee, Jae-Won (1992) "Factors Affecting Gatekeepers' Selection of Foreign News; A National Survey of Newspaper Editors", *Journalism Quarterly*, vol.69, no.3 pp. 554-561.

Donohue, G.A; Olien, C.N. & Tichenor, P.J (1989) "Structure and Constraints on Community Newspaper Gatekeepers," *Journalism Quarterly*, vol.66, pp. 807-812.

Eldrige, John (1993) *Getting the Message: News, Truth and Power*. London: Routledge.

Fukuyama, Francis (1999) *The Great Transformation*. New York: Free Press.

Galtung, Johan et al. (1965) "The Structure of Foreign News", *Journal of Peace Research*, no.2, pp. 64-91.

Geoff, Peter (ed.) (1999) *The Kosovo News and Propaganda War*. Wien: The International Press Institute.

Giddens, Anthony (1996) *Introduction to Sociology*. New York: Norton.

Giddens, Anthony (1998) *The Third Way. The Renewal of Social Democracy*. London: Polity Press.

Ginneken, Jaap van (1998) *Understanding Global News*. London: Sage.

Graham Holm, Nancy (1999) "US Influence on Danish TV journalism", in Kabel, Lars (ed.) *Nye Nyheder*. Aarhus: Ajour.

Grunwald, Henry A. (1993) "The Post-Cold War Press", *Foreign Affairs*, vol.72, no.3, pp. 12-16.

Held, David; McGrew, Anthony; Goldblatt, David & Perraton, Jonathan (1999) *Global Transformations*, Cambridge: Polity Press.

Hirst P. & Thompson G. (1992) "The Problem of Globalization", *Economy and Society*, no.4.

Hjarvard, Stig (1999) *TV nyheder i konkurrence*. København: Samfundslitteratur.

Hjarvard, Stig (1996) *Grænseløse medier – Nye sociale fællesskaber?* København: Media Committee.

Holm, Hans-Henrik & Sørensen, Georg (1995) (eds.) *Whose World Order*. Boulder: Westview Press.

Holm, Hans-Henrik; Kabel, Lars; Kitaj, Torben; Møller, Lars & Ytzen, Flemming (2000) *Verden på tilbud. Om udenrigsjournalistik og mediernes udenrigsdækning*. Aarhus: Ajour.

Hutchinson, David (1999) *Media Policy*. Oxford: Blackwell.

Kabel, Lars (ed.) (1999) *Nye Nyheder*. Århus: Ajour.

Jackson, Robert & Sørensen, Georg (1999) *Introduction to International Relations*. Oxford: Oxford University Press.

Jensen, Klaus Bruhn (1994) *Verdensnyheder*. København: DR (Report 2 B).

Lund, Erik (1975) "Nyhedsstrukturer og redaktionsprocesser i TVA 1964-1974", in Skovmand (ed.) *DR50*. København: DR.

Medieudvalget (1996) *Betænkning om medierne i demokratiet*. København: Statens trykningkontor (Betænkning nr. 1320).

Morley, David & Robins, Kevin (1995) *Spaces of Identity. Global Media, Electronic Landscapes and Cultural Boundaries*. London: Routledge.

Moeller, Susan D. (1999) *Compassion Fatigue. How the Media Sell Disease, Famine, War and Death*. New York: Routledge.

Ougaard Morten (1999) "Globalisering: myter og realiteter". København: Business School.

Paterson, Chris (1998) "Global Battlefields", in Boyd-Barret, Oliver & Rantanen, Terhi (eds.) *The Globalization of News*. London: Sage.

Pew (1999) *Striking the Balance. Audience Interests, Business Pressures and Journalists' Values*. Washington D.C.: PEW.

Pittelkow, Ralf (1986) *TV avisen set indefra*. København: DR, (Report 7).

Stephenson, Hugh & Bromley, Michael (1999) *Sex, Lies and Democracy. The Press and the Public*, Harlow: Longmann.

Taylor, Phillip M. (1997) *Global Communication. International Affairs and the Media since 1945*. London: Routledge.

Tuchman, Gaye (1978) *Making News: A Study in the Construction of Reality*. New York: Free Press.

Utley, Garrick (1997) "The Shrinking of Foreign News", *Foreign Affairs*, vol.76, no.2, pp.2-9.

van Dijk, Teun (1988) *News Analysis. Case Studies of International and National News in the Press*. Hillsdale: Lawrence Erlbaum Publ.

White, David Manning (1950) " The 'Gate Keeper'". A Case Study in the Selection of News", *Journalism Quarterly*, vol.27, pp. 383-396.

Willis, Jim (1990) *Journalism: State of the Art*. London: Praeger.

Williams, Kevin (1998) *Get Me a Murder a Day. A History of Mass Communication in Britain*. London: Arnold.

Volkmer, Ingrid (1999) *News in the Global Sphere. A Study of CNN and Its Impact on Global Communication*. Luton: University of Luton Press.

Transnational Politics and News Production
Norwegian Correspondents on the Brussels Beat

Tore Slaatta

Introduction

How do European integration processes influence news production and the political role of the news media? New strategies for transnational news production are presently being developed as responses to increased competition in the global news market. As technological improvements for transnational and global news production and distribution speed up towards convergence, international news media organisations are increasingly struggling to position themselves within the European and global media orders. In this situation, the idea of developing particular routines and sections for news on European, transnational politics has emerged as an important competitive strategy. Thus, we are witnessing the pro-liferation of a market-driven communicative space in Europe that, to some ex-tent, can be said to function as a media public sphere for the European political and economic elite (Schlesinger 1999a).

However, this process is not solely driven by the market. It is also initiated and inspired by the changing institutional frameworks of transnational politics within the European Union. Seen from an institutional perspective, the framework needed for a transnational, as opposed to national, political order in Europe is largely already in place. This demonstrates the need for a European public sphere, within which the news media must play a pivotal role. In practice, however, the traditional idea of the political role of the news media is as a Fourth Estate within the nation state framework. And the link between media markets and national political cultures creates strong imperatives for the continuing development of news production strategies and routines that correspond to a national, rather than transnational, frame of reference (Keane 1992, Slaatta 1999).

In this perspective, it becomes interesting for media scholars to see how the traditionally nationally oriented news media in different European countries are presently formulating news production strategies and routines focussed on Europe and the European Union. Questions can be formulated as to what degree and how the national news media are changing or maintaining national frames of reference in their practices of producing political news; how and to what degree these frames can be said to open the mediation of transnational rather than national political discourse; and to what degree possible changes can be seen as predominantly market driven or resulting from shifting considerations regarding new political and institutional contexts.

This essay discusses how political changes and events in the relationship between Norway and the EU in 1990s influenced the strategies of Norwegian news production on the Brussels news beat. Focus is set on the period following the referendum in November 1994, when the majority of the Norwegian electorate voted "no" to full membership in the EU. It is argued that interpretations of the political situation after the referendum on Norwegian membership, along with the institutional framework of the EEA Agreement (European Economic Area), significantly influenced the assignments, priorities and work conditions for Norwegian EU correspondents on the "Brussels beat". Hence, compared to the situation in the years before the referendum, the period following the referendum was marked by a shift of interest away from the EU and a strengthening of the national, as opposed to European, frame of reference in Norwegian news production practices.

The empirical findings reported here are part of a research project on the changing relationships between news media and politics in Norway[1]. The project has been based upon a wide range of empirical data and the use of multiple methods: quantitative and qualitative content analysis of news media content, interviews with editors and journalists, interviews and observations on the Brussels news beat, and interviews with political agents and sources involved in political discourses on EU politics (Slaatta 1999).

The Norwegian case

In many ways, Norway represents a special case as regards issues of European integration and the media. Norway did not become a full member of the EU after the '94 referendum, and the divisions among the electorate still cut across traditional party alignments. Moreover, the history of the Norwegian media order has an important political aspect, which along with its geographic peculiarities and sparse population explains the strong regional and national links between media, markets and politics in Norway.

Between 1986 and 1994, the Norwegian news media became increasingly engaged in coverage and reporting on negotiations with the EU, first on the EEA negotiations and, from 1993, on the issue of full EU membership. Media activity peaked with the coverage of the long lasting referendum campaign period in the fall of 1994 (Slaatta et al. 1998). After the Norwegian electorate voted "no" to full membership in the European Union, the news media tried to adjust to a new political context. In particular, they tried to make sense of the importance of the EEA Agreement for future Norwegian – European relations.

The EEA Agreement presently regulates the relations between EU and the EFTA (European Free Trade Association) countries: Iceland, Liechtenstein, and Norway. Briefly, the EEA lets the EFTA countries (but not Switzerland) into the

European Single Market. Although a wide-ranging treaty, the Agreement remains an international trade agreement between two multinational organisations: EU and EFTA. The institutional framework of the EEA Agreement is carefully designed to ensure the member states of EFTA their sovereignty and right to veto ratification of EU acts of the single market. Through the EEA Agreement, Norwegian governmental representatives are allowed consultations with the European Commission and representation in various EU Commission policy expert committees. But, as they belong to a non-member state, Norwegian officials and ministers are not represented in the Council or in the European Parliament.

Although it is an interstate agreement designed to preserve nation state sovereignty, it is an open question how and to what extent the EEA Agreement will affect political developments within the Norwegian state. The treaty is inherently linked to the general processes of integration between the member states, and allows only small measures of participation and influence on decision-making processes within the EU. Thus, it is more than just a trade agreement, and Norway's position in the European political order has become ambiguous.

In this situation, Norwegian relationships to Europe and the EU can be described as being in a state of 'identity crisis'. In political discourse, the meaning of the Norwegian position in the European order is continually being contested and negotiated by competing political agents. Norway is, thus, presently being defined as both 'inside' and 'outside' the EU, and one continuing debate in the public political discourse involves defining just how far inside or outside we actually are.

This has particular consequences for the way political knowledge on Europe and the EU became produced and mediated in the Norwegian news media during the post-referendum period. As an 'outsider', Norway might be seen as a non-member state, and as being very different from other European countries, emphasising 'facts' about Norway being a small, homogenous nation state, with a highly developed economy and well-organised welfare state and a historical record of stable, democratic political institutions. As an 'insider', the emphasis can be put on how Norway is historically part of international and European politics, culture and economy, and how the EEA Agreement presently constitutes an institutional framework for a transnational, rather than national, political order.

This volatile situation gives the Norwegian news media an important role in actively constructing and mediating, for Norwegian citizens, political knowledge and symbols concerning European politics. In public political discourse, the national news media are active agents in the symbolic contest for defining the meaning of Europe and the changing relationships between EU and Norway.

Domestication and the construction of political knowledge

The concept of domestication has recently been introduced in studies of international news production to explain the narrative differences that appear in national broadcasting of international events (Gurevitch et al., 1996). Mostly in suggestive terms, it is argued that although events and news are seen as "international", it is through a process of "domestication" that foreign and transnational events and news stories are made relevant and meaningful to domestic readers and viewers. An event or news story can be said to be "international" through its consequences and causes, or because international crisis news appeals to empathic reactions and reactions from informally or formally legitimated voices of the 'international society'. Still, when comparing the differing presentations within national-oriented news media, it is observed that journalists use frames that reflect the cultural and political idiosyncrasies of their domestic and local audiences. In this way, the term 'global news' or 'international news' becomes ambiguous, and it becomes important to analyse exactly how different news media are domesticating 'facts' and 'events' from a presumed 'global' news environment.

My approach to analysing domestication and the role of the news media reflects a different expectation of the probable outcome of the research. Rather than seeing domestication as a residual category that explains differences appearing in national news media reports on international or foreign events, I see domestication as both a sociological and ideological structure. Historically, there is a strong connection between the practice of news production and the political order of the nation state. This is observable in the way the profession of journalism was established and how norms and considerations regarding newsworthiness and news production routines became connected to interpretations of national interests and identities. What I find particularly important is the way political institutions of the democratic nation state became the institutional framework for correspondents' beat routines and source-journalist relations. Considerations of political institutions and situations have always been important parts of the organisational and professional knowledge that defines and makes sense of organisational priorities and news production routines.

Generally, I will argue that European integration, or what I will call "Europeanisation", produces new conditions for news production by 1) establishing new political arenas, procedures and practices whereby transnational political discourses are constructed, mediated and thereby domesticated; 2) redistributing symbolic powers and redefining regions of disclosure and enclosure where political information can be accessed and made public, thereby; 3) changing the routines of news production and source – journalist interaction (Slaatta 1999). In theory, the European Union could be seen as an emerging institutional framework for a transnational, political field, in relation to which the present structures and orders of European and national news media constitute a complex and contradictory media public sphere. Thus, it is an empirical question as to how, and to what degree, these new conditions are actually influencing various news media's practices of news production focussed on EU-related matters.

Instead of observing how domestication appears as a bias in "international news", I want to analyse how and to what degree the changing relationships between EU and Norway during the 90s became interpreted as changing contexts for Norwegian foreign news production focussed on EU and EEA. Rather than analysing crisis news and international event news, I focus on the systematic, routine reporting of transnational politics between Europe and Norway.

In the following, I will discuss how Norwegian editors, journalists and Brussels correspondents were constructing theories and images of the political situation and the role of the news media during the post-referendum period (1994 – 1997). Among many interesting questions are: How did they interpret the new political situation and its significance for EU coverage and newsworthiness? How did the media organisations define assignments and allocate resources as a response to the new situation? And how did the relationship between home journalists and Brussels correspondents change? At the Brussels beat: How did beat work change, and how did relationships between Norwegian correspondents and the international press corps change? And, finally, how did relationships to sources and the EU institutions change?

Interpreting the Post-Referendum Situation[2]

In the period immediately following the referendum, the correspondents and their editors in the major Norwegian news media formally reformulated their considerations of newsworthiness and redesigned organisational routines for news production. In their considerations, journalists and editors formulated overall theories and interpretations of the European order and the position of Norway as being outside or inside the political, cultural and economical spaces of Europe. Also important were considerations of the domestic climate of debate and the consequences of the referendum for political culture.

Interpreting the field: newsworthiness and political discourse

Journalists and editors interpreted the new political and economic relationships between Norway and EU, based on EFTA and the EEA Agreement, as having important consequences for the organisation of news production after the referendum. In their understanding of the changing political context, considerations of story suitability were connected to redefinitions of foreign policy orientations and interpretations of national interests and identities in a new situation. The membership discourses were seen as dissolving into separate, but connected news discourses, and what was seen as a new consensus in the foreign policy orientations towards Europe reduced the level of newsworthiness. On the Brussels beat, interpretations of the outside, non-member position as being less involved and less interesting reduced newsworthiness similarly.

In 1995 and 1996, home journalists, editors and Brussels correspondents argued that the threshold for news on EU and EEA issues was getting high, some would say extremely high. Asked to comment on why, they almost unanimously argued that the logic of news production focussed on Europe was now completely changed compared to the pre-referendum situation. Journalists as well as editors felt that EU and EEA stories had lost their 'appeal' and interest, since '...we are not a member'. Thus, considerations of newsworthiness were based on theories of changes in official foreign policies and in the political context and its 'implications for Norway'.

133

The EEA Agreement was seen to define a political context with very different implications for news media discourse production than would have appeared in a membership situation. Not being a full member was taken as a sign that Norway was 'not involved any more', and there was a general understanding of the 'realpolitik' in the present situation: 'If we had been a member...' the situation would have been different, many argued. According to those interviewed, their media organisation still would have to cover the 'major political events', and the summits and major events within the EU would be considered newsworthy. But the everyday flow of news from the EU was now seen as being of little interest.

When reflecting upon the political order in Europe, journalists and editors constructed theories of the 'Norwegian condition'. The recent boom in the Norwegian economy was suggested as particularly important. The theory was that since everything was going so well, nobody really had to bother about the problems in Europe or Norway's lack of influence due to its non-member status. Norway was, somewhat ironically, pictured as a different society with a quite different political agenda than the rest of Europe. This was seen as a disconnection of the news discourse in Norway from that of other countries.

More generally, home journalists and editors made professional judgements on newsworthiness on the basis of commonsensical interpretations of the domestic public political agenda. As a sign of a shift, the sudden stop of the referendum debate became an occasion for rethinking journalistic strategies and correspondent networks. A sense of 'loss' seemed to prevail among the political elite, of which journalists and correspondents are a part. Several used the metaphor 'dead' to describe the present climate for news production. An 'exhaustion' was observed in the political system. The EU membership question had occupied politicians, experts, editors and journalists for so long that it was now seen as natural to reduce the activity. In the eyes of the editor, high levels of coverage could provoke resentment rather than mobilise a new interest in the EU. Implied in this is both a concern for sources as well as the general public. One should 'bother' neither sources nor the public with 'unnecessary coverage'.

Interpreting the field: the new consensus

The home journalists generally expressed a dependency on reports on conflicting issues from the political opposition in the Storting. When opposition sources presented a conflict, news discourse was generated. But if no one was willing to break a consensus, news stories were expected to be hard to generate.

The referendum and the EEA Agreement were viewed as producing a new consensus in the foreign affairs arena. The conflict on EU membership was non-existent, as was the need for political parties to comment and formulate policies on European issues. This was seen to influence news production strategies and possibilities. For instance, news stories on the EU were not considered to have high potential for conflict, which was needed if they were to be 'dramatised' through agent reactions (Cohen 1963; Eide and Hernes 1987). As the membership issue was settled, public attention was thought to shift to other conflicts. The heat of the debate had subsided, and excessive reporting on peripheral events was viewed as equally bad journalistic work as was not covering the major news stories of the day. Articulating editorial views on EU issues was no longer considered important or relevant.

Although some small variations were observed depending on when the interviews were conducted, all interviewees mentioned the same selection of political discourses as the most important. In 1995, the continuous ratification of Single Market legislation and the flow of 'acquis communautaires' into the EEA Agreement were seen as constituting the major news discourse. In 1996, new legislation was expected to be less frequent, but still newsworthy and important to follow. Considerations of newsworthiness from the Storting depended on the degree of conflict within that body. At that time, high newsworthiness connected to EU events was seen as unlikely. According to one journalist, a potential big story could only be expected if a future conflict with the EU involved major, national enterprises and political agents, which could then call the entire EEA Agreement into question.

The foreign news agenda of EU politics and European integration itself were seen as generally less important, and increasingly difficult to report on. Some issues were characterised as 'major issues'. The EMU process (European Monetary Union) was seen as particularly important, because it was expected to have an impact on Norway, despite its non-member status. But as a complex and financial matter, it was considered difficult and of low newsworthiness to the average reader. The project of European integration itself, for instance related to the problems of the new member states and the discussion on EU expansion towards Eastern Europe, was seen as less interesting, as was the IGC process (Inter-Governmental Conference), though some coverage on the major summits might be considered[3]. For the journalist and editors whom I interviewed since April 1996, the outbreak of the BSE crisis (Bifunginal Spinal Epidemic)[4] in Europe was to a surprisingly small degree thought of as a typical EU story, although they remembered the events as somewhat EU related. The EU was now predominantly seen as important for the Norwegian business community. To bring the political sides of EU issues more into the news discourse, a redefinition of the 'realpolitik' situation was thought to be necessary.

Constructing the national interests

A major element of foreign news newsworthiness was based on considerations of what EU issues are connected to 'Norwegian interests'. The crucial frame for news production would then be the 'Norwegian perspective' through which international events and discourses became domesticated. In news media discourse from political beats, one particular way of producing this domestication effect textually was through 'sourcing' of national sources. However, a problem appeared in the post-referendum situation since the 'national interest' was not represented by Norwegian officials within the major EU fora. Thus, Norwegian journalists lacked 'their own' national sources in the EU institutions.

Lacking a Norwegian COREPER (Committee for permanent representatives) delegation during the post-referendum period, the foreign affairs journalists and Brussels correspondents found themselves searching for news with a particular emphasis on the Norwegian perspective through the EEA Agreement. The political processes and institutions that were defined in the EEA Agreement created new routines for news production, for instance when Norwegian ministers travelled to EEA and EFTA meetings, or when conflicts of interest could be found, among Norwegian interests, the EU and other member states, over the implementation and practice of Single Market legislation. But news stories on the EEA Agreement were seen as a dull material. As several (male) editors and journalists put it, '...EU and EEA have no sex appeal', and such assignments were not seen as particularly interesting for a general reporter. Perhaps more interesting in terms of commentary than news: domestication could also be produced through a frame of anticipating and analysing the consequences of the referendum result. Based on an initial definition of Norway's position as outside or inside the EU, the consequences of European integration and EU policies for Norwegian interests were considered to be newsworthy.

Considerations regarding news production

In addition to considerations of the political context and the national interest, journalists saw several explanations concerning news production itself as important for newsworthiness. First of all, there was a lack of significant events and drama: The slow and often boring way in which the continuing political processes developed made them difficult to report on. Second, the same background information was required: Recapitulating former stages in the processes, presenting the agents, the institutions and the detailed workings of the political processes and procedures as well as the conflicting interests that were represented, often had to accompany each of the news stories. Without such information, continuity in the news stories was easily lost. At the same time, always having to 'educate the public' was seen as burden, and for elite audiences, this was believed to be redundant information.

The routine flows of information from Brussels also created particular problems for the correspondents when newsworthiness was lowered. When all the obvious, prescheduled news stories had to be covered, it was hard to find time to work on more exclusive stories. The complexity of the beat created a problem of news selection and of being able to follow up properly; one had to decide well in advance which stories were newsworthy and which were not. This was seen to create a mainstreaming effect on the correspondents' reports, lowering the importance of employing an independent, permanent correspondent and highlighting the efficiency of using agency news from home. Connected to these points was the impression that political bureaucrats and EU institutions had a low image factor: The low availability of interesting picture opportunities from the political processes made newsworthiness even lower. The need for pictures was of course most important for the television journalists and the tabloids.

Repeated portraits and talking heads of EU Commissioners would easily take up space in the limited number of pages available for international news coverage.

The Changing News Production Routines at the Brussels Beat

The changes in evaluations of story suitability and newsworthiness had immediate effects on the organisational routines of news production both on the national and the Brussels beat. In Brussels, it became harder for correspondents to justify their physical presence. The lack of a national delegation within the COREPER and the EU Commission reduced newsworthiness and also made access to EU sources and information more difficult. As a result, the role and function of the Brussels beat changed. For the remaining correspondents, the Brussels beat became a more traditional foreign news beat in Europe.

Redefining the sense of place: changing beat assignments

In 1995, the number of permanent correspondents for Norwegian news media in Brussels fell from 11 to 4. The importance of 'being there' was to some degree still acknowledged, but the need for *permanent* correspondents varied. The mere cost of having a permanent correspondent was a constant reason to search for alternative models of news production[5]. It could be argued that it was just as easy to follow the EU from home through *Reuters* and other online services as it was to cover it on the Brussels beat. The correspondents themselves had differing opinions on the matter, but they generally agreed that Brussels and the EU beat had become a more boring place to be. The time when everything they wrote was of major interest to Norwegian readers was absolutely gone.

The correspondents all believed that their permanent offices were upheld because they now covered other European regions and issues as well. Brussels was seen as 'a central place in Europe' rather than an EU beat. Their work became more similar to other, non-member state journalists, as they increasingly found themselves covering the Central European region rather than EU agencies. The concept of news itself was seen to be changing: it was not confined to news on transnational politics and international relations. Increasingly, cultural and sports events now had to be covered as well.

Thus for the Norwegian correspondents, the EU beat was becoming neither a general, agency beat focussed on EU nor a substantial beat on European affairs. Apart from the geographical dimension that was now most important in defining the Brussels beat, it was something in between. As agency beat reporters, the correspondents primarily covered the EU institutions and NATO in Brussels, involving regular contact with sources and stable routines for news production. And since the EU institutions also moved around, with conferences, summits and changing locations of the Council presidency, the location of the EU beat was not fixed. The EU beat reporters travelled to where the action was. As substantial beat reporters, they saw European politics as their speciality and often defined their role as ambassadors to the lay world on the specialities they covered. They had particular knowledge of the workings of the EU institutions, not of the particular issues at stake. Thus in terms of specialist knowledge, they were generalist who had to assemble information on things they knew little about from the outset. The correspondents believed themselves to be generalists on most issues, as well as specialising in one or two particular issues.

Changing social contexts of news production on the Brussels beat

In 1996, it was common knowledge that the EU beat had surpassed Washington D.C. in terms of number of accredited journalists. Brussels was said to be the world's biggest location for news production, and the EU was the major international correspondent beat. According to my informants in the EU Commission, they had over 1000 accredited journalists registered, from newspapers all over the world. The member state journalists dominated, but journalists from countries outside Europe were also well represented.

The Norwegian correspondents still had their offices among the international press, close to the EU buildings, but they now found themselves representing an outside, non-member country, which made their reporting more similar to that of other journalists from non-member states. Most important was the lack of domestic sources: Norwegian politicians and parties were no longer required to have opinions on the major EU issues, and the political processes of the EU were not reflected in domestic political discourse. Moreover, since a Norwegian national interest was not clearly expressed or represented within the EU fora, there was no reason to report from the meetings. Another effect of non-membership was seen to be a more limited access to EU sources. This in turn altered the collegial relationships to the other international journalists, since sharing information became difficult.

Being reduced in numbers, there was less of a corps feeling among the Norwegian journalists now than before. During the negotiations and the interim period, there was little competition and getting your news stories published at home hardly required exclusivity. Everything they sent home was printed and it was natural to share information and services with national colleagues. Now, during the post-referendum period, exclusivity was seen as an important factor in successful negotiations with the home editor. The low level of newsworthiness made the scope for originality small, and competition among the correspondents increased.

Negotiating newsworthiness

Negotiations between foreign correspondents and home editors were constant, and mainly occurred through daily telephone calls to the foreign affairs editor. During the membership negotiations and the so-called "interim period" (marking the period until the referendum, when Norway was treated as a member and therefore had full access to internal EU meetings and information), contacts were also frequently made with other editors. But since the referendum, the correspondents again connected more exclusively to the foreign affairs editor.

Negotiations took place within the framework of established professional norms and tacit understandings regarding the correspondents' need for autonomy and simultaneous obligations to their news organisation. It was seen as a delicate art, and one taking the two of them, although the home editor was usually 'given the last word'. It was also seen as a professional truism that the home office 'always knew best'. Still, the correspondents usually found it easy to communicate and work with their editors, although misunderstandings and conflicts could occur. The correspondents generally appreciated how the home contacts enabled them to construct the relevant, national perspective on international events.

In principle, there was leeway for following independent tracks, but if these became too time consuming, they had to be discussed with the editor. However, the correspondents generally admitted they had limited spare time for the investigative journalism needed to produce exclusive stories. Exclusivity on the EU beat could most efficiently be obtained through source interviews, not through investigative journalism.

The bilateral, national perspective was considered most important. It connected the single events to the continuous construction of national interests. Often, news stories would be dramatised as continuing reports on signs of loss or victory for national interests during the process, with a final crescendo on the basis of the political results.

Different considerations applied for news stories generated from 'the EU mill', which in 1996 was primarily seen as related to the extension to the Eastern European countries, the EMU process and to some extent the IGC process (Inter-Governmental Conference). These were seen as processes and events that '...we cannot disregard, they are self-evident', as the *NRK* correspondent (Norsk Rikskringkasting, the Norwegian public service broadcaster) expressed it. A general interest in the continuing ups and downs of the European integration project and long trends in European history was reflected here. It was considered as requiring a particular professional knowledge to turn these events and issues into news stories. In constructing the international perspectives on these stories, European post-war history was often reflected upon and constructed as an important background. More recent crisis situations and important incidents in Europe, such as the BSE crisis and the war in the former republic of Yugoslavia, were reported within this long-term frame.

The need for detailed coverage of the minute dealings of EU processes was gone. With more sporadic coverage came the need to repeat and provide background information to each story. Thus, the frame often became more general comments, with an educational element rather than a news story. Often, the correspondent would make a comment on the situation of a particular, long lasting political process, based on a day's work of updating comments from official sources.

The 'view from Brussels' was increasingly given symbolic significance, becoming as important as 'the view from Washington and Moscow' used to be during the Cold War period. At particular events, *NRK* would set up 'live conferences' among studio staff and correspondents, and the Brussels correspondent would be aired on radio news programs together with other correspondents and "internal pundits" (Schlesinger 1978: 79 and 153). In the few newspapers with several correspondents and stringers abroad, a similar, combined effect could be obtained through editing of international news coverage, where for instance comments from several points of view could be combined to form a 'collage' with news, pictures, graphic figures and comments on the same page.

Being part of the press corps

Journalists in Brussels willingly comment upon the peculiarity of the place and the intense political activity every day, every hour, every minute. An enormous 'pressure' is felt there, with an immense and speedy flow of information on sources, issues and events. Thus, for EU correspondents, the problem is often that there is too much information at the doorstep, but too little information upon which to base a good choice. The problem is to choose the 'right' story of the day. Therefore, it is important to be part of the international press corps. Sharing among international colleagues is seen as the most important way of becoming informed in Brussels. The different nationalities are not really competitors, so sharing is not harmful to their own struggle for exclusivity, unless it is passed on to their own, national competitors. Sharing between different nationalities takes the form of systematic trading, since the various nationalities have systematic access to different sources and kinds of information. Because of this, any additional language that an EU correspondent can make use of is an important resource for acquiring tips and information.

However, in the period after the referendum, the position of the Norwegian correspondents vs. the international corps of correspondents had changed. They thought back on the interim period and the membership negotiations as a time when their news stories had an international audience and their inside information from Norwegian sources could be swapped with inside information from international colleagues. As it was now, the Norwegian sources were of no particular interest to international colleagues, and only in rare cases could they exchange information.

Still, since they were not seen as competitors, the Norwegian correspondents could receive tips and information from international colleagues. But one-way relationships were considered embarrassing, and there were perceived professional norms about how far one could go in terms of receiving free services from international colleagues. The relationship to Nordic colleagues was seen as particularly vulnerable with respect to these professional practices and norms. One correspondent claimed that the Swedes, who were considered to be very helpful during the negotiation period, had become more difficult to approach, and that the Danish and the British now were 'better colleagues'. The British correspondents were generally considered to be on good terms with the Norwegians and also of particular value and relevance, because their style of reporting was seen to reflect the same, critical attitude towards the EU that the Norwegian correspondents had tried to achieve.

Sharing, but not trading, also took place among the Norwegians, mostly when they met at conferences and summits where simultaneous press briefings could be covered through co-operation. The international corps would go, more or less 'en bloc' from Brussels to IGC meetings and the special summits set up by the EU Presidency in their national capitals. On many occasions, the Norwegian correspondents would also co-operate with Swedes and Danes. Again, the advantages for the Norwegians were considered to be greater, since the Swedish and Danish colleagues had access to their COREPER delegations, ministers and EU nationals.

The density of sources made it easy to gather information on particular issues. But the problem was to simultaneously keep up with events and changes in all other political processes and to be able to act and choose – based on relevant information – the right stories to develop at the right time. It was therefore seen as favourable to have an office in the International Press Centre, where colleagues were always available. The same correspondent could not telephone a source too often, and colleagues could co-operate on covering a particular source.

Changing Relationships with Sources

In the post-referendum situation, the Norwegian Brussels correspondents felt that their relationship with sources had completely changed. The issues they were pursuing on the beat were thought to differ increasingly from those of member state journalists, and their relationships to sources were altered because of this. But more directly, the "no" vote had an immediate effect on the correspondents' access to information from the EU institutions. According to the NTB correspondent, the flow was '...literally turned off' when the interim period was over. As mentioned earlier, this was felt to completely change their position in the international press corps, making them different from other Nordic colleagues.

Since there were no Norwegians working within the EU institutions, the correspondents felt as if they lacked 'their own' bureaucrats and politicians on the inside. The contrast to the membership negotiations and the interim period was considered to be decisive. At this point, the Norwegian correspondents were important targets for EU spokespersons and the commission officials. Now, a request for an interview or a comment from someone in the EU commission was harder to get. As a result, the use of documents, newspapers, agency reports and peer sources had now become more important than oral sources.

It was also felt that Norway and Norwegian journalists were considered as less important to the EU: EU sources were seen as harder to access because it became harder to legitimise spending their attention and time on Norway. And NATO again surfaced as a more important agency beat: compared to the EU, NATO still offered Norwegian correspondents their own national sources, and thus a direct bilateral connection to Norwegian national security interests was more easily established.

Staying informed on the Norwegian perspective

As an 'outside' nation state, staying informed was a challenge. The Norwegian correspondents found themselves working in similar ways as the Norwegian diplomats. The problem for both was to find out when and where Norwegian interests were connected to the EU processes. According to the NTB correspondent, the result was that they were now working more or less '...as the Norwegian diplomats: going in the same circles, seeking the same sources'.

The importance and role of the Norwegian Embassy and the staff at the EEA delegation as information sources were seen as having changed after the referendum. The correspondents found it much easier to work with them, interviews were more easily given and the delegation staff was seen as being more professional towards the media than before. The EEA specialists at the Norwegian delegation were considered to be excellent sources for updates and background on complex matters under negotiation.

The correspondents sensed a danger in becoming too close, and expressed a need for autonomy from the EEA delegation. For instance, all the correspondents expressed the view that visiting ministers could no longer count on coverage. The ministers on their side still planned their visits so that they were available to the press, coming down in the evening to meet the press before the meetings the next day. And the correspondents all admitted that they would still usually show up, although allegedly, sometimes more out of politeness than of genuine interest. And depending on whether they could get an exclusive interview, at least one of them would still end up covering the visit. The impression was that newsworthiness as concerned EU was considered to be so low, that any minister that could bring some 'glamour' to the beat was still welcome. Although their assignments had changed, the presence of the EEA delegation legitimated their existence and offered the most immediate and obvious link to domestic politics. Thus, autonomy on the beat was hard to maintain, and the EEA delegation seemed to have a strong position in defining the news.

Compared with the negotiation period, the Norwegian correspondents believed that Norwegian interest organisations and lobbies now were fewer. They were also believed to be more discrete than during the negotiations. Still, the correspondents were aware of recent incidents when they had been exposed to attempts to get coverage or news stories on their behalf. For instance, the correspondents still received telephone calls or met lobbyists at receptions and social gatherings. And the various interest organisations still present in Brussels were sometimes invited to talks or expert meetings arranged particularly for the press and the Commission staff.

Legitimacy and the national web of facticity

A dominantly national perspective was maintained and reconstructed in the news through the frequent use of authoritative, official sources from the Norwegian government and the delegation in Brussels. As Tuchman has argued, the correspondents' way of establishing facts often went through interviewing and checking with different sources, creating a particular 'web of facticity' in the news stories. Hence, in the post-referendum situation, this became an increasingly national web.

In consequence, National and EU official sources were more automatically held to be legitimate and credible, whereas others to a larger degree had to '...demonstrate their relationship to a more amorphous entity – the public' (Tuchman 1978: 92). The sheer number of bureaucratic and elected officials, both representing national delegations and European institutions, turned Brussels into a beat where official sources were best seen and heard. Whereas the national, official sources had a predefined, unquestionable legitimacy as authoritative sources, lobbyists were seen as informers, sometimes as important experts on particular issues, but always as potential manipulators of the correspondents' obligations to objective reporting. Thus when selecting authoritative sources, correspondents tended to reconstruct a public arena of representational, domestic politics. Civil society groups were increasingly seen as lobbyists, having less legitimacy as major sources in the news stories.

The official, governmental bias of the source web was additionally strength-ened through the lack of opposition to foreign policy orientations in the domestic political discourse. Compared to the negotiation period and the interim period, there was now, among editors, journalists and correspondents, anticipation of a national consensus about Norwegian foreign policies towards EU. Thus, as also argued in other research projects on the use of authoritative sources in foreign affairs news, a national consensus had a structuring effect (Sahr 1993; Giffard 1996).

However, an assumption of a continued, national conflict on the membership issue also existed among home-based EU journalists, editors and correspondents on the Brussels beat. Gans has argued that high proximity is what gives more balanced news to domestic than to foreign affairs news (Gans 1979). In traditional foreign news, sources are 'distant others', and more ideological biases can be used to stereotype their behaviour. But news production on the Brussels beat was characterised by high proximity and a deliberate attempt to balance and present the news as 'objective'. In this respect, the beat news from Brussels was treated like domestic news.

Changing relations to EU sources

The most important source on the EU beat was the Commission briefing, occurring every day, from Monday to Friday at 12.00. Since the news agenda of the Nor-wegian journalists had shifted as compared to the member states, the need to go to the Commission briefings was seen as less urgent. On the other hand, neither *Reuters* nor *FT*, which would inform the member state journalists on the most important topics, were considered able to cover the special Norwegian agenda. Thus, there was still some need to be around. And the Commission was other-wise seen as more difficult to access since the different DGs no longer informed the Norwegians on a general basis. Thus, they had to make continuous phone calls to the various offices in order to keep up with their stories. To make things even worse, the turnover of officials and spokespersons made contacts that were useful two months ago useless at the time of print. Thus regular contact with the EU institutions and EU officials was considered necessary.

For the member state correspondents, the most important official source related to the Council meetings was their respective COREPER staff and the ministers participating in the meetings. Although the Norwegian journalists lacked a COREPER delegation to go to, they were now sometimes let in on the Swedish briefings, and to some extent also on the Danish and British. Most important, the Norwegian correspondents had 'a secret friend' in the press officer at the Swedish delegation, and in the close connections between nationals, personal friendships were often seen as more important than formal networks.

For the general international press corps of member state journalists, there were several other important agencies connected to different issues and political processes, both inside and outside Brussels. For instance, the international press corps would usually follow the monthly Strasbourg meetings in the European Parliament, although some had stringers there to do the job for them. Back in Brussels, the Regional Committee and the Economic and Social Committee were important sources in their respective fields. In addition there was the European Investment Bank, the Court of Justice, and the Court of Auditors – all three in Luxembourg. And finally, the Union Council meetings were the 'moveable beat' in Europe for the Brussels correspondents and provided a welcomed occasion for everyone to leave the Breydel quarters. To the Norwegian correspondents, these sources had somewhat less importance now, depending on the stories they chose to cover.

The Norwegian correspondents' view on the European Parliament was dualistic. On the one hand, it was acknowledged that the Parliament was mostly powerless and not very interesting as an institution. The low estimation of the EP's powers made the Parliament region less interesting than the Commission. And since the Norwegians lacked their own elected officials, their motivation for going to EP sessions was very low. On the other hand, it was acknowledged that there were skilled people there who were well informed on certain issues. Particularly the Danish delegates were mentioned as being good sources of information from time to time. But there was a well-known catch connected to the use of European MPs as sources. They were sources available for any opinion between heaven and earth, and they sometimes seemed only too willing to come forward. It was also seen as problematic to define whom they represented and on whose behalf they were speaking. The MPs were thus considered best as background, expert sources, and less credible and useful as political sources for the headlines (see also Morgan 1999).

Of greater interest to the Norwegian correspondents now were the EFTA organisations, and particularly the ESA (EFTA Surveillance Authority), which played an increasingly important role within the framework of the EEA Agreement. But being judicial processes, access was strictly regulated by delicate rules of secrecy, and the ESA was not considered an easily accessible source of tips and informal information.

Conclusion: Domestication and the Practice of News Production

The empirical research on the news media in Norway has shown that changes in the institutional framework and political relations between Norway and the EU in the 90's were interpreted as an important context for changing foreign news production practices focussed on EU- and EEA-related issues. The present research project has focused on the post-referendum situation, and I have argued that the major frame of reference in Norwegian news media is still predominantly connected to interpretations of national interests and identities, corresponding to the view that Norway is "outside" the European Union.

Despite its transnational implications, the institutional framework of the EEA Agreement was seen as a reason to reduce, rather than increase, journalist activity on the Brussels beat. After the referendum, when a majority of the Norwegian electorate voted "no" to membership, the membership issue disappeared from public debate. Soon, the interpretation of newsworthiness and the assignments for EU specialists and correspondents changed. Editors, home specialists and Brussels correspondents interpreted the referendum result and the EEA Agreement as defining a situation with lower newsworthiness than the interim and campaign period. Thus, beat assignments, working conditions and source relations changed accordingly. The reduced number of Norwegian correspondents present in Brussels after 1995 had their beat assignments redefined – from being EU specialists, they became more general, all-round Europe correspondents.

The research provides an example of how interpretations of the changing institutional context of transnational politics are important for the organisation of news production routines in a national news media order. It shows how "domestication" should not only be understood as a rhetorical strategy or narrative frame for the mediation of international and foreign news stories, but rather as a sociological and ideological structure underlying the organisational priorities and routines of foreign news production. As such, domestication has important political and cultural consequences for the construction and mediation of transnational political discourse in Europe.

The findings leads one to question how the Norwegian news media, and other nationally oriented media orders in Europe, are presently functioning as part of a European media public sphere. This is an empirical question, and more research is needed on the way the changing European and international media orders are presently structuring news flows and on the mediation of knowledge and symbols in different parts of Europe[6]. At present, the promotion of transnational institutions and politics in Europe seems to go hand in hand with driving forces in the political economy of the media. One consequence of this would seem to be the proliferation of an elite, financially oriented news media order in Europe, which to some degree could be said to constitute an elite public sphere

(Schlesinger and Kevin 1999). Changes in the institutional frameworks of national and European media policies are allowing increasing cross-ownership and formal co-operation among European media organisation. As media technology and markets increasingly traverse national borders, Europe is becoming a battlefield for media markets. The traditionally nationally oriented news media will therefore, sooner or later, be forced to position themselves within an increasingly open, European and international media order.

Thus, the mediation of political knowledge and symbols in Europe is already being structured in new ways. However, we can expect that the national frame of reference will continue to constitute the major market for popular, national print and broadcast media, and the European media order will continue to create and sustain contradictions in the integration processes of Europe.

Notes

1. The essay is based on a research project titled "Europeanisation and the Norwegian news media: political discourse and news production in the transnational political field" (Slaatta 1999); Department of Media and Communication, University of Oslo. The project was developed within the cross-disciplinary research program ARENA (Advanced Research on the Europeanisation of the Nation-State), funded by the Norwegian Research Council. I want to express my special thanks to Philip Schlesinger for inspiring and supporting this work.

2. Qualitative interviews were conducted by the author between 1995 and 1997 in the major Norwegian news media organisations, both with editors and home journalists with particular EU or EEA assignments. Interviews with Brussels correspondents were conducted on the Brussels beat in November and December 1997. Interviews with various sources and source organisations were conducted in Brussels during the same period. On the national news beat, source interviews were mainly conducted in the MFA (Ministry of foreign Affairs) and with party leaders and staff at the Norwegian parliament, Stortinget. Interviews were usually set up as personal, face to face conversations, which were either taped and transcribed or monitored and reconstructed on the basis of extensive notes.

3. In connection with the research project (see note 1), both quantitative and qualitative content analysis was conducted. The sample period included 6 weeks of news media output, and coincided with the IGC summit in Turin, and with the outbreak of BSE.

4. BSE is also known as CJD (Creuzfeldt Jacobs Disease) or popularly known as Mad Cow Disease.

5. It is an international trend that foreign and international news correspondents are becoming less permanent and more often operate from a home base. Also, foreign news coverage in Norway is more often put together from secondary sources, bureau news, stringers and syndicates. Thus, Brussels is still the major permanent foreign news beat for Norwegian correspondents, although the assignments have changed from being predominantly political, EU assignments, to more all-round, Europe assignments.

6. Only a few studies on the European news beats exist at present. Among the most important is the work of Schlesinger (1997, 1999a and 1999b) and David Morgan (1995 and 1999).

References

Boyd-Barrett, O. & Rantanen, T. (1998) *The Globalization of News*. London: Sage.

Braman, S. & Sreberny-Mohammadi, A. (eds.) (1996) *Globalization, Communication and Transnational Civil Society*. New Jersey: Hampton Press (IAMCR series).

Bruhn Jensen, K. (ed.) (1998) *News of the World*. London: Routledge.

Carlsson, U. (1998) *Frågan om en ny internationell informationsordning*. Göteborg: JMG (Doctoral dissertation).

Cohen, B. (1963) *The Press and Foreign Policy*. Princeton: Princeton University Press

Eide, M. & Hernes, G. (1987) *Død og Pine*. Oslo: Fafo.

Ericson, R.V.; Baranek, P.M. & Chan, J.B.L. (1989) *Negotiating Control*. Milton Keynes: Open University Press.

Gans, H. (1979) *Deciding What's News*. New York: Pantheon Books.

Giffard, A. (1996) "International News Coverage of the Rio Earth Summit", in Braman, S. & Sreberny-Mohammadi, A. (1996) *Globalization, Communication and Transnational Civil Society*. IAMCR, N.J: Hampton Press

Gurevitch, M. et al. (1996) *Global Newsrooms, Local Audiences*. London: John Libbey.

Hjarvard, S. (1995) *Internationale TV-nyheder*. København: Akademisk Forlag.

Keane, J. (1992) "The Crisis of the Sovereign State" in Raboy, M. & Dagenais, B. (eds.) (1992) *Media, Crisis and Democracy*. London: Sage

Morgan, D. (1995) "British Media and European Union News: The Brussels News Beat and Its Problems", *European Journal of Communication*, vol.10, no.3. London: Sage.

Morgan, D. (1999) *The European Parliament, Mass Media and the Search for Power and Influence*. Aldershot: Ashgate.

O'Heffernan, P. (1993) "Mass Media and U.S. Foreign Policy: A Mutual Exploitation Model of Media Influence in U.S. Foreign Policy", in Spitzer, R.J. (ed.) (1993) *Media and Public Policy*. London: Praeger.

Olsen, J.P. (1995) *Europeanization and Nation-State Dynamics*. University of Oslo (ARENA Working Paper 95/9).

Sahr, R. (1993) "Credentialing Experts: The Climate of Opinion and Journalist Selection of Sources in Domestic and Foreign Policy", in Spitzer, R.J. (ed.) (1993) *Media and Public Policy*. Westport, Connecticut: Praeger.

Schlesinger, P.R. (1978) *Putting Reality Together: BBC News,* London: Constable.

Schlesinger, P.R. (1995) *Europeanisation and the Media, National Identity and the Public Sphere*. University of Oslo (ARENA Working Paper).

Schlesinger, P.R. (1997) "From Cultural Defence to Political Culture: Media, Politics and Collective Identity in the European Union", *Media, Culture and Society*, vol.19, no.3, pp. 369–391. London: Sage.

Schlesinger, P.R. & Kevin, D. (1999a) "The European Union – A sphere of Publics", in Eriksen, E.O. & Fossum, J. (eds.) *Democracy in Europe, Integration and Deliberation*. London: UCL Press.

Schlesinger, P.R. (1999b) "Changing Spaces of Political Communication: The Case of the European Union", *Political Communication,* no.16, pp. 263-279.

Slaatta, T. (1998) "Media and Democracy in the Global Order", *Media, Culture and Society*, vol.20, no.2, pp. 335-344. London: Sage.

Slaatta, T. (1999) *Europeanisation and the Norwegian News Media: Political Discourse and News Production in the Transnational Field*. Oslo: UiO, Department of Media and Communication (Report no.36, Doctoral dissertation).

Tuchman, G. (1978) *Making News*. New York: The Free Press

Striving for Credibility
News and Current Affairs on Star TV India

Norbert Wildermuth

A Changing TV-Newsscape

In India, news and current affairs (n&c) have been the de facto monopoly of the state broadcaster Doordarshan (DD) much longer than any other genre of television. Apart from the commercially unattractive genre of educational and development-oriented programming, domestically produced and distributed n&c were, in fact, one of the last citadels of government control over the content of television to fall. While a wide choice of general entertainment programming and non-domestically produced n&c were provided (via cable and satellite) in English, Hindi and a number of regional Indian languages, from 1991 onwards, a combination of financial and regulatory constraints delayed the commercial broadcasters' entry into the field of Indian produced n&c for almost half a decade. Yet with Rupert Murdoch owned Star TV and Murdoch (until October 1999) co-owned Zee TV moving into this field in late 1996, the Indian 'news on television' sector has changed almost beyond recognition. Gone are not only the days of the public broadcaster's uncontested monopoly as the nationwide programme carrier of privately and in-house produced n&c, but also the days when the threat of the 'Murdochisation' of Indian (news on) television could be mobilised in an attempt to ward off the widespread criticism of the inefficient, amateurish and hegemonic character of n&c produced by DD. With the end of the state broadcaster's monopoly and with the entry of the private sector, Indian satellite and cable audiences were to judge for themselves the potential gratifications, the journalistic and the service 'quality' of the factual programming offered by competing newscasters. In consequence, a predominant attitude of (foreign and private media) scepticism and concern – informed by a set of more or less pessimistic speculations about the consequences of non-state controlled tv-news and current affairs – was effectively challenged by a much more pragmatic, "what you see is what you get" approach.

So, what have the private satellite channels, and especially Star TV, on offer? Are Indian c&s homes provided with a meaningful alternative or do they get just more of the same? Are the n&c shown by private satellite channels as socially relevant as they obviously are entertaining and attractive? Do these non-state-controlled n&c live up to a level of professional media performance, not only in terms of viewer address and audiovisual presentation, but also with regard to their journalistic practice? In other words, are these new programmes able to provide their limited and privileged audience with a substantial and critical view on the social realities of India? These are some of the central questions we should keep in mind when we discuss the 'modernisation', 'westernisation' and/ or 'globalisation' of the Indian electronic news media. Furthermore, in terms of evaluating these changes and in terms of the challenge they constitute to the dominant discourse on the normative role of broadcasting news in post-colonial India, such a 'critical' (social and political consequences-oriented) perspective may finally lead us to question some of the prevalent views and commonplace notions, regarding the relation between (news) media and society, under circulation in India. What if the final de-monopolisation of the Indian n&c sector qualifies as a change for better and not for worse, as predicted by its early opponents? And what if the journalistic and editorial standards practised by (some of) the Delhi-based newcomers and their regional-language imitators have proved to be higher than the questionable public service standard Indian tv audiences had to make do with, watching DD's in-house news bulletins over three decades? Obviously, a positive answer would raise a number of crucial questions and suggest a reconceptualisation of the tv-mediums ongoing proliferation, in the commercialised and globalised/localised context of contemporary India. As evidently, a positive answer must be substantiated by a systematic textual and institutional-market analysis, exploring both, the representational and discursive properties of the private and Doordarshan produced n&c coverage and the political and economical conditions for their production, distribution and reception.

In the following, I will describe and discuss the proliferation of commercially produced n&c programming for transmission on Doordarshan and the Star TV network. In this context I will ask three basic questions: 1. Based on which particular strategies has Star TV (successfully) entered and positioned itself in this field? 2. What makes its n&c not only more entertaining and attractive, but also more credible and trustworthy than DD's in-house productions? 3. How has DD reacted to this challenge? Central to my endeavour is, furthermore, an attempt to understand these developments in a wider perspective in which television is conceptualised as both determined by India's contemporary modernisation and being a determining agent in this process of change. The 'new' n&c coverage, I will argue, is reflective of the ongoing transformation of the social, economic and political sphere observable in India, as it plays a growing institutional role in the imagination and negotiation of this 'development'. This leads me to the central question of whether, under which particular socio-historic conditions and in which form of strategic co-operation with the Indian private tv sector, a transnational satellite broadcaster like Star TV has been able to occupy the communicative space and to fulfil the service obligations of 'broadcasting in the public interest', at least partially. This discursive space, defined by a set of particular tv-journalistic and representational practices, has been 'neglected' and at least partially 'abandoned' by state broadcaster Doordarshan and is consequently, I will argue, still in the process of being defined and fully realised.

Starting with an outline of the 'early period' of satellite television news transmission to India and a consideration of some of the predicaments raised against satellite and cable tv in general and transnational newscasters in particular, I will continue to show how this 'criticism' has informed Star TV India's strategic efforts to make a 'smooth' and 'successful' entry into this field. An aim that has been realised on the level of n&c programming as well as on the level of a projected, responsible and credible channel identity, which was, however, not primarily informed by the wish to offer more 'high-quality', public service-oriented n&c. Professional coverage of n&c is a costly venture.[1] Murdoch's financial engagement must therefore be understood, I argue, as an attempt to gain political clout and to influence in his favour the overall image of the Star TV network's brand image in India. Although no money-spinner in itself, the corporate importance of Star News lies in its potential to boost the brand value of the Murdoch-owned network as a whole, to attract additional viewers, subscribers and revenues and to make the Star TV India platform profitable.

After this 'historical' view on the emergence of a private news production and transmission sector, I will move on to examine the 'success' of NDTV, Star TV's major franchisee for n&c, through a content and textual analysis of the aesthetic and discursive forms of news mediation, news selection criteria etc. by which 'credibility' with and 'appeal' to educated upper and middle-class viewers are aspired to. For this purpose, I have analysed some dozen (English) news bulletins recorded in India in January 1999 and February 2000. In order to understand the 'relative' significance and communicative space occupied by Star news in Indian society, my sample includes the news coverage by its main (Hindi and English-lingual) contenders, DD and the Zee TV network. Here, I will, however, confine myself to contrasting the characteristic features of *Star News* and *The News* on DD. Based on analysis of this comparative data, I will basically argue *firstly* that a combination of institutional and representational strategies, as realised in the journalistic practices of Star TV India, has created the widely accepted, public image of Star News as an attractive, popular, credible and influential provider of n&c with Indian decision-makers, the people who do matter in politics and economy; and *secondly* that the continued lack of the same representational properties has been crucial for the competitive 'failure' of DD to occupy a strong market and/or public service-oriented position.

I will finish my paper with a consideration of the inherent 'limitations' of commercially produced n&c programming in its public service function, which will bring me back to the question of who is going to profit from the new n&c programmes shown in India.

Early Transnational Contenders

CNN International and the BBC World Service, available via satellite from 1991 onwards, carried news on international events – like the Gulf War – and occasional reports on India. Yet neither of these global broadcasters has been sufficiently 'Indianised' to attract more than a marginal share of Indian cable and satellite audiences over an extended period of time. Other satellite networks endowed with 'deep pockets'- such as Star TV, Sony Entertainment Television (SET) and popular Zee TV – had less of a niche character and were able to reach the majority of Indian c&s homes on a regular base. Yet in their first years of activity, these networks were eager to position themselves primarily as English or Hindi general entertainment channels. Subsequently, they were carrying no, or almost no, n&c that "were not considered popular genres and were therefore no priority areas" (Thussu 1998b: 280). Their prolonged 'reluctance' to move into n&c can be clearly seen, if we take a look at the following numbers (Table 1), showing the share of factual programming on these channels in September 1995 and September 1996.

Table 1.   News and current affairs of overall programming (percent)

	Sept. 95	Sept. 96
Star Plus	1.7	2.5
Zee TV	3.9	2.9
SET	0.0	0.0
DD1	29.3	30.5
DD2	23.9	23.4

Source: Cable Waves, 1998: 105ff.

Compared with DD's national network (DD1) and its Metro channel (DD2), the picture becomes pretty clear. More than five years after the arrival of satellite television, n&c were more or less non-existent on the private networks – DD's de facto monopoly seemed to be (still) unchallenged.

In an article published as late as 1998 (based on research done in the summer of 1996), Sandhya Rao claimed correspondingly:

> Star TV and private regional Indian language channels do have news programs but for a limited time, whereas Doordarshan covers local and national news extensively (Rao 1998: 54).

Yet Rao was not only wrong – the Delhi-centred state broadcaster can hardly be said to cover local news extensively – but her assessment was also outdated by the time her article appeared in print. The reason is that from 1996 onwards, the situation had changed swiftly, as indicated by the continuous increase in tv channels carrying n&c receivable in India. By the end of the decade, the number of private news services had multiplied, their programme output 'exploded' and

DD's de facto monopoly been replaced by a multitude of news providers and an abundance of programmes. In just three years, the Indian television news sector had moved, so to speak, from an era of scarcity to a state of plenitude. Let me recall the major steps of this deregulation.

The Predicaments of Satellite Television

With the arrival of three international n&c broadcasters, the proliferation of three 24-hour Indian news channels and the incorporation of informational programming – in English, Hindi and a number of vernacular Indian languages – on more than a dozen privately owned channels, the Indian television newsscape has changed rapidly, too rapidly some may say, over the last decade. According to advocates of the cultural/media imperialism thesis[2], the presence and operations of both international news and current affairs services (i.e. the BBC, CNN, CNBC) and the Rupert Murdoch owned, 'Indianised' Star Plus/News channels, constitute a potential threat to the cultural diversity, national unity and sovereignty of India. In this scenario, the logic of global consumerism will eviscerate national identity and culture, thereby undercutting national integration projects. Triggered by a 'revolution of rising expectations', conflicts may arise between the audience's wants and needs: between the English speaking urban middle classes and the rural non-English speaking majority, so their argument goes. Furthermore, people with a higher socio-economic status will have more avenues and better access to external information (and entertainment) programming, thus widening the gap between the 'media-rich' and the 'media-poor'. In consequence, the government's role of strengthening national integration and promoting development through television is potentially jeopardised. The 'Murdochisation' of Indian television – 'Murdochisation' defined as "a combination of the following factors: a convergence of global media technologies; a tendency towards market-driven journalism ...; transnationalisation of US-inspired media formats, products and discourse; and lastly, an emphasis on infotainment, undermining the role of the media for public information" (Thussu 1998a: 7) – and the 'fragmentation' of Indian society, in terms of social and cultural identities, are the inevitable, long-term consequences of the Indian broadcasting sector's liberalisation and deregulation, these critics conclude.

Yet there are good reasons to question this scenario. Almost a decade after the arrival of CNN on the Indian subcontinent, it has become evident that the prevalent discourse on the 'effects' of India's 'invasion from the sky' by transnational media – a discourse based on the 'cultural imperialism' paradigm and the free flow of information debate of the 1980s – is characterised by serious inadequacies, both in terms of theory and in terms of the reality that these discourses purport to explain. Based on an ideological model of globalisation rather than on concrete empirical evidence the programming character and profile of international and 'Indianized' but foreign controlled, (n&c) channels have been taken for granted and based on a political economy analysis of their institutional position and structural features alone. Subsequently, the ongoing national debate about 'necessary' media policies for the regulation of the Indian broadcasting sector has too often been solely based on a superficial evaluation of existing programmes as well as on the speculative anticipation of emerging trends in satellite television programming.

Ironically, this pessimistic (its proponents may say 'cautious' or 'critical') attitude towards and assessment of n&c programming produced and/or carried by commercial satellite broadcasters – articulated in public by a large and influential segment of India's cultural, administrative and political elite – has always been contradicted by the same elite's preference for these services as regards their own tv consumption. The demonisation of Murdoch, CNN-bashing and the prevalent criticism of the BBC's 'post-colonial' bias went consequently – and especially in the early years of the satellite television boom in India – hand in hand with the distinct interest of the educated, upper-class audiences to have 'free' and unlimited access to these channels as far as their own households were concerned.[3] The receptivity for 'foreign propaganda', 'consumptive lifestyles' and for the transnational's 'distortion' of the Indian social and political realities was, with the typical attitude of the patronising nationalist, projected on an unknown but supposedly deceivable Other. Hence, while the majority of Indian cable and satellite viewers welcomed the emergence and expansion of a discursive space for non-state-controlled broadcast journalism as a long awaited boon, successive Indian governments were demonstratively concerned – or at least inclined to articulate such a grave 'concern' in public – with how transnational media services available via cable and satellite "are bound to report India from their perspective to Indian audiences" (Kishore 1994: 101).

Yet the state authorities' position was far from uncontested and monolithic – the ruling government and its state apparatuses far from unified in their judgement of the magnitude of the satellite (news) threat. This became all too evident when the Congress Government decided to ignore its former 'reservations' and to opt for a strategic alliance with some of these 'alien' forces shortly afterwards. Early in 1995, DD joined hands with Ted Turner, the owner of CNN and TNT, to launch a joint satellite channel on the national, state-controlled INSAT network. This decision points not only to some of the striking inconsistencies of Indian media policy but also to an ongoing struggle between competing interest groups in DD, the Ministry for Information and Broadcasting, the India Parliament etc. To simplify matters, we may state the existence of two opposing camps advocating almost contrary positions with regard to broadcasting regulation and the 'necessary' reform of the state broadcaster DD.

Privately Produced News and Current Affairs on DD

So far I have outlined some of the contradictions and tensions, anxieties and expectations created by the 'deregulation' of television (news) transmitted from and to India in the 1990s. Yet the picture is far from complete if we do not take into consideration a parallel and certainly no less significant dimension of change during the 'early stage' of satellite television in India: the emergence and growing integration of privately produced n&c on Doordarshan's so-called Metro channel. A trend with long roots in DD's first wave of 'modernisation', 'popularisation' and 'commercialisation' realised from 1984 onwards. In this process one name in particular played a central role.

In 1984, Dr Prannoy Roy, a renowned psephologist (and a former World Bank consultant), got into broadcasting, producing the first non-stop live coverage of parliamentary elections for DD. Four years later, New Delhi Television (NDTV), established by Prannoy Roy and his wife Radhika (a former journalist with *India Today* and *The Indian Express*), was formally incorporated as a video production venture. In November 1988, NDTV was granted telecast facilities on DD's national network, for the first and so far only independently produced and commercially sponsored current affairs series on international news, called *The World This Week* (*TWTW*). The programme, which ran until 1994, became tremendously popular, due to its "extended visual coverage" (Kumar 1996: 299), providing "a dose of professionalism to news and current affairs on the state broadcaster" (Thussu 1998b: 281). By June 1990, *TWTW* had proved such a commercial success that it was shifted into DD's highest sponsorship category. For Prannoy Roy, its sole presenter, this meant more than unprecedented financial success alone. Successively he also developed into what we may call India's first and foremost news media personality. Based on this unique combination of televisual popularity and media professionalism, Roy made further 'exclusive' inroads into the monopolistic sphere of state broadcasting. From 1989 onwards, NDTV produced, on a regular base for DD, live coverage of the annual government budget session and a journalistic analysis of special events like parliamentary elections. Finally, in 1995, NDTV made a venture into domestic news with *Tonight*, the first privately produced, daily newscast to be shown on the state-controlled network.

The logic behind DD's cautious deregulation made (economical) sense and was part of a multidimensional strategy to reorganise a 'public' broadcaster under increasing financial pressure. In an attempt to halt the loss of audiences and the flow of television advertising revenues to the private satellite services, Doordarshan, an organisation notorious for its indifference to the currents of opinion and social change, had to face the challenging task of being attractive, not just with the bulk of tv audiences but also in well-off c&s homes. To target and reconquer this important and lucrative audience segment, the Indian Government launched its first entertainment satellite venture, called the Metro channel, in January 1993.[4] In contrast to the national network channel (DD1), the Metro channel (DD2) was planned as an entertainment channel with segments of current affairs and business programmes thrown in. Unable to buy or commission enough programmes to fill the available air time on DD2, Mandi-House decided to lease portions of the channel to some of India's most notable independent production houses. Regarding n&c, a 'renewed' public broadcaster aimed at building the credibility it so clearly lacked in the eyes of the viewer. To this

end, DD started two privately produced and sponsored half-hour news magazines, *Newstrack* and *Eyewitness*, on its Metro channel, in 1994. Not surprisingly,
both these programmes were soon to command a popularity and journalistic
credibility with c&s audiences, considerably higher than that of the in-house
produced DD news bulletins. As popular were the highly acclaimed NDTV productions.

To sum up: The consecutive incorporation of private producers in 1994/95,
indicates the cautious deregulation of n&c shown on DD – a development set off
and motivated by the arrival of its commercial competitors. While *The World
This Week* was "banned from reporting on Indian news" and while its reporting
of political stories focussing on India's neighbours had "to be handled with care"
(Kumar 1996: 299), this 'second generation' of outsourced n&c products was
allowed to focus on the major political issues of the day. As were of course, at
least in theory, DD's in-house produced news bulletins. Yet in practice, DD's
news staff was shying away from reporting whatever could be deemed controversial by the government of the day. Government control for more than three
decades had turned the state broadcaster's n&c department into a loyal and
unquestioning offshoot of the ruling political machinery. This state of affairs
existed not only in the eyes of most Indians, but it was also indicated and
reprimanded by a judgement on the highest juridical level.[5] The 'opening up' of
n&c shown on DD, though limited to the satellite-distributed Metro channel,
made a profound difference and had far-reaching consequences. It not only
contributed to the emergence of a competitive domestic television production
sector, specialised on n&c,[6] it also helped to carve out and strengthen a journalistic space for critical and investigative tv journalism, not very proliferate in India
until then.[7] Not less important and to be understood in response to the extended
exposure of c&s audiences to privately produced n&c, viewer expectations and
criteria for the judgement of 'quality' in Indian news reporting can be assumed to
have changed profoundly. Though the immediate impact of the 'private' programmes on their audience is hardly documented,[8] their pronounced popularity
indicates that they took up, served and furthered a growing 'demand' for profes-
sionally made and service-oriented alternatives. Furthermore, it showed that
television was welcomed and expected to constitute the mediated arena for
public debate, on political and other issues. Last but not least and as seen from
the perspective of the ambitious Star TV and the ever expansionist Zee TV, the
popularity of Prannoy Roy & Co. with an English and Hindi speaking audience
demonstrated the commercial potential of n&c distributed via cable and satellite.

By the mid 1990s Rupert Murdoch and Subash Chandra (the majority owner
of Zee TV) had obviously decided that it was time to challenge DD's monopoly
and that there was a realistic chance to carve out a niche for n&c on the private
television market.[9] In just a year, Star Plus and Zee TV multiplied their factual
programming (see Table 2). A trend that becomes even clearer if we also take El
TV, the Zee network's second entertainment channel, into consideration.[10]

Table 2. News and current affairs of overall programming (percent)

	Sept. 97	differences to Sept. 96
Star Plus	19.7	+ 17.2
Zee TV	8.0	+ 5.1
EI TV	22.0	+ 22.0
SET	0.0*	–
DD1	16.7	- 13.8
DD 2	10.9	- 12.5

* No news and current affairs but 3.0 % infotainment according to source.

Source: Cable Waves, 1998: 105f.

Seen in a wider media sociological perspective, we can state that television in India has undergone a fundamental change over the last ten to fifteen years, with regard to its institutional character and normative role in society. The tv medium's consecutive transformation from a pure transmission channel, used to represent and articulate the agendas set by the dominant political and social actors, to a market-, viewer- and consequently service-oriented media institution which striving to set its own, 'independent' agenda, has been described extensively in the context of other (Western) countries. However, as Stig Hjarvard among others has emphasised, this does not mean that the television medium has become completely market-oriented and market-driven in its institutional character (Hjarvard 1999: 41). The market's demands and possibilities are rather to be understood as being in continuous tension with the demands and possibilities created by the logic of the tv-medium's ongoing 'professionalisation' in terms of its representational and journalistic practice.

Late Commercial Contenders

In October 1996 the Indian broadcasting sector was taken by surprise. Rathikant Basu, the former, highly acclaimed director general of DD, announced that he was willing to change sides to become Star TV's newly appointed Chief Executive Officer in India. Accompanied by his former 'A' team of DD administrators, Basu was brought in by Murdoch to head an ambitious plan to reposition Star Plus. And indeed, barely three weeks after Basu took over, Murdoch's South Asian flagship entertainment channel started to abandon its image as an exclusive English channel, in order to go more and more *deshi* (Indian) with a mix of news, films, Hindi and dubbed Western serials.[11] Not surprisingly, a crucial brick in Star Plus' ongoing 'Indianisation' (or rather 'Hindi-isation') strategy was the excellent rapport the new CEO commanded with some of the major Indian tv production houses. This in addition to his intimate knowledge of government policies, programmes and strategies designed to cope with the challenges of satellite television. With Basu crossing over, well-funded and ambitious Star TV

157

became the new Mecca of the Indian television software industry. It was accepting programme ideas, and it had money to give advances and strike profit-sharing deals with major production houses. Finally, Murdoch seemed in many ways easier to deal with than Chand Mahal Ibrahim, the then Minister for Information and Broadcasting.

Most prominent among the programmers whom Basu brought along was Prannoy Roy's NDTV, a company that had already built itself a reputation as the best n&c production house available on the Indian subcontinent. With NDTV producing *Star News*, a daily prime time news bulletin, in both Hindi and English, and *Good Morning India*, a daily two-hour breakfast show, for transmission on Star Plus, the transnational satellite broadcaster was able to boost its journalistic reputation. Embodying, so to speak, Star TV's 'Indianisation' strategy, the brand image value of Prannoy Roy was deemed crucial for the repositioning of Star Plus.[12] Offering a popular fare, characterised by high production values and a high journalistic profile, Roy & Co. were expected both, to consolidate Star TV's primary audience – educated, upper income c&s homes – and to get hold of the broader Indian middle class.[13]

Zee and Star TV: Striving for Prestige and Political Clout

Well aware of the fact that control over n&c on television harbours not only prestige, but also enormous political influence, Zee TV moved in earnest into factual programming right on the heels of Star TV.[14] This, not at least, with the intention to influence political decision makers regarding the overdue regulation of broadcasting in India, the so-called Broadcasting Bill, first projected in autumn 1996.[15] When Subash Chandra's Zee TV moved into n&c, however, it did so only *after* it had consolidated itself sufficiently as a general entertainment network and it did so with caution, step by step, based on its experiences with Election and Budget Day coverage, a hybrid talk-current affairs show, and various forms of infotainment. These programmes may have provided Chandra with a feel for the 'political' potential of factual programming. To quote from a Zee TV strategy paper, published in October 1997:

> In any media business, clout and market respectability flows from control over news and current affairs. Every successful entertainment products company looks at entering news and current affairs (*An Approach to Business*: 37).

But the entry made business sense too, given the need to expand the Zee network's airtime sells and to build up a 'bouquet' of channels to counter the growing success and competition of Indianised Sony Entertainment Television and Star Plus. A more popular, softer and viewer-oriented package of national news, talk shows and current affairs, had its own viewer potential, in the eyes of India's shrewdest media tycoon.

> News is fast emerging as programming options and viewership draw. In coming years it will come to be identified as 'televisions noblest service' and source

of its prestige. In Western countries the television news has come to be identified as most trustworthy source of news. In the coming years broadcast news
could be made into an incompatible combination of show business, advertising
and news. Once you get all the three elements under one roof the dust will
never settle. (*An Approach to Business*: 50)

By 1997, both Star and Zee TV were striving to define their journalistic role in
the public sphere of India, though with a different audience focus and strategy
in mind. India's (party) political and administrative elite came to rely and depend increasingly on these networks as the mediators of their views and actions.
However, compared with Doordarshan, the commercial broadcaster were institutionally more independent and not as easily pressured, and thus dictated the
conditions of this interaction. Gaining viewers, revenues, power and recognition
were part of one and the same proliferation process. But where did this leave
Doordarshan?

Competing for Cable and Satellite Homes: DD Versus Star TV

In less than a year (from October 1996 onwards), DD's Metro channel had not
only lost some of its most prestigious current affairs programmes to its commercial contenders, but the public broadcaster had also kicked off NDTV's news
bulletin *Tonight* in retaliation. Left with DD were – apart from its in-house productions – only *Aaj Tak* and *India this Week*.[16] Furthermore, deserting the state
broadcaster were not only the Indian producers, but also the sponsors and advertisers who followed the bulk of the c&s viewers.[17] As Murdoch and Basu had
reckoned, Prannoy Roy proved to be the name that sold Indian n&c, even on a
'foreign-owned' channel.[18] Yet the Roy-popularity argument should not be over-
emphasised. If Star News has made a successful entry into the field of n&c in
India, then this 'popularity' with Indian c&s homes has a number of other, complementary reasons, one being the high production values and digital transmission standard offered by Star News but not by Doordarshan.

The news on Doordarshan, was – and still is – "remarkably unimaginative,
with very limited visuals and little on-the-spot reporting" as Daya Thussu among
many others has remarked (Thussu, 1998: 28). DD's news announcers, in 1997,
were placed in front of a plain light blue background similar to the backdrop of
a photo studio. Voicing over even the original sound of video footage and com-
menting on still photographs, the bulk of the news was simply narrated by the
news presenters.

> Often the visuals would show a speech being made at a press conference, but
> instead of broadcasting the speech itself, the commentary would paraphrase
> what was being said,

reports Daya Thussu, from his August 1997 sample, to continue with his critical
comments:

159

The quality of visuals and the production values were inferior to those of Zee. Despite facing competition from transnational and private Indian news organisations, the state broadcaster continued to display an amateurish approach to news delivery: at times there was a gap of several seconds between the visuals and the start of the commentary; the graphics were basic and at times there were no visuals at all (Thussu 1998b: 286).

NDTV had started with a small team of researchers, producers and technicians, in a small but well-equipped studio, developed its own graphics software, and had done all its editing with the aid of computers, while still on the government channels. With the financial input of Star TV, Prannoy Roy's software production house soon owned more state-of-the-art equipment than the news departments of Doordarshan and Zee TV together.[19] A development that was further accelerated by the launch of the Star News channel in February 1998, when Star TV India came to invest "approximately USD 10 million in hardware" (*Business Standard*, 05.02.98) and NDTV was able to bag a USD 20 million profit-sharing contract to deliver the bulk of programming over the next three years. By the end of the millennium, NDTV claimed to command the "largest nationwide news gathering network of producers, correspondents, camerapersons and editors, linked by satellite connection", and to continue in the complacent style of its homepage:

> Fifteen bureaus across the country, one in every major state capital; a dedicated team of 95 reporters, and production crews of over 400 people, who work round the clock to bring you the most accurate and credible news in the country. New Delhi Television, the news people you can trust.[20]

Judging by the financial performance of the n&c programmes produced for Star Plus and Star News, the top advertisers and sponsors have put their trust (and money) into the 'professionalism' and 'credibility' of NDTV. While most of the big brands jumped on the Star News bandwagon, neither the Zee nor Doordarshan news bulletins were able to attract comparable names. Correspondingly, advertising rates were reported four to five times higher on Star TV than on Zee India and the DD Metro channel in early 1998.[21]

Success through Westernisation

It can be argued that NDTV's (widely acclaimed) journalistic and editorial professionalism has been achieved based on its reflexive adoption of Western broadcasting codes, programming formats, production techniques and 'best' tv journalistic practices. Thus, through the adoption of a set of professional routines and operations – originating in the Western developed societies – which themselves have undergone a fundamental process of modernisation and reorientation during the last two decades (see Hjarvard 1999). The DD in-house produced n&c have on occassion also been advertised as 'modernised' and 'further professionalised'.[22] However, in contrast to the private news production sector, the public broadcaster's projected modernisation has been overtly focussed on the hardware side of innovation, neglecting the news staff's human qualification. In terms of DD's journalistic practice, very little observable change and improvement has been achieved during the last decade. Hampered by heavy institutional traditions and organisational routines, the state broadcaster – compared to its private counterparts – has largely proved to be less responsive both to the efficiency and viewer orientation demands caused by an increasingly competitive environment and to the standardising and reflexive forces of India's news Westernisation. So while DD's programming policy has generally become more oriented towards the viewer's assumed entertainment expectations, its in-house produced n&c programmes have remained remarkably 'conservative' in form and content.[23] Certainly, the news department of a 50,000 head strong former state bureaucracy is not 'turned around' without a committed effort on all levels. The co-operation between DD management and staff to reach this goal was, however, hampered by a number of unresolved conflicts, involving, for example, some 'necessary' (from the perspective of mangement) but highly 'unpopular' (among the journalistic staff) decisions with regard to the news department's manpower policy.[24] Considering, furthermore, the lack of political will – signalled by consecutive central governments – to demand and support a thorough re-organisation of DD's news department in earnest and considering the fact that the state broadcaster has not been managed by a team of tv professionals but by a group of administrative government officers,[25] the state broadcaster's 'failure' to reform throughout the 1990s can hardly come as a surprise.

In the genre of n&c a high level of trust and credibility with the viewer is understood to constitute a crucial parameter for the (perceived) 'quality' of programming. Especially since the de-monopolisation of television in the 1990s, the professionalisation of a tv-channel's news coverage – professional defined along the paradigmatic lines of the international standards and 'best' practices set by a handful of European and American, national and transnational market leaders – has been defined in terms of a broadcaster's communicative ability to create these parameters through a set of viewer-oriented, representational routines and medium-conscious practices.

As suggested, NDTV's 'image' as a highly credible, trusted and viewer-oriented news provider has been achieved and discursively constructed step by step over more than a decade. This process of brand image construction has paralleled the slow but consecutive internationalisation and commercialisation of Indian television starting with the cautious 'modernisation' of DD way back in the 1980s. It is important to note, in this context, that Prannoy Roy's growing (individual-led) credibility was far from achieved easily, neither with regard to his programmes shown on Doordarshan nor on Star Plus. Both these networks had a rather low, institutionally given (journalistic) authority, were generally 'mistrusted' and commanded no distinctive (channel-led) credibility in the eyes of the Indian public when NDTV started to cover n&c for them.[26] Displaying an above – average standard for fairness, impartiality and non-corruptness, NDTV's journalistic and editorial performance, was, nonetheless, perceived to make the crucial difference.

The continued association of NDTV with the BBC World has not only increased the experience and competence of India's 'leading software production house', but has also improved NDTV's leading market position and furthered its professional tv-journalistic reputation. From November 1997 onwards Roy has anchored and produced *Question Time India*, an one-hour talk show that followed format-wise the British original, which it came to replace on the Asian BBC World service.[27] Finally, in 1999, NDTV secured itself an additional stake in the global newscaster's 'Indian-band' strategy, when Roy's software house was commissioned to produce the weekly magazines *Out of India* and *India Business Report*.[28] Not surprisingly, NDTV is perceived, by the Indian public, as *the* domestic incarnation of a Western-style n&c programmer: "Our BBC", as many Indians say.

An empirical determination of the precise impact of Western standards, formats and models on the 'modernisation' of n&c as shown on Indian television is, however, impossible. Neither can we identify how change and innovation occurred, nor can we know to what extent they are caused by institutional cooperation and/or by individual media professionals' increased access and exposure to Western broadcast services. In fact, the changing face of tv journalism, as practised in India, is the result of several independent forces, only one of which can be classified as the deliberate adoption of international standards, based on professional values and role models. Technological change, the deregulation of the Indian broadcasting sector and a general change typifying the dominant journalistic discourse, are among the determining factors. However, having outlined the changing market forces that have encouraged and enabled the successful emergence of 'Western-style' n&c, we can describe and identify how this 'modernisation' has materialised on a textual and aesthetic (format) level.

Towards the Democratisation of the Indian News Coverage

A major strength of *Star News*, compared with the 'journalistic form' practised by *The News* on DD1, lies in NDTV's aim and capability to present both a more comprehensive and a more easily consumed political news coverage. This fundamental difference can be seen in the use of language, in the journalistic and editorial perspective, in the use of sources and cases, in the way the news is presented and addresses the viewer, as on many other levels.

The English used on DD1's news is formal, unemotive and for the most part more complicated than necessary, both whether phrased by a reporter or in the news announcements read by a news presenter. The viewer is addressed in the objectified, bureaucratic and patriarchal language known from the public proclamations issued by Indian authorities. In consequence, the viewer is easily left with the impression of being communicated to and not with, thus being relegated to the position of an anonymous and voiceless citizen. NDTV, in contrast, has understood the importance of enabling what Horton and Wohl (1956) have labelled as (the illusion) of para-social interaction created between the viewer, the media personality addressing the viewer and the individuals he interacts with on screen. Using a language that establishes the temporal and spatial relations of co-presence with the viewer, the newsreader/anchor reaffirms a sense of shared participation, as (s)he seemingly engages in a conversational discourse with the viewer (see Allan 1999: 100). In the news shown on Star TV, the English is polished and precise (close to the BBC's *received pronunciation* and with less of an Indian accent than the newsreaders on DD or Zee News), but colloquial and far more informal – with casual remarks and so-called 'happy talk' thrown in – than the English typical for the majority of Indian bureaucrats and officials alike. Crucially, Roy and his team demonstrate, on the one hand, their ability to express themselves in a confident and socially correct but not subservient manner, trying to keep the communication as simple as possible – conversational in the sense of Norman Fairclough's (1995) well-known conversationalization thesis – given the intended subject and message. On the other hand, they demonstrate their journalistic capacity to go beyond the various (economic, political, bureaucratic etc.) discourses they are confronted with. They project, in other words, the image of a group of educated and sharp-minded persons, who are able to engage in a reasonable argumentation, on equal footing with the 'experts' and 'politicos'. This, in a communicative set-up of interaction, where the sources are expected to articulate their interests, views and decisions in a proper but 'ordinary', non-privileged and non-insider language.

Obviously, the outlined role-model and mediated image of the 'powerful' tv journalist provides the viewer with a more attractive and arguably empowered focus of identification, than the image of the polite but 'impotent' and harmless DD reporter. The Indian tv viewer expects, probably more than ever, a tv reporter or anchor to be sufficiently articulate and willing to control a given interview situation and to respond with an adequate professional stature to the viewpoints and arguments he encounters. Whereas the news staff of NDTV seems to make a serious attempt to question, challenge and deconstruct the discursive articulations they are confronted with, the DD news staff generally represents a far less independent journalistic position. Journalist-driven interviews – conducted with an awareness for the expressive and discursive possibilities of tv journalism – are at best mimicked by the DD news personnel, so as to project the image of being a professional and modernised, credible newscaster. Yet what the Indian tv audience is confronted with, day after day, is the prolific performance of a news department whose reporters and journalists give the impression of lacking communicative authority and who show only a weak initiative whenever they interact on screen with the Indian establishment. With their news reports and news announcements merely 'echoing' official positions, the particular English used by DD news is indicative of the state broadcaster's communicative position regarding the coverage of (political) news. Basically, in this role-model, the tv-medium is defined as a vehicle to transport the messages politicians and authorities are eager to distribute among (the affluent sections of) Indian society. Editors and journalists are supposed to play a 'neutral', meaning uncritical and helpful, role in this process of mediation and to restrain from attempts to identify or decide for themselves (based on journalistic criteria) the political news agenda. The DD news department may have resisted the competitive urge towards a more populist news discourse practice – and this is the good message – but to date it has failed to develop into an independent and credible journalistic critic of the existing power relations and tremendous socio-economic inequalities characteristic for Indian society – and that is the bad message.

Budget Day

When comparing DD and Star TV, the scope of difference in function and communicative role the tv-medium and its journalists occupy in relation to the political system becomes even more apparent, if we look at the network-specific comprehensiveness and analytical 'depth' of their news coverage. *Samachar* and *The News*, shown on the national network (DD1), frame their news reports in the rhetoric style of reference, protocol and the factual, which only allows for a very particular, one-dimensional form of comprehensiveness. To give an example: When the annual Union Budget was announced on February 29, 2000, Doordarshan's English early evening news bulletin used nine out of fourteen minutes on a single report summing up the various financial schemes and allocations in great numeric detail. After a short visual introduction, showing the Union finance minister during his speech in Parliament, text plate after plate is displayed and read aloud by the reporter in the off. The 34 text plates (!) are sparsely intercut by half a dozen brief, 'illustrative' archive clips (showing a power plant when the power sector is mentioned etc.), four more overvoiced footage scenes and one soundbite from the finance minister's speech in Parliament, positioned about mid-way in the report. Informing the viewer about as many details, exact amounts and financial decisions as possible seems to be the public broadcaster's best bet regarding the coverage of such an important political event. After the (three-minute) commercial break, the newscast is completed with a (one-and-a-half minutes) second news item. Presented by the newsreader with the brief remark that the prime minister, Atal Bihari Vajpayee, has called the finance minister's piece of work a 'good budget', this final report consists of the statement Vajpayee had given in a non-exclusive meeting with the press some hours earlier, in a hardly edited and non-commented format. Following this was a reminder of the headlines (including two more text tables) and *The News* on DD1 was finished.

In comparison, the evening news bulletin shown on Star Plus and Star News, was a very different affair. The half-hour news programme (consisting of about 20 minutes of news and 10 minutes of commercial breaks) also starts out with an outline of the central financial decisions and allocations taken in the budget, though in a much shorter (two-minute) summarised form of presentation, limiting itself to seven text plates to give the viewer the major (numerical) information. This summary report is followed by half a dozen short reports exploring the assumed consequences and impact of the budget on (i) the consumer and subsidised goods prices, (ii) the Indian industry, (iii) the Defence sector, (iv) Indian farmers, (v) Olympic athletes etc., starting with a report on the nose-diving Bombay stock market. Each of these brief (two- to three-minute) items includes comments and reactions made by professional experts, members of the national opposition parties and/or ordinary people. Vajpayee's press statement is also covered (using excerpts), but as it is placed between the criticism of a 'weak and unbalanced budget', expressed by a majority of the mentioned (non-government) sources, his remarks create the impression of being of a less affirmative and much more defensive character than in the DD news bulletin. Last but not least Star News has a report from a remote village without electricity, but with a single battery-operated community television set. The villagers are questioned and express, not surprisingly, their complete lack of understanding and interest in the announcement of the budget and in the extensive live coverage the event has received on the national network and half a dozen private tv channels. In fact, the some-dozen head strong village audience decided to watch a Hindi feature movie instead.

Viewer-Orientation, Proximity and Credibility as Indicators of Professionalisation

The comparative example may illustrate why NDTV is known for its ability to provide news coverage that is comprehensive in the sense of including considerable in-depth analysis, debate and background. On the Star TV channels an effort is made not only to inform the viewers about the facts, but also to help and guide them in their efforts to figure out the consequences and meaning of Budget 2000 for their own lives and for the lives of others. *Star News* demonstrates a considerable concreteness, uses case stories and is generally characterised by a representational practice that gives more of a face and voice to a multitude of non-official perspectives and discursive positions. *The News*, in contrast, shows DD's continued preference for news as authoritative summaries and its complete ignorance of the need to be viewer-oriented – to create 'intimacy on a distance' and the impression of a high degree of proximity on all levels of the broadcaster's mass mediated interaction with the viewer.

The demand for proximity has been described as *the* guiding frame for the conceptual (re)orientation observable in the ongoing 'modernisation' and diversification of the tv-news genre by Western channels, irrespective of their local, regional, national or transnational character. In other words, in an increasingly competitive broadcasting environment we are faced, with a more explicit viewer-orientation which has been understood to cut across the multitude of channel-specific strategies and representational discourses. Doordarshan's news department, however, seems neither able nor willing to fully use and explore the communicative potential of the medium. It is, therefore, foremost in this sense that the state broadcaster's news coverage is perceived as less 'professional' by the Indian public.

165

As I have argued, what is demonstrated here – through DD's news selection criteria, its particular journalistic perspective and discursive practice – is its notorious reluctance to transform its news bulletins into an arena for investigation, public debate and the televisual mediation of political and other, more individualised, conflicts occurring in Indian society. This is apparent, not least, in DD's almost complete lack of live reporting and live interviews, given its extensive networking infrastructure. Whereas studio guests, the invitation of opponents and the live interview of distant sources (including other NDTV journalists) via cable and satellite link are commonplace on Star News, they are more or less absent from the national network's news bulletins. The interviewed person may shed an additional perspective on the news issue at hand, opponents may help to identify and present a conflict's antagonistic positions, the live form may contribute to the 'immediacy effect' (Ellis 1982) of n&c on television. Yet live interviews and debates do not provide the interviewer (and editor) with the same degree of journalistic control, do not allow for selective quotation and are in general more demanding than their pre-recorded and pre-edited counterparts. Things may go wrong, get out of hand, so why take a risk? Put in slightly exaggerated terms, this seems to be the common sense rationale behind DD's 'reluctance' to make use of its extensive technological facilities in order to include more live elements in its news coverage. The notorious Delhi-centrism of DD's news coverage and slow, bureaucratic allocation procedures may be other crucial reasons.[29]

Regarding the coverage of 'breaking news' the state broadcaster has an equally poor record. To give just one example, a major train accident in West Bengal in August 1999 was covered on the spot and every hour by the Press Trust of India as well as by the Indian tv news agency ANI. The state broadcaster, on the other hand, did not even bother to rush a SNG unit or (at least) one of its own reporter and camera teams to the scene.[30] This despite the fact that Doordarshan has a full-fledged studio and regional programming centre in nearby Calcutta.

Given DD's command over a nation-wide terrestrial and satellite network including more than two dozen regional *Kendras* (the regional broadcasting centres that run the vernacular language channels and that are supposed to provide regional-specific programming to the national broadcaster in Delhi), the public broadcaster could be expected – and basically is expected by the majority of Indians – to reflect the tremendous size of India, the cultural and ethnic diversity of its one billion people, and the multitude of their actual life circumstances on a more comprehensive scale than do its private competitors. Judging by the range of news issues covered, however, this assumption does not hold true. Regional issues are either ignored and relegated to one of DD's fourteen regional tv channels, or they are reported from the point of view of the nation's Capital, on the national news bulletins – a fact which has led to an almost complete rejection of the Hindi *Samachar* and of *The News* in India's North East and South. While NDTV tries to counter its former image as a Delhi-centric programmer, for example, by screening a daily prime time news hour on Star

News called *Nationwide,* which consists of reports and live interview links with the NDTV studios in Bombay, Calcutta, Delhi and Madras, DD1's n&c department has so far shown no comparable efforts to make use of its much denser All-Indian newsnet.

Nor does the Doordarshan news staff have a favourable record of bringing the 'invisible' parts of life and struggle in India to the small screen. Whereas Star News takes up issues that may exemplify some of the less known and media-covered conflicts and existential problems of India's disadvantaged majority, e.g., in a weekly investigative magazine called *Assignment* and in a special daily news-item called *India Matters,* such stories are less prominent on the national news bulletins. Officially bound and normatively defined by its public service obligation, the state broadcaster may cover comparable (socio-economic and socio-political) issues too. Yet Doordarshan does so, typically, using a less advocatory but more benevolent and patronising discursive style, a journalistic angle that too often projects the state institutions' agency not as the cause of, but as the solution to the problem. Furthermore, these items are relegated primarily to the educational and development-oriented (non-prime time) programme slots, as these kinds of issues are seldom deemed 'relevant' enough to be taken up during national (prime time) coverage. Finally, Doordarshan in its discursive news practice favours to represent ordinary people with a focus on their collective and 'anonymous' properties. They are, in other words, not 'imagined' as

Table 3.   News characteristics in comparison

	DD 1	Star TV
language	formal	informal
live interviews & coverage	occasional	regular
actuality	low	high
immediacy effect	limited	increased
time & space construction	there & then	here & now
studio guests	seldom	often
analytical reports & debate	few	many
presenter & anchor role	institutionalised	personalised
address	indirect	direct
news selection criteria	narrow	broadened
feedback & direct response from the viewer	neglected	pursued
pluralism	restricted	extended
integrity/credibility	disputed	acknowledged
proximity	limited	heightened
communicative relation with the audience	paternalism	mediation & advocacy
role identity for viewer	collective subject	viewer/consumer/individual
institutional role	news transmission	news making
discursive orientation & focus on the demands of	state/government	audience/advertisers

individuals (exemplifying a case story) but as the voting, demonstrating, victimised, consuming, religious etc. numerous masses ever present in India.

For the sake of comparison, the differences between *Star News* and *The News* (on DD 1) could be presented in the following dichotomic form (Table 3). Yet it must be mentioned that the contrast may not be as clear, the two news bulletins not always as strikingly different as suggested, if we look at a more comprehensive sample. It has been my explicit purpose to select and present two news bulletins as distinct as possible – an example which I found in the early evening newscasts on Budget Day. The differences may therefore be over-emphasised and the similarities somehow neglected, but the general tendency, I claim, is far from distorted and has been validated by watching, taping and analysing more than 50 hours of n&c programming.[31]

To sum up: Concerning the choice of images, DD is still very restricted in its representation of the state. What Doordarshan lacks is not only a law (the still pending Broadcasting Bill) that would have enabled competition, but also a clear-cut, yet flexible policy concerning the content and images of the software. As Britta Ohm (1999) has remarked, "such a policy was never formulated and its non-existence could be read as a sign of a fear of the uncontrollable image" (Ohm 1999: 75). In consequence, the state broadcaster's news department was left without an elaborated, journalistic and audiovisual strategy. Its staff, instead of being encouraged to explore the mediums intrinsic qualities – to challenge and transcend an established frame of orientation – was socialised to a working culture where 'playing it safe' seems to be the foremost guiding principle. After all, anything shown in the news could be accused of being 'wrong'.[32] The 'realistic' image that DD tries to project comes therefore close to a non-image, in the sense that there are hardly any images in real life that might not be prone also to encourage an 'other', potentially subversive and oppositional, interpretation and thereby to question the state institutions' hegemony, agency and power structure. The images and visuals offered by DD's new department are, in consequence, framed and selected so as to be *recognised* and *believed*, not *understood* and *explored* in a human sense. Slowed down by its bureaucratic, institutional heritage the state broadcaster's news coverage has yet to overcome its historical preference for the 'denotative' use of the image. As long as DD is bound by a 'tradition' of political control and protocol journalism, and as long as it limits its journalistic scope and role to the reporting and referring of the 'factual', it will never fully explore or exploit the medium's communicative capacity.

At NDTV, on the other hand, technological possibilities, institutional independence and representational practice go hand in hand to live up to a professional standard set by global news services, especially the BBC. The Indian market leader has demonstrated how to create 'convincing' audiovisual narratives and how to create 'trust' in its journalistic performance. NDTV's news personnel/anchors function as the visible prestigious symbols of network identity; branding and personalisation are used as representational strategies to re-embed the social interaction with the viewer. In a media environment where only a very few tv-journalists and production houses have been in the business for more than half a decade, and where the demand has increased tremendously, NDTV is continuously re-creating its brand image as the leader of a handful of professional and established programmers. "Rely on us, we rely on experience" a self-assured Prannoy Roy tells the viewer at the end of one of NDTV's promos which are part of each and every commercial break on Star News.

Inherent Limitations

As I have tried show, Star TV among other commercial networks has made a successful entry into Indian n&c. NDTV's experience and reputation as India's most credible and professional n&c programmer has been utmost crucial in this process. NDTV's image as market leader has been actively constructed over more than a decade and furthered when Prannoy Roy was given the chance to build up the highly acclaimed Star News channel. Not surprisingly, success breeds envy but also blatant imitation. Surfing the Indian cable tv channels in February, March and April 2000, I was able to witness more Star News 'clones' than ever. Clearly, the news bulletins of commercial Jain and Sahara TV, recently (re)launched, have developed their aesthetic 'look' (i.e. dress code, studio set-up and decorations, opening sequence, camera set-up, musical introduction etc.) and 'representational' strategy (i.e. anchor personality, viewer address etc.) with a close eye on the media performance displayed by NDTV. Although financially less generously endowed than their well-established role-model, and journalistically less experienced, professionalised and/or independent,[33] these newcomers sometimes give a more ambitious than actually successful impression in competing with the market leader on its own terms. The 'best practice' and 'standard setting' role of NDTV in an increasingly competitive Indian tv environment can, none the less, be observed to have a profound influence on even traditionally complacent and self-centred Doordarshan. This can be seen most clearly on the newly started 24-hour DD News channel which obviously felt in dire need of inspiration in terms of how to popularise such an ambitious endeavour among a reluctant c&s audience.[34] At the moment, the Indian television newsscape is (still) highly fluid and DD may be forced to reorient its n&c operations much faster and more radically than suggested by my ('dichotomic' style of) presentation. Yet the crucial question remains as to whether the state broadcaster will not only be eager, but also able – given its institutional ponderousness – to transform swiftly into an autonomous, credible and viewer-oriented public service broadcaster in order to gain back a substantial share of the c&s homes (and consequently advertisers) it lost to its private competitors.

What seems to have emerged at this point, is a newsscape where the c&s viewer has the chance to make a (complementary) choice. She, but most likely he, may turn to CNN International and the BBC World for immediate (most up-to-date) and comprehensive coverage of international news. He may watch CNBC India to satisfy his growing interest in Indian and international business news. He may turn to the vernacular language newscasts on one of Doordarshan's regional channels, and he may watch the national Doordarshan news bulletins to get the 'official' (Delhi-centric) position. He may check and evaluate these news bulletins by turning to the Star TV channels, which he perceives as more 'slick', comprehensive, credible, non-biased, useful and entertaining, but market-driven in their representation. Finally, he may watch the more down-market Zee News and he may enjoy some of the privately produced late evening news shows on DD News (*Nightcap*), on the Star Plus (*Aaj Ki Baat*) or on the Metro channel (*Aaj Tak*). If the viewer is not from the Hindi-belt, however, his first choice will most probably be the news coverage shown on a commercial vernacular language channel. Yet no matter how wide the choice, even for a non-English speaker, the majority of all tv homes and c&s homes will see no news at all. On an average day – though of course not during major news events like military conflicts, general elections etc. – all the newscasts together reach, reportedly, less than half of the c&s and terrestrial homes alike turning on their tv sets.

While n&c matter, they do so primarily for the highly educated and affluent, upper middle and upper classes. It is mainly for this group of powerbrokers, decision-makers, professionals, intellectuals and opinion leaders that the increased and diversified choice, offered, for example, by NDTV is of immediate relevance. Yet though NDTV seldom comes above a share of three to four per cent of c&s viewers – that means less than one million of India's approximately 25 million c&s homes and less than 0.5 per cent of the overall population – its influence should not be underestimated. As mentioned above, it provides a 'model' of tv-journalistic and representational practices monitored by all the other n&c producers and channels in India. Western 'best practices' and informational tv-formats are, so to speak, passed down via the market leaders, although they become 'Indianised', localised and customised in this process. NDTV's relevance is consequently not confined to c&s homes. In the long run it also has an indirect but powerful influence on terrestrially transmitted n&c programming shown on DD's national network. Furthermore, NDTV reaches a small but influential and powerful segment, 'the people who matter', both via Star TV and the BBC World India band.

The deregulation of the Indian newsscape has created, that is crucially enlarged, a democratic and journalistic space for debate, accountability and critical investigation almost non-existent on television prior to 1996. Basically this phenomena reflects on (and contributes to) India's transformation from a 'mixed' model of governance, economy and planned development (with capitalistic enterprises besides an almost socialist dominance of the public sector), to a more deregulated, privatised and liberal economical system in the 1990s.[35] The proliferation of Star News, I want to argue, represents the communicative dimension of a changed authoritative relation between the Indian state and its (educated, upper-class) citizens which is expressed in the paradigmatic change from a 'collectivist' to a more 'individualist' notion of modernisation. What we have seen since the start of India's market liberalisation – coinciding not accidentally with the arrival of c&s television in India in 1991 – is an attempt on the part of the reconfigured 'transnational' elite and middle classes to claim television as a vehicle for representing themselves, not only to themselves but also to the nation and the world. Crucially, the members of the Indian elite and the middle classes are no longer identical with the once so powerful guardians of the Nehruvian 'socialist' welfare state, i.e. the civil servants, politicians, professionals and intellectuals who were eager to determine and control the state broadcaster's discursive practice for more than three decades. Correspondingly, in the privately produced n&c shows, the c&s viewer is faced, above all, with the 'new heroes' of a booming Indian economy: the businessmen, 'techno-entrepreneurs', market-oriented government functionaries, 'progressive' political leaders, software engineers and people working in the media. That is India's 'cosmopolitic' and 'modern' elite and the upward-mobile middle-class professionals associated with them who have aggregated, over the last two decades, to constitute a nationalist-modernising hegemonic bloc.[36]

The changing journalistic and representational practices of television signify, furthermore, a parallel (to the ongoing economic liberalisation and intrinsically linked with this process) trend towards greater informational 'openness' and political accountability (see Ninan 2000). We can talk – borrowing an adequate phrase from John B. Thompson (1995) – of the contemporary emergence of a 'mediated transparency in politics'. Television, not least in its commercial satellite incarnation, has come to play an increasingly important role for the mediation of competing ideological, political and economic discourses. Furthermore, as the medium, more than ever, reflects on (and contributes to) the notion of an individual's legitimate claim to be served and to have a mediated 'direct' voice – direct in contrast to the 'indirect' articulation of his interest via the elected members of the political system – (satellite) television has become a major ideological 'definer' in the ongoing process and negotiation of India's 'modernisation'.[37] Institutionally, this shift in the medium's communicative role – from being the mere transmitter of development-oriented, educational and other government- and bureaucracy-disseminated messages, to being an agenda-setting institution on its own – has invested (commercial) television with a considerable amount of ideological and, as a result, bargaining and political power.

So far, Rupert Murdoch, the prolific owner of the Star TV network, has made no overt attempt to exploit the Indian situation. This, presumably not because this global media marauder is too scrupulous to intervene with the editorial policy of his associates and companies, if deemed necessary and possible,[38] but due to Murdoch's realisation that his Indian operations are so economically vulnerable that he dare not antagonise either the Indian government or the Star TV audience, who might overwhelmingly sympathise (and shift to another channel) with Prannoy Roy in case of a major conflict. Murdoch's demonstrative detachment from NDTV's editorial decisions makes therefore sense for both sides. Star TV India refrains from the attempt to politicise via direct control over the journalistic content on its Indian n&c shows. Hence, it does not have to take any 'flak' – negative responses intended to influence the news organisation – nor is it held directly responsible for the antagonisation of powerful interest groups caused by these programmes. However, there is no guarantee for a continuance of the present agreement between Murdoch and Roy, which comes up for renewal in January 2001.

The co-operation between a n&c programme producer (NDTV) and a carrier (Star TV India), who markets the commercials and sponsorships with a minimum of interference in programming and editorial decisions, may be a worldwide unique form of strategic alliance between a transnational network and its domestic partner. As a result, NDTV, a private n&c programmer, may play something close to a public service role. However, NDTV can be said to be limited in this function, not only by its (non-terrestrial) distribution and restricted access to the Indian viewer, but also by its (indirectly) advertising-financed revenue base. Whereas NDTV might be called less pro-government than Doordarshan's n&c department, it certainly shares a stronger pro-business attitude with its private contenders, especially Zee TV and CNBC India, both in its programming produced for Star TV and the BBC World.

The Indian 'public sphere', constituted by the citizens who take part in the public articulation of the dominant discursive formations, has clearly become less based on mass-rallies, -speeches, -mobilisations, etc. – although this political mass culture still plays a more central role than in Western democracies – and has become more dependent and focussed on the electronic media. Compared with the former extremely elitist base of the Indian public sphere, circumscribed by the (English) print media, television has indisputably enlarged this narrow, social base. After all, even an illiterate person can now follow the political process and its public debate, provided he has tv access. Furthermore, satellite on the heels of terrestrial television is fast gaining ground, both among the lower middle classes and in rural areas. Still there is a long way to go. Audience studies show that, among the disadvantaged segments of the population, television is primarily used for entertainment. In consequence, even the Hindi and English news shown on terrestrial DD1 reaches only a fraction of India's one billion people. This uneven (media) news consumption reflects India's uneven socio-economic structure, characterised by the co-existence of a small but growing, wealthy, highly modernised, transnational-oriented, urban sector and its vast, marginalised, traditional, locally-oriented, rural counterpart.

No matter how fundamentally the Indian tv-newsscape may have changed under the conditions of *uneven development and modernisation*, India's so-called silent majority is still far from equally represented and served by the commercial satellite n&c services. Star News, CNBC India and the BBC World – targeting and oriented primarily towards c&s homes with a high purchasing power – are from the point-of-view of the disadvantaged masses far too 'elitist' and 'high-brow', whatever their philanthropic intentions. It is, therefore, the 'low-brow' and 'populist' Zee News and some of the vernacular language channels that may be able – over time and with the continued increase of number of television set – to reach a majority of the Indian population. Given the contemporary non-viability of commercially financed n&c directed towards these viewer segments and given the hollowness of DD's claim to have the entire Indian population (already) in mind in their news coverage, this would, however, demand yet another viewer-oriented 'modernisation' and democratic enlargement of India's tv-journalistic space.

Notes

1. In India news and current affairs programmes are still far from being money-spinners. Star News earned around $ 1 million during Elections in February 1998 – 25% of the amount actually spent on airing the programme (*Business Line*, 03.03.98). Zee India TV, by the end of its first year as a 24-hour infotainment channel, reportedly incurred a loss of over USD 600,000 a month (*Business Standard*, 23.11.98) on estimated USD 800,000 per month production costs (*The Hindu*, 18.01.98).
2. See e.g., Kishore (1994), Nanjundaiah (1995), Rughani (1996), Sahay (1993), Thomas (1993a & 1993b), Thussu (1998b) regarding India, and Herbert I. Schiller's (1992) attempt at a theoretical reformulation of the cultural imperialism thesis.
3. 'Free' in this context does not mean free-to-air, that is, without additional costs involved, but unchecked and uncensored by Indian authorities.
4. Initially the Metro channel was limited to the metropolises of Delhi, Bombay, Madras and Calcutta but as the venture turned out to be a success with audiences and advertisers alike, it was extended to all the major cities in India (Agarwal 1996).
5. In February 1995, the Supreme Court delivered a landmark judgement in the so-called *Ministry of Information and Broadcasting vs. Cricket Association of Bengal* case. The Court ruled that airwaves constitute public property that must be utilised for advancing the public good. In two separate concurring judgements, the Supreme Court said that, the airwaves being public property, it was the state's duty to see to it that they were utilised so as to advance the free speech right of the citizens, which was served by ensuring plurality and diversity of views, opinions, and ideas. This could not be ensured by a medium controlled by a monopoly, whether the monopoly was of the state or of any other individual, group, or organisation. Chief Justice Jeevan Reddy observed, "Government control in effect means the control of the political party or parties in power for the time being. Such control is bound to colour and in some cases, may even distort the news, views and opinions expressed through the media. It is not conducive to free expression of contending view points and opinions which is essential for the growth of a healthy democracy" (quoted in Arun Mehta, 1998). Subsequently, the Supreme Court ruled that "the broadcasting media should be under the control of the public as distinct from Government" (quoted in Ninan 1998: 13). See also Sinha, 1998; Ghosh, 1998; Petrazzini & Harindranath, 1996.
6. According to *Business Standard* (16.10.97), the number of Indian tv software production houses has increased from about 100 in 1992 to more than 900 in 1997. Since then the private tv production sector has, however, witnessed a process of concentration and consolidation.
7. This development in the Indian tv sector should, however, not be seen in isolation. Journalism, as practised in India, has in general undergone a fundamental transformation from the 1980s onward. This has been expressed most strikingly in the emergence of a number of weekly and fortnightly illustrated magazines like *India Today, Outlook, Frontline, The Week* etc. which have introduced investigative, critical and civic, service-oriented forms of journalism, as developed abroad, in India. The emergence of these media ventures and their commercial success with a 'new journalism' has had not only a profound influence on the Indian print media sector, but on tv journalism as well. And it is hardly surprising that some of these print media houses were the first to move into the production of n&c programmes whether distributed on video or commissioned by Doordarshan.

8. In October 1994, a qualitative reception study of current affairs programmes, shown on television, was prepared for the Delhi-based Media Advocacy Group by MBL Research and Consultancy Group Ltd, New Delhi. The study is based on twenty-two in-depth interviews, conducted in the capital, focussing on how people were responding to *Newstrack* and *Eyewitness*. Its major findings are presented and discussed in Ninan (1996: 62) and can be seen to reinforce the notion that one thing Indian tv viewers principally expected from news and current affairs programming, at the time, was that they make Indian politicians more accountable.

9. The proliferation of n&c on Star TV can be seen as part of an overall effort to offer the Indian viewers a 'complete portfolio of services' on the Star TV South platform which already roomed a music channel (Channel V), two sports channels (Star Sports and ESPN), an English movie channel (Star Movies), an English general entertainment channel (Star World), and an international news channel (BBC WS). The Zee TV network correspondingly included a music channel (Music Asia), a Hindi Movie channel (Zee Movie) and a Hindi general entertainment channel (El TV) by the end of 1996.

10. Launched in November 1994 as a 'Channel for the Youth', El TV was gradually repositioned as a Hindi/English 'infotainment' channel throughout 1997. To start with, this was achieved by shifting/retransmitting the Zee TV news bulletins and other factual programmes to/on El TV. With the transformation into a 24-hour 'infotainment' channel in January 1998, El TV was renamed Zee TV India. The year after, reformatted as a back-to-back n&c only channel, it finally became Zee News.

11. The repositioning of Star Plus as a *deshi* ('domestic') channel was effectuated from October 21, 1996 onwards. In order not to clash with Zee TV's prime time, the indigenisation of Star Plus began cautiously with the creation of a non-prime time 'Hindi band'. With a duration of four (weekdays) to seven (Saturdays) hours daily, this initial Hindi-lingual segment included, among other programme slots: a Hindi news bulletin (7.00 pm), an afternoon hour of old DD soaps (*Buniyaad, Khandaan*), an early evening slot for established Hindi serials (*Meri Awaz Suno* and *Imtehan*), a Saturday Hindi film slot, a film-based show, and the screening of the popular DD mythological *Chandrakanta* on Sunday mornings (see Doctor, 1996; IPAN BC Review, October 1996).

12. Prior to the restructuration, Star TV had been branded the archetypal cultural alienator in India on various occasions. In May 1995, for example, a guest on a Star TV talk show (*Nikki Tonight*) described Mahatma Gandhi as a 'bastard bania' (bastard trader). Gandhi's great-grandson, Tushar Gandhi, sued Star TV, TV 18 (the show's producer) and the participants, for Rs. 500 million (USD 15 million). An Indian court issued a warrant against Rupert Murdoch after the filing of a complaint that Star TV had defamed Mahatma Gandhi, and Bombay's Chief metropolitan found that this constituted a prima facie case of insult and defamation (see Sinha 1998: 36; Indian Express 03.10.98).

13. The STAR News channel will target a wider middle class/lower middle class market and will focus essentially on the Indian subcontinent, Star TV officials said in February 1998 (see *Business Line* 05.02.98). The likely explanation: The News Corporation, Murdoch's holding company, had sunk an estimated USD 1.2 billion into buying and developing the Star TV network by the end of 1996, and was still estimated to be underwriting annual losses to the tune of at least USD 90 million. There was, hence, an acute need to increase Star TV's revenues, on its second largest market (the Chinese Republic, being the largest one), beyond the Rs 850 million (approximately $ 25 million) it was supposed to have earned in 1995. According to the rationale of Rathikant Basu: "We have done the current sort of programming for several years and the results have not been great ... this is because the English audience is too small. It's not that an English only channel is unviable, but the advertising it gets will always be limited. ... Star Plus saturated this market and still didn't find it adequate" (quoted in Doctor, 1996).

14. One of Zee TV's early programmes *Aap Ki Adalat* (Your Court), a mock trial show which put many politicians in the dock before the law actually did, "gave the channel considerable clout and raised its profile beyond a merely entertainment network" (Thussu 1998: 280).

15. "Subhash Chandra thought of doing a programme like *Aap ki Adalat* in the early days of the channel and persuaded Rajat Sharma to join him and make it happen. Later, when it became a widely-known show, he used Sharma to open political doors for him. Still later, he would use his own political clout to scupper partner Murdoch's Direct To Home plans. Or so the latter's men believe" reports Ninan ("Murdoch's match", *The Hindu*, 03.10.99). And indeed, as has become clear over the last three years, Murdoch's ambitious plans for South Asia, announced by the end of 1996, have failed due to a comprehensive ban for DTH (Ku-band) services issued in July 1997 and prolonged by successive Indian governments since then. Though financial partners in Zee TV until October 1999, Subash Chandra Goel has vehemently opposed any move of Rupert Murdoch and his Indian team to get this ban lifted. See *The Hindu*, 08.02.98; *Connect Magazine*, July 1998.

16. Mistrusting the 'disloyal' private producers, Mandi House officials by summer 1997 contemplated to axe even these remaining and popular shows in an effort "to reverse the brain drain from Doordarshan" (Prasar Bharati CEO, S.S. Gill quoted in *Business Standard* 27.11.97).

17. In an unprecedented rush, Star TV India was able to sell the advertising slots of Star News "even before it went on air because Prannoy was anchoring it" remarks Sushil Pandit, Associate Vice-President, Contract (quoted in Indian Express, 14.07.97).

18. As early as December 1996, the IPAN Broadcasting Review made a substantiated claim that Star TV's English news bulletins were weaning away viewers from Doordarshan:

    According to MARG's findings, viewers, particularly men over 25 years of age, have now started spending more time with STAR Plus than with Doordarshan. The total viewership between 9.00 p.m. and 9.30 p.m. has increased substantially (70 per cent in Mumbai and 14 per cent in Delhi) and most of this increased viewership has gone to STAR Plus. In the four weeks after Prannoy Roy and his NDTV moved to the Murdoch-owned channel, STAR TV has managed to capture 60 per cent of all viewers of the 9.00 pm slot in Mumbai and 54 per cent in Delhi (IPAN BC Review, December 1996)

19. The exemption being OB vans and other uplinking facilities, which are a continued monopoly of Doordarshan and state-owned VSNL. So far, Star and Zee TV have been reluctant to acquire this expensive technology as long as their right to uplink from Indian territory has not been secured.

20. See http://www.ndtv.com/others/about.htm 20.02.00.

21. See *Business Standard*, 27.12.97, 25.02.98 and 23.11.98.

22. As happened last in November 1999 by the newly appointed Minister for Information & Broadcasting, Arun Jaitley (see *Business Line*, 17.11.99). See also Ninan, "DD to hire experts for anchoring news", *The Hindu* 25.01.00.

23. Serious attempts to accelerate the pace of DD's tv journalistic 'professionalisation' have been made, then and now. Yet they were regularly shot down by the respective Indian governments in power. In December 1997, Prasar Bharati (the formally 'independent' broadcasting organisation under which Doordarshan operates) CEO S.S. Gill announced "uncensored" news on DD from then on (see *Business Standard*, 29.11.97 and 27.12.97). Just a year later, however, Gill was kicked out by the then ruling National Democratic Alliance (NDA). Furthermore, the (then) new Minister for Information and Broadcasting, Pramod Mahajan, had DD officials instructed to telecast programmes about the BJP government's achievements under prime minister Atal Bihari Vajpayee (*Business Standard*, 15.12.98). By March 1999, Mahajan had the head of DD news transferred who "still had some misguided notions about (Prasar Bharati) functioning autonomously", claiming that "autonomy is no longer an issue when so many private channels exist" (Ninan, "Lock and key", *The Hindu* 28.03.99). With the ruling NDA's attack on Doordarshan's institutional autonomy and journalistic independence, the professionalisation of the state-broadcaster's n&c practices is still caught in the outlined contradiction between a public service and a propagandistic role.

24. The dismissal of some senior women newsreaders from prime time DD1 newscasts in June 1998, for example, has caused the Supreme Court to issue notices to Prasar Bharati CEO S.S. Gill, to DD and the Information & Broadcasting Ministry, directing them to explain the decision. Some newsreaders had petitioned the court alleging gender bias (see IPAN Industry

Watch, July 1998). The removal of more than a dozen regular newsreaders in January 2000, some of whom have been around for over two decades, led also to a public controversy, but was less vehemently resisted ("DD to hire experts for anchoring news", *The Hindu*, 25.01.00). This might indicate a growing readiness inside the DD workforce to accept some unpopular but competition-oriented measures.

25. The contemporary Prasar Bharati CEO Rajeev Ratna Shah, for example, comes from the Indian Administrative Service, Deepak Sandhu, head of Doordarshan's news and current affairs department from the Indian Information Service.

26. Doordarshan, due to its notorious non-public service and non-autonomous character and a news performance record which aspired rarely to a journalistic stature above that of an "electronic extension of the (the government's) Press Information Bureau" (*The Hindu*, 18.10.98) disseminating official policies and limiting itself to the coverage of state visits and functions. Star TV, due to its prolific owner, the notorious media marauder and archetypal 'cultural imperialist', Rupert Murdoch.

27. See "BBC to introduce India-specific programme band" *Business Line*, 11.09.97; *Business Line* "More India on BBC World", 13.11.97; Ninan, "A policy Guide" *The Hindu*, 06.12.98.

28. For a detailed account of the BBC World's Indianisation strategy see *Business Line*, 20.08.98; *Business Line*, 16.10.97; *Business Standard*, 16.01.99.

29. The slow and highly bureaucratised procedure to book a live link within Doordarshan is another reason, according to Bhaskar Rao, Centre for Media Studies (personal conversation 03.03.00)

30. See Ninan, "Made-up gods" *The Hindu*, 08.08.99.

31. As part of my PhD research project, the data sample was gathered in January 1999 and February/March 2000 during my field work in New Delhi. N&c programming was furthermore watched (though not recorded) extensively for analytic purposes in February/ March 1999, June/July 1999 and March 2000 during extended periods of stay in Simla and Bombay. Finally the n&c programming shown on Star News and DD1 was followed regularly via the Internet video streams (http://www.ndtv.msnbc.com/live/video.htm and http://www.ddindia.net/real/real.html).

32. 'Wrong' in this context means not only contrary to the political and economic interests of powerful pressure groups in Indian society, but also inappropriate and populist in the sense of the basic Nehruvian assumption that the audiovisual images seen on tv and cinema are able and intended to seduce a vulnerable audience. As Britta Ohm, among others, has pointed out, "the perception of the image and the visual as being dangerous, irresistible, escapist and intrinsically capitalist was created by the pre-definition of the image in the West and by the extrovert use of images in the commercial Hindi film industry" (Ohm 1999: 75). DD's (historical) task was therefore to 'civilise' the audiovisual image in contrast to its' vulgar' exuberance elsewhere – abroad and in the country. "This taming included contrasting the image to its capitalist use. ... Science, civilisation and socialism were seen as one and meant to exclude any 'barbaric unruliness' of which the image with its multilayered nature is *the* representative" (Ohm 1999: 75f).

33. Jain TV, for example, is widely regarded as the biased mouthpiece of the Sangh Parivar. Its owner, Dr. Jain, has not only contested as BJP candidate to the Lok Sabha on several national elections, he is also the entrepreneur behind the BJP's video-bus election campaigns in the late 1980s (see Brosius 1999).

34. The hiring of Sanjay Nigam, former TVI, as a special consultant for the development of n&c on Doordarshan, overriding to a certain degree the programme development competence of Deepak Sandhu, head of Doordarshan's n&c operations, can be interpreted as another indicator of an increased 'competitive' and 'professionalised' orientation gaining ground among the decision-makers of Prasar Bharati.

35. For a comprehensive account of India's market-oriented reform see e.g. Jenkins 1999.

36. Compare in this context Ronald Inden's (1999) illustrative account of the emergence of a new type of hero in Bollywood Cinema in the 1990s.

37. See also Arjun Appadurai (1996) who sees "the megarhetoric of developmental modernization
     ... punctuated, interrogated, and domesticated by the micro narratives of film, television, mu-
     sic, and other expressive forms, which allow modernity to be rewritten more as vernacular
     globalization and less as a concession to large-scale national and international politics"
     (Appadurai 1996: 10).
38. When carriage of the BBC World Service threatened the advance of Star TV in the republic of
     China in 1994 by reporting on human rights violations, the popular news service was taken off
     the Murdoch-controlled Asiasat-platform to accomodate Bejing.

References

Agarwal, Amit (1996) "Questioning the Legacy." *India Today* (15 August).

Allan, Stuart (1999) *News Culture*. Buckinham: Open Univ. Press.

Appadurai, Arjun (1996) *Modernity at Large*. Delhi: Oxford Univ. Press.

Brosius, Christiane (1999) "Is This the Real Thing? Packaging Cultural Nationalism", in Christiane
     Brosius & Melissa Butcher (eds.) *Image Journeys: Audio-visual media and cultural change in
     India*. New Delhi: Sage.

Cable Waves (1998) *Yearbook 1997/98*. Delhi.

Doctor, Vikram (1996) "Plus or Minus?", *Business India* (21 October).

Ellis, John (1982) *Visible Fictions*. London: Routledge & Kegan.

Fairclough, Norman (1995) *Media Discourse*. London: Arnold.

Ghosh, Rishab Aiyer (1998) "Trends in Indian Media and Prospects for Broadcasting Reform", in
     Monroe, E. Price & Verhulst, Stefaan G. (eds.) *Broadcasting Reform in India*. Delhi: Oxford
     Univ. Press.

Goswami, Anupa (1997) "Message for the Media." *Business India* (24 March).

Hjarvard, Stig (1999) *Tv-nyheder i konkurrence*. København: Samfundslitteratur.

Horton, Donald & Wohl, Richard (1956) "Mass Communication and Para-Social Interaction: Obser-
     vation on Intimacy at a Distance", in Gumpert & Cathcart (eds.) *Inter/media: Interpersonal
     Communication in a Media World*. Oxford: Oxford Univ. Press.

Inden, Ronald (1999) "Transnational Class, Erotic Arcadia and Commercial Utopia in Hindi Films",
     in Brosius, Christiane & Butcher, Melissa (eds.) *Image Journeys: Audio-visual Media and Cul-
     tural Change in India*. New Delhi: Sage.

Jenkins, Rob (1999) *Democratic Politics and Economic Reform in India*. Cambridge: Cambridge
     Univ. Press.

Kishore, Krishna (1994) "The Advent of STAR TV in India: Emerging Policy Issues", *Media Asia*, pp.
     96-103.

Kumar, K.J. (1996) "International News on Indian Television: A Critical Analysis of the World this
     Week", in French, David & Richards, Michael (eds.) *Contemporary Television: Eastern Perspec-
     tives*. Thousand Oaks: Sage.

Lo, Terence (1996) "No News is Bad News: 4 June and Individualism in Hongkong", in French,
     David & Richards, Michael (eds.) *Contemporary Television: Eastern Perspectives*. Thousand
     Oaks: Sage.

Mehta, Arun (1998) *Media Regulation in India*. http://www.cerfnet.com/~amehta

Mrinal Pande (1999) "News, Views and Abuse", *The Hindu* (19 September).

Nanjundaiah, Shashidhar (1995) "Deregulation of Television Broadcast in India. Cultural and Infor-
     mational Impacts", *Asian Journal of Communication,* no.1, pp. 71-87.

Ninan, Sevanti (1996) *Through the Magic Window: Television and Change in India*. New Delhi:
     Penguin.

Ninan, Sevanti (1998) "History of Indian Broadcasting Reform", in Monroe Price & Stefaan G. Verhulst
     (eds.) *Broadcasting Reform in India*. Delhi: Oxford Univ. Press.

Ninan, Sevanti (2000) "Analysis with an Accent", *The Hindu* (27 February).

Ohm, Britta (1999) "Doordarshan: Representing the Nation's State", in Brosius, Christiane & Butcher,
     Melissa (eds.) *Image Journeys: Audio-visual Media and Cultural Change in India*. New Delhi:
     Sage.

Petrazzini, Ben & Harindranath, G. (1996) *Information Infrastucture Initiatives in Emerging Econo-mies: The Case of India*. Occasional paper. Harvard Information Infrastructure Project. http:// ksgww.harvard.edu/iip/GIIconf/petpap.htm.

Rao, Sandhya (1998) "The New Doordarshan: Facing the Challenges of Cable and Satellite Net-works in India", in Melkote, S.R.; Shields, P. & Agrawal, B.C. (eds.) *International Satellite Broadcasting in South Asia: Political, Economic, and Cultural Implications*. Oxford: Univ. Press of America.

Rughani, Pratap (1996) "Collecting Orbital Junk", *Himal South Asia*, June, pp. 12-18.

Sahay, S. (1993) "Invasion from Sky", *The Hindustan Times*, 4 November.

Schiller, Herbert I. (1992) *Mass Communication and American Empire*. Boulder: Westview Press.

Sinha, Nikhil (1998) "Doordarshan, Public Service Broadcasting and the Impact of Globalization: A Short History", in Price, Monroe E. & Verhulst, Stefaan G. (eds.) *Broadcasting Reform in India*. Delhi: Oxford Univ. Press.

Subrahmanyam, K. (1995) "Facing the CNN and BBC Challenge", *Times of India* (5 July).

Thomas, Pradip N. (1993a) "Broadcasting and the State in India: Towards Relevant Alternatives", *Gazette*, 19-33.

Thomas, Pradip N. (1993b) "Informatization and Change in India – Cultural Politics in a Post-Modern Era", *Asian Journal of Communication*, no.1, pp. 64-83.

Thussu, Daya Kishan (1998a) "Infotainment International", in Thussu, Daya Kishan (ed.) *Electronic Empires: Global Media and Local Resistance*. Oxford: Oxford Univ. Press.

Thussu, Daya Kishan (1998b) "Localising the Global: Zee TV in India", in Thussu, Daya Kishan (ed.) *Electronic Empires: Global Media and Local Resistance*. Oxford: Oxford Univ. Press.

Zee TV (1997) An Approach to Business (Unpublished strategy paper).

Frames in Television News
British, Danish, and Dutch Television News Coverage of the Introduction of the Euro

Claes de Vreese

Much attention in political communication research has been devoted to the political and social role of news and its potential for democratic processes. At the core of this research is an interest in the relationship between the production of news, its content, and its implications for public understanding of political, economic, and social issues. Whereas the 'production – content – effect' interaction has been studied from many angles, very few approaches encompass an integrated view of the multi-layered, reciprocal processes. The notion of framing offers such a perspective, in which the interaction between journalists, sources, news content, and the audience in constructing meaning is essential.

Framing is conceptually indebted to work by Goffman (sociology) and Kahneman and Tversky (psychology). Although not concerned with media as such, Goffman, in his work on frame analysis, argued that frames are important in processing and interpreting unmediated events because they allow individuals to "locate, perceive identify, and label" (Goffman, 1974, p. 21). Kahneman and Tversky's (1984) seminal experimental study effectively demonstrated the effects of framing on the perception of a pre-defined problem[1]. Their findings provide the fundament of *prospect theory*, which holds that people are risk seeking when framed to consider losses and risk averse when considering gains. Their study suggested that a frame may determine *if* and *how* people understand and evaluate a problem.

Building on research in other disciplines, framing made its way into political communication research. The growing body of research on framing can be divided into studies examining *media* frames and studies focusing on *audience* frames (Entman, 1993; Scheufele, 1999). The first line of research has focused primarily on the ways in which issues are presented and covered in news (e.g. Entman, 1991; Norris, 1995; Patterson, 1993; Semetko & Valkenburg, 2000). Tuchman (1978) examined antecedents of news frames by looking at frames as "the negotiation about newsworthiness of an occurrence as a news event", a process that "imports" a character to an occurrence (Tuchman, 1978, p. 193). The second line of research, focusing on audience frames, has primarily dealt with the effects of specific frames on how individuals perceive, organise, and interpret events and issues (e.g. Domke, Shah & Wackman, 1998; McLeod & Detenber, 1999; Nelson, Clawson & Oxley, 1997; Price, Tewksbury & Powers, 1997; Rhee, 1997; Valkenburg, Semetko & de Vreese, 1999). In a seminal study, Gitlin (1980) demonstrated the profound implications media frames can have for public opinion and public policy making, and Iyengar (1991) documented the impact of news frames on the attribution of responsibility for social issues to either individuals or systemic factors.

This chapter aims at synthesising a number of previous studies of *frames in the news*. It does not address processes of production, through which frames emerge, nor are the complex processes of framing effects explored. Based on a review of studies of news frames, important distinctions for understanding this research are suggested. In the second part of the chapter, the notion of news frames is explored in a study of British, Danish and Dutch television news coverage of the introduction of the common European currency, the euro, on January 1, 1999.

Media Frames

The central dimensions of a frame are the selection, organisation, and emphasis of certain aspects of reality, with the exclusion of others. Research on frames in the news has defined frames as an 'organizing idea' (Severin & Tankard, 1997), an 'organizing theme' (Gamson, 1992), and "patterns [...] of presentation, of selection, emphasis, and exclusion" (Gitlin, 1980, p. 7). A news frame provides "a template that guides journalists in assembling facts, quotations, and other story elements into a news story" (McLeod & Detenber, 1999, p. 4). A frame may, thus, be thought of as a device that contributes to the process of selecting and packaging plentiful and diverse information into relatively short time or limited space. Frames in the news can be examined and identified by "the presence or absence of certain keywords, stock phrases, stereotyped images, sources of information and sentences that provide thematically reinforcing clusters of facts or judgements" (Entman, 1993, p. 52). Entman's (1993) definition suggests the ability of frames to provide audience members with a tool kit to be employed in processing information. This definition is the most frequently cited in the framing literature. It, however, is very broad and suggests that frames can be interpreted as very specific, concrete, and formalised textual manifestations and as part of a larger political or socio-cultural context.

Framing has acquired an important position on the international communication research agenda, especially within North-American research traditions. It extends research on the influences of news media beyond the well-defined agenda-setting function, which purports the news media's ability to define what issues will be on the public's mind (McCombs & Shaw, 1972; for an overview of agenda-setting research, see Dearing & Rogers, 1996). Framing focuses not only on the topics and issues selected for coverage in the news, but more importantly on the particular ways in which such issues are presented and which aspects of an event are made salient. In the early 1990s, framing was characterised as a promising approach to studying news (McQuail, 1994), presumably given the prospect of its parsimonious character. More recently, it was acknowledged as an important emerging concept in communication science (McQuail, 2000). However, previous framing research has also been described as an incoherent and fractured paradigm (Entman, 1993).

Framing provides, theoretically and conceptually, a context for defining research questions and hypotheses as well as interpreting results from content analyses. Applying framing as a guiding concept for conducting a content analysis of, for example, news coverage is no different from other approaches to content analytic studies. It involves drawing a meaningful sample of content, developing an appropriate and pre-tested codebook, training and supervising coders (or developing software), testing reliability, and ultimately drawing conclusions about structures and patterns in the content under investigation (Krippendorf, 1980; Riffe, Lacy & Fico, 1998).

Framing research suffers from shortcomings in formal definitions and concise operationalisations – a criticism and reflection also recently voiced by the renowned scholars Cappella and Jamieson (1997). The semantic confusion is fuelled by interchangeable use of terms such as frame, theme, script, schemata, discourse, and presentation. Frames guide the selection of aspects of reality and provide a structure for determining what information is presented and emphasised. They help journalists and editors to organise and evaluate new information so that it dovetails with established perceptions and patterns of reporting. A frame is a template defining the structural components of news stories, the selection of sources to be included, and the choice of words and phrases used to describe, analyse, and interpret.

Research on news frames is conceptually and theoretically associated with various other areas of research within (political) communication studies. The process of selecting information and bits of reality for packaging in the news is linked to the notion of newsworthiness and news values (e.g. Galtung & Ruge, 1965). The concern with structure in news stories is linked to narrative theory and the idea of discursive macro-propositions in news texts (e.g. van Dijk, 1988). The choice of words and phrases is linked to work on the use and function of metaphors and symbols (e.g. Edelman, 1964). Whereas the strength of framing may lie in its over-arching nature, the common ground and potential overlaps with other approaches stress the need for framing research to recognise its theoretical and conceptual antecedents as well as to explicate any operationalisations used for empirical observations. In other words, the use of frames as a concept must be justified, the definition validated, the measures concise, and the explanatory power immanent.

Frames in Political and Economic News

In reviewing research on frames in the news, a distinction can be made between *issue-specific news frames* and *generic news frames* (de Vreese, 1999). Issue-specific frames pertain to specific topics or news events, whereas generic frames can be found in relation to different topics, some even over time and, potentially, in different political and cultural contexts. An issue-specific approach to the study of news frames allows for a high level of specificity and detail relevant to the issue under investigation. It has the potential to capture specific aspects of selection, organisation, and elaboration that are present in news coverage and that pertain specifically to a well-defined issue. However, analyses drawing on issue-sensitive measures have the inherent disadvantage of limiting the scholar's ability to generalise, compare and test hypotheses. Generic frames are more general and may not capture all the specifics of an issue. Therefore they may be less useful for studying all issues in their full depth. This, however, is compensated by the universality of generic frames, which allows for comparisons between frames themselves, issues, and space.

One study of *issue-specific* news frames was based on a content analysis of several major US newspapers' coverage of the US national budget deficit (Jasperson, Shah, Watts, Faber, & Fan, 1998). Four frames were identified, and these were labelled 'talk', 'fight', 'impasse', and 'crisis'. The four frames reflected the chronology of the development of the issue in the news coverage. The frames deduced were highly issue-sensitive and pertained specifically to the chronology of the topic examined. This is also the case in Entman's (1991) study of the news media coverage of two airline accidents. He demonstrated how a US accident was framed in terms of 'tragedy' and 'mistake', whereas a comparable Soviet accident was framed in terms of 'attack' and 'deliberate.'

In another study of press and US network news coverage of the closing of a General Motors plant, it was found that a 'no option' frame dominated over an 'alternative frame' that challenged and offered alternatives to plant closure (Martin & Oshagan, 1997). Two studies in the realm of electoral processes have investigated issue-specific frames in the news. In one study of the 1988 national Canadian election, Mendelsohn (1993) identified three frames used in the television news coverage of the election: 'tactical motivations', 'performance', and 'leaders' moods.' In a European context, a content analytic study of news coverage during the campaign towards an urban planning referendum in Amsterdam, the Netherlands, revealed two predominant, polarised frames in the news: an 'environmental' frame, emphasising the impact on the environment of the building of a new living area, and a 'residence frame', emphasising the consequences for the housing situation (Neijens, 1999). Some studies of frames in the news move beyond the level of issue specificity. In an investigation of Cold War and Post-Cold War US television news, Norris (1995) identified a 'cold war' news frame. This is an example of an issue-related, context-bound frame. However, given the more general nature, durability, and visibility of the 'cold war frame' over several decades, we move beyond the purely single issue-specific news frame towards a more generic notion of news frames.

An example of generic news frames that transcend issue and time is Iyengar's (1991) distinction between 'episodic' and 'thematic' frames. The episodic frame focuses on particular cases, whereas the thematic frame "places political issues and events in some general context" (Iyengar, 1991, p. 2). Iyengar found the episodic frame to dominate US network news. He further suggested that the frame could have implications for how the audience makes sense of social issues, such that episodically framed news stories lead viewers to assign responsibility for social issues to individuals rather than to the 'system' or society at large. Cappella and Jamieson (1996, 1997), in their analysis of political and in particular campaign news, identified 'strategically' framed news, that is, news framed in terms of winning and losing in the 'game of politics', emphasising the style and presentation of parties and politicians rather than substantial elements of the issue at hand. They found strategically framed news to dominate US news coverage of politics.

Neuman, Just, and Crigler (1992) suggested a number of frames used by the news media and the audience. They derived a typology of frames used by the audience when discussing current affairs and found that the frames deduced from interviews with audience members were also present in the news media coverage of a number of contemporary issues. They identified 'human impact', 'powerlessness', 'economics', 'moral values', and 'conflict' as common frames (Neuman et al., 1992, pp. 74-75). The generic nature of these frames is suggested in that they are not confined to a specific issue. The frames overlap with and receive empirical support from research identifying personalisation and human interest as important dimensions of news. Bennett (1996, p. 48), for example, suggested that personalised news can be defined as "the journalistic bias that gives preference to the individual actors and human interest angles in events while downplaying institutional and political considerations that establish their social context". This identification of a mode of news reporting bears great resemblance to Neuman et al.'s (1992) human impact frame.

In a content analysis of television news and newspapers in the Netherlands, Semetko and Valkenburg (2000) suggested a number of generic news frames. In this study, five frames were identified: 'conflict', 'human interest', 'attribution of responsibility', 'economic consequences', and 'morality'. The human-interest frame brings a human face, an individual's story, or an emotional angle to the presentation of an event, issue or problem. The responsibility frame presents an issue or problem in such a way as to attribute responsibility for cause or resolution to either the government or an individual/group. The morality frame emphasises religion, God or certain prescriptions for social behaviour.

Whereas the responsibility frame was found to be the most prevalent in Dutch news overall, two of the most common frames in economic and political news were the conflict and economic consequences frames. The prevalence of the conflict and economic consequences frames in the Dutch news is in line with findings from previous studies suggesting that news about politics and the economy is often framed in terms of *conflict* or in terms of the *economic consequences* of events, issues, and policies (see Gamson, 1992; Graber, 1988; McManus, 1994;

Neuman et al., 1992). The *conflict frame* refers to disagreement between individuals, groups, institutions or countries, and emphasises the diverging opinions/approaches of conflicting parties (see e.g. Cappella & Jamieson, 1997; Patterson, 1993; Price, 1989). Research on news values in different journalistic cultures supports the notion of framing news in terms of conflict. The presence of conflict is consistently listed as an essential criterion for a news story to make it into the news (see e.g. Eilders, 1997; McManus, 1994; Price, 1989). The *economic consequences frame* reflects a "preoccupation with the 'bottom line', profit and loss" (Neuman et al., 1992). It has been suggested that news producers often use the consequence frame to make an issue relevant to their audience (Gamson, 1992). By framing news in terms of its consequences and the wide impact of an event, the journalistic goal of proximity is reached (Graber, 1993; McManus, 1994).

Several studies have supported the notion of generic frames, such as the conflict and economic consequences frames, as present in news coverage. Whereas previous research suggests that the conflict and economic consequences frames may be found in different countries, the necessity of integrating the political, economic, and social context of news frames has been argued (see, for example, Gamson, 1992; Neuman et al., 1992). Such a perspective enriches the understanding of news frames and acknowledges that frames are the result of interactions between journalists, sources, and the broader political and media system context (Pan & Kosicki, 1993).

Framing the Introduction of the Euro

Exploring the conflict and economic consequences frames in the context of an international event provides an opportunity to gauge both how these generic frames compare cross-nationally and how news in different countries is provided with a specific spin. In an on-going research project at The Amsterdam School of Communications Research *ASCoR*, the production, content, and effect of news coverage of European affairs on public opinion is investigated[2]. Integral to this project is a study of the news coverage of the introduction of the common European currency, the euro. One study specifically explores the framing of the euro and the use of the conflict and economic consequences frames (de Vreese, Peter, & Semetko, 2000).

Besides a number of country-specific studies, there is relatively little research on how the European Union is covered in the news, despite the fact that the media are consistently mentioned by European citizens as the most important sources of information about the European Union (Eurobarometer, 52, 2000). One exception is a cross-national comparative study of the television coverage of the 1979 European Parliamentary elections (Blumler, 1983), which was followed up in a few studies investigating the 1989 and 1994 election in one or more countries (see, for example, Leroy & Siune, 1994). The few other studies dealing with the media coverage of the European Union in a cross-national comparative perspective are limited to media monitoring projects. These projects provide only simple measures of the visibility, topical focus, and positive/negative slant of 'European' news (see e.g. Fundesco 1996, 1997; Euromedia Monitoring, 1995-1997). News about the same issues or events may be very different in different European countries. For example, news in countries that are net-contributors to the EU countries may be different from news in net-receiving EU countries. Similarly, news in European countries not participating in the European Monetary Union (EMU) may have a different emphasis and framing of European affairs as compared to news in more pro-European countries.

In the following, the framing of the January 1999 introduction of the euro in television news in Britain, Denmark, and the Netherlands is discussed. These three countries are different in terms of size and support for the euro / EMU: The Netherlands is a small European country participating in the EMU, and traditionally in favour of advanced European integration. Britain and Denmark are rather euro-sceptic, non-euro / EMU participants. Based on a content analysis of the main evening television news, the framing of political / economic news in general and news about the introduction of the euro in particular was examined. The analysis is focused on an investigation of the conflict and economic consequences frames. For Britain, the news programs included in the analysis were BBC's *9 o'clock News* and ITN's *News at Ten*, for Denmark DR's *TV-Avisen* and *TV2 Nyhederne*, and for the Netherlands NOS *8 uur Journaal* and *RTL4 Nieuws*[3]. The analysis showed that the introduction of the euro received extensive coverage in the days surrounding the launch of the new currency, taking up more than 20% (Britain and the Netherlands) or 25% (Denmark) of the total broadcasting time. The coverage of the euro completely vanished in the immediate aftermath of the launch.

In terms of the framing of the news stories, the presence of different dimensions of the conflict and economic consequences news frames was investigated. For the conflict frame, these dimensions were 'disagreement', 'reproach', and 'reference to two or more sides of the issue'. For the economic consequences frame, they were 'costs/expenses', 'explication of economic consequences of an action', and 'reference to losses/gains'. The content analysis suggested that the conflict frame was more prominent in general political / economic news stories as compared to the economic consequences frame (see Table 1). This pattern was found in all three countries. In stories about the introduction of the euro, however, the economic consequences frame was more visible than the conflict frame in all countries except Britain. The economic consequences frame was most visible in Denmark in comparison with the other countries. News about the euro in Britain and Denmark was also more often framed in terms of conflict as compared to news in the Netherlands.

Table 1. Percentage of news stories containing different dimensions of a conflict or economic consequences frame

	Britain		Denmark		The Netherlands	
	General political news	Euro news	General political news	Euro news	General political news	Euro news
	n = 94	n = 23	n = 67	n = 22	n = 114	n = 31
Conflict:						
Disagreement	44	17	68	32	53	13
Reproach	40	22	31	18	35	13
Two or more sides	59	26	37	23	34	7
Economic Consequences:						
Costs/expenses	14	13	19	32	19	19
Economic Consequences of actions	6	9	10	27	21	13
Gains/Losses	3	4	18	32	12	16

Note: The content analysis covers the period of the launch of the introduction of the euro (December 31, 1998 – January 4, 1999) and five weekdays in January 1999. n refers to the number of stories in each country[4].

The Context of News Frames

The analysis suggested presence of both the conflict and, albeit on a more modest level, the economic consequences frames. Whereas a quantitative measurement of the prevalence of certain frames in the news is an appropriate and comparable approach to studying the prevalence of news frames in a (cross-national) comparative fashion, it has been emphasised earlier that an exclusively quantitative approach may be an insufficient measure in itself. Specifically, when investigating the launch of the euro, the national economic and political context constitutes an important interpretative perspective in which to fully understand the notion of frames. Whereas frames may be generic in nature and draw on similar devices cross-nationally in terms of selecting, emphasising, and packaging certain types of information above others, understanding the national spin on such frames is equally important.

The news programs in all the studied countries organised their coverage of the introduction of the euro according to the chronology of events: the euro was followed as it appeared on the stock markets in Asia, then Europe and then the U.S. All networks carried identical footage of the Asian Stock Exchanges, champagne corks popping among EU finance ministers in Frankfurt, and the first trading on Wall Street. All provided coverage of a public euro event in Frankfurt, which was a major public relations effort involving more than 10,000 people forming the Euro symbol. All mentioned the considerable costs covered by companies and governments for conversion to the new currency, and described how companies were working through the night to be ready for the launch. Finally, all news programs stressed that the launch signifies the existence of a currency to compete with the US dollar.

British and Danish news gave the impression that the launch of the euro was viewed with some anxiety. News about the launch was presented in terms of the potential economic repercussions for the domestic macro-economy and for individual businesses. British and Danish news had certain similarities in the extent to which news appeared to be framed in terms of *conflict*, although conflict did not surface on the day of the launch itself. At the time of the launch in January 1999, the Danish and British Labour governments had not officially called for a referendum to determine each country's position on the euro. In both countries, much political tension was focused on disagreement over EMU membership among members of the government and the opposition and within the largest political parties.

In Britain, when reporters mentioned conflict on this issue, it was largely depicted as disputes within the Conservative Party, or between Labour and the Tories. In Denmark, leading politicians were openly in favour of joining the common currency as soon as possible. Clashes were reported with members of the opposition and public opinion showing reluctance towards joining the EMU. One story carried quotes from the Danish Prime Minister: "We need to be in and the sooner the better" with the Minister of Finance echoing this view: "We do not want to have another referendum until public opinion says the answer will be 'yes'". The juxtaposition of Danish pro and con views on EMU entry included a demonstration of Danish workers and a story about opposition groups demanding a special commission to investigate the effects of introduction of the euro.

In framing the launch of the euro, conflict was hardly visible in the Netherlands and of an international rather than domestic nature. *NOS News* opened with the headline "Spectacular Introduction of the euro" but the lead story began "The most spectacular (with a visual of corks popping) was that there was nothing spectacular at all". Dutch *RTL4 News* headlined "A cake overtakes the successful launch of the euro" and opened with a pie thrown in the face of the Dutch Finance Minister. Dutch news looked for conflict and found it in the 'political disagreement' surrounding the Wim Duisenberg 'issue'[5]. *NOS News* described the problem in this way: "The Duisenberg issue is a typical example of the European Union. The economy is fine, but the political disagreement constantly threatens to disrupt things." *RTL4 News* reported similarly: "The turbulence surrounding Duisenberg does not say a lot about the stability of the new currency, but it does say a great deal about the political weaknesses in this co-operation. The big test will come when one country fails to follow the agreements on finance policy, creates disputes, and threatens the euro."

The conflict frame was present in the news in the three countries, albeit on different levels. Conflict, however, was presented differently. In Britain it was within one political party, and in Denmark as disagreement between the government and Danish political and non-political 'anti-Europeans'. The Dutch focused on the conflict between a small country and a large country (France) as well as within the Dutch coalition government.

In framing the introduction of the euro in terms of *economic consequences*, Danish news reported reticence related to the launch of the euro. The event was presented in terms of the potential economic repercussions for the domestic macro-economy and for individual businesses. Danish *TV-Avisen*, for example, opened its bulletin on January 4, 1999 with a story about a company whose competitive position was allegedly threatened by the introduction of the euro, which would give international competitors an advantage in terms of currency stability and savings on money transfers.

News in both Britain and Denmark noted how the common currency would be more powerful than their own. One Danish journalist put it this way: "The debut of the euro on the world stage marks one of the most important steps towards a United States of Europe." Though the economic consequences frame was not strongly present in British news, the euro was viewed as having the potential to diminish the global importance of the Pound, with future battles being waged between the dollar and the euro. In that way, British news reporters noted, it represented a much greater step towards integration than Britain wanted to take, and it was a fundamentally important step over which Britain had no control. Dutch news, by contrast, was less concerned with the implications of the euro for the Dutch economy or consumers, and instead framed the launch in terms of the economic implications for businesses forced to devote extra hours to complete conversion and software.

In sum, whereas news about the introduction of the euro was framed in terms of economic consequences in all three countries, this frame was applied quite differently. Britain was concerned about the diminishing role of the Pound as a world currency, in Denmark, however, it was seen as a disadvantage for Danish businesses on the international market, and Dutch journalists considered it an extra, but necessary, expense for businesses.

Conclusion

As final remarks to this chapter synthesising previous work on frames and discussing findings of a recent study of frames in television news in Europe, a number of points are important. The analysis of the framing of the introduction of the euro suggested that similar news frames are found across different countries in both political and economic news generally and in relation to a special event. The conflict and economic consequences frames identified in other research on political and economic news were also found in the news coverage of the launch of the euro. This supports the notion that certain frames are of a generic nature and also indicates a certain element of universality in journalistic reporting of economics and politics. Although generic frames may be found to operate in different political and economic settings, it is also important to consider the national spin.

The analysis of news coverage of the euro launch indicates a dual trend in news also observed elsewhere. Research has suggested that news is simultaneously becoming increasingly 'global' and 'local'. The use of the economic consequences frame supports studies showing the domestication of news. The process of 'making the international national' is a well-known phenomenon (see, for example, Cohen, 1996). The 'internationalisation – domestication dynamic' inherent in news production is particularly visible in studies of news coverage of European affairs. First, Europe is becoming increasingly visible on the national news agendas (an indication of internationalisation). Second, pan-European issues (such as the euro) are, on the one hand, domesticated in order to conform to the important 'proximity' news value. On the other hand, a number of areas and issues that have traditionally been confined to the nation state are becoming 'European'. Debates on welfare policies, immigration, and the environment are examples of discursive areas to which an increasingly important European dimension has been added. The domestication of 'European news' has also been observed during elections for the European Parliament. Rather than being a shared pan-European event, these elections have been characterised as isolated, national, second-order elections (Reif, 1984). The low visibility of a distinct European dimension in news coverage of this inherently European event has been suggested as one of many factors explaining the relative absence of a European identity and public sphere.

Future research must address how national news media 'make sense of Europe' and further develop cross-national investigations of news coverage. In line with other research (Fundesco, 1997; Norris, 2000), the analysis of news coverage of the launch of the euro suggested that coverage of European Union affairs is cyclical, peaking around major events (such as the introduction of the euro) and largely disappearing during routine periods. More research is needed to fully explore the cross-national differences and similarities in framing Europe in the news, and the implications of these differences for public opinion formation.

In subsequent research on framing, there would also seem to be a need to explore more than the two frames investigated in the present study. As research has shown (Neuman et al., 1992; Semetko & Valkenburg, 2000), other frames such as 'attribution of responsibility' or 'human interest' have also been found in national news. Additionally, it would seem natural to explore differences in the framing of news between, for example, the US and European countries. The focus on 'game' and strategy, which is well documented for news in the US (see e.g. Cappella & Jamieson, 1997; Patterson, 1993), may only apply to a limited extent to European news produced in a multi-party system with different political traditions. A systematic cross-national assessment of different political and media systems' influence on news coverage would be enriching (see e.g. Blumler & Gurevitch, 2000). For understanding the differences in news coverage, research-ers have also pointed out the importance of the national institutional, political, and social contexts in which news is produced and the cross-cultural differences in journalistic practices, norms, and roles (Patterson, 1998; Weaver 1998; Weaver & Wilhoit, 1996). Linking these contextual factors specifically to empirical research on framing would be beneficial.

Future research on framing may also explore more closely the link between frames in the news and framing effects (Scheufele, 1999). Some studies offering evidence of framing effects on public perceptions of current issues support the claim of effects based on frames specifically designed and applied in, for example, experimental research (see e.g. Domke, McCoy, & Torres, 1999). Other studies emphasise the validation of the type of frames through literature reviews (e.g. McLeod & Detenber, 1999) or via content analyses of news (see e.g. Cappella & Jamieson, 1997; Iyengar, 1991, and Valkenburg et al., 1999). In these studies of framing effects, the frames tested were investigated and found in actual news coverage. The justified argument has been made that a valid study of the effects of news frames must be preceded by systematically collected knowledge about the way events and issues are framed in the news. Along these lines, Cappella and Jamieson (1997) suggested that frames must have identifiable conceptual and linguistic characteristics and must be commonly observed in journalistic practice. Consequently, content analyses of news may be considered an important prerequisite for the study of effects of news frames.

In this discussion of research on frames in the news, a number of areas to be further explored in future research have been introduced. Research on news frames in political communication is still in its 'infancy', and as such, demarcations as well as overlaps with other traditions of news analysis and audience research are still to be explicated. Broadening the scope of research on frames, both geographically and conceptually, will enable us to further refine, develop, and apply the concept.

Notes

1. Kahneman and Tversky (1984) sketched two differently framed, hypothetical scenarios concerning an unusual Asian disease, expected to kill 600 people. In two experiments, they offered two scenarios for participants to choose from: If program A is chosen, 200 people will be saved. If program B is adopted, there is a one-third probability that 600 people will be saved and a two-thirds probability that no one will be saved. 72 percent chose Program A, 28 percent Program B. In the second experiment, the scenarios were: If Program C is chosen, 400 people will die. If program D is adopted, there is one-third probability that nobody will die and a two-third probability that 600 people will die. The preference for scenarios was reversed by the framing: Program C was chosen by 22 percent, though the identical Program A was chosen by 72 percent. Program D was chosen by 78 percent, though the identical Program B received only 28 percent.

2. The research project at The Amsterdam School of Communications Research ASCoR, University of Amsterdam, includes the author's Ph.D. project which is supported by The Danish Research Academy and the Netherlands Organisation for Scientific Research [NWO]. This research is integral to a larger project chaired by Prof.dr. H.A. Semetko, Prof.dr. K. Schönbach, and Prof.dr. C. v/d Eijk.

3. On January 1, 1999, the euro was officially launched in 11 of the 15 countries of the European Union (including the Netherlands, but excluding Denmark and Great Britain). On January 4, 1999, the euro was officially traded as currency on the international stock markets. The period included in the content analysis covers the launch of the euro (December 31, 1998 – January 4, 1999) and five weekdays in January 1999 (January 5 – 8 and 11, 1999). For more information about the content analysis, see de Vreese et al., 2000.

4. The presence of the conflict and the economic consequences news frames in the news stories was measured by adapting more recent methods of Semetko and Valkenburg (2000). The

conflict frame was operationalised with three items: "Does the news story reflect disagreement between parties/individuals/groups/countries?", "Does one party/ individual/group/country reproach another", and "Does the story refer to two sides or to more than two sides of the problem/issue?". The *economic consequences frame* was measured with three items: "Is there mention of the costs/degree of expense involved?", "Is there a reference to economic consequences of pursuing or *not* pursuing a course of action?", and "Is there mention of financial losses or gains now or in the future?". These questions were answered with yes or no, and were applied to all political and economic stories. Each item was designed to measure a different dimension of the news frame. Trained and supervised MA students in the International School of University of Amsterdam carried out the analysis. The percent agreement between coders ranged from 73-100% for all questions in the three countries.

5. The Dutchman, Wim Duisenberg, was appointed to lead the European Central Bank (ECB) for a term of eight years. His appointment was the subject of considerable debate in the EU because he was supported strongly by most countries but initially rejected by the French, who insisted that a Frenchman have the seat after only four years.

References

Bennett, W.L. (1996) *News: The Politics of Illusion*. New York: Longman (3rd ed.).

Blumler, J. (ed.) (1983) *Communicating to Voters. Television in the First European Parliamentary Elections*. London: Sage.

Blumler, J.G. & Gurevitch, M. (2000) "Rethinking the Study of Political Communication", in Curran, J. & Gurevitch, M. (eds.) *Mass Media and Society*. London: Edward Arnold.

Cappella, J. & Jamieson, K. (1996) "News Frames, Political Cynicism, and Media Cynicism", *The Annals of the American Academy, AAPSS, 546*, pp. 71-84.

Cappella, N.J. & Jamieson, K.H. (1997) *Spiral of Cynicism. The Press and the Public Good*. New York: Oxford University Press.

Cohen, A.A. (1996) *Global Newsroom, Local Audiences: A Study of the Eurovision News Exchange*. London: John Libbey.

Dearing, J.W. & Rogers, E.M. (1996) *Agenda-setting*. London: Sage.

Dijk, van T.A. (1988) *News as Discourse*. Hillsdale, NJ: Lawrence Erlbaum.

Domke, D., McCoy, K. & Torres, M. (1999) "News Media, Racial Perceptions, and Political Cognition", *Communication Research,* no.26, pp. 570-607.

Domke, D., Shah, D. & Wackman, D.B. (1998) "'Moral Referendums': Values, News Media, and the Process of Candidate Choice", *Political Communication,* no.15, pp. 301-321.

Edelman, M. (1964) *The Symbolic Uses of Politics*. Urbana, IL: University of Illinois Press.

Eilders, C. (1997) *Nachrichtenfaktoren und Rezeption. Eine empirische Analyse zur Auswahl und Verarbeitung politischer Information*. [News factors and reception. An empirical analysis on the selection and processing of political information.] Opladen: Westdeutscher Verlag.

Entman, R. (1991) "Framing US Coverage of International News: Contrasts in Narratives of the KAL and Iran Air Incidents", *Journal of Communication,* no.41, pp. 6-27.

Entman, R. (1993) "Framing: Toward Clarification of a Fractured Paradigm", *Journal of Communication,* no.43, pp. 51-58.

European Commission (1997) *Euromedia Monitoring 1995-1997*. Union for Public Opinion and Research. Brussels, Belgium: Directorate-General X.A.2.

Eurobarometer/European Commission. (2000) *Eurobarometer: Public Opinion in the European Union*. Brussels, Belgium: Directorate-General X (Rep. No. 52).

Fundesco/AEJ Annual Report (1996) *The European Union in the Media 1995*. Madrid.

Fundesco/AEJ Annual Report (1997) *The European Union in the Media 1996*. Madrid.

Galtung, J. & Ruge, M. (1965) "The Structure of Foreign News", *Journal of Peace Research,* no.2, pp. 64-91.

Gamson, W.A. (1992) *Talking Politics*. New York: Cambridge University Press.

Gitlin, T. (1980) *The Whole World is Watching*. Berkeley: University of California Press.

Goffman, E. (1974) *Frame Analysis: An Essay on the Organisation of Experience*. Cambridge: Harvard University Press.

Graber, D.A. (1988) *Processing the News. How People Tame the Information Tide*. New York: Longman (2nd ed.).

Graber, D.A. (1993) *Media Power in Politics*. Washington: CQ Press, (3rd ed.).

Iyengar, S. (1991) *Is Anyone Responsible?* Chicago: University of Chicago Press.

Jasperson, A.E.; Shah, D.V.; Watts, M.; Faber, R.J. & Fan, D.P. (1998) "Framing the Public Agenda: Media Effects on the Importance of the Federal Budget Deficit", *Political Communication*, no. 15, pp. 205-224.

Kahneman, D. & Tversky, A. (1983) "Choices, Values, and Frames, *American Psychologist*", no.39, pp. 341-350.

Krippendorf, K. (1980) *Content Analysis. An Introduction to Its Methodology*. London: Sage.

Leroy, P. & Siune, K. (1994) "The Role of Television in European Elections: The Cases of Belgium and Denmark", *European Journal of Communication*, no. 9, pp. 47-69.

Martin, C.R. & Oshagan, H. (1997) "Disciplining the Workforce: The News Media Frame a General Motors Plant Closing", *Communication Research*, no. 24, pp. 669-697.

McCombs, M. & Shaw, D. (1972) "The Agenda Setting Function of the Mass Media", *Public Opinion Quarterly*, no.36, pp. 176-187.

McLeod, D.M. & Detenber, B.H. (1999) "Framing Effects of Television News Coverage of Social Protest", *Journal of Communication*, no.49, pp. 3-23.

McManus, J. (1994) *Market Driven Journalism. Let the Citizen Beware?* Thousand Oaks, CA: Sage.

McQuail, D. (1994) *Mass Communication Theory. An Introduction*. London: Sage, (3rd ed.).

McQuail, D. (2000) *McQuail's Mass Communication Theory*. London: Sage, (4th ed.).

Mendelsohn, M. (1993) "Television Frames in the 1988 Canadian Election", *Canadian Journal of Communication*, no.18, pp. 149-171.

Neijens, P. (1999) "Campagne, media en publieke opinie" [Campaign, media and public opinion], in P. Neijens & Ph. van Praag (eds.) *De slag om Ijburg* [The battle over Ijburg]. Amsterdam: Het Spinhuis.

Nelson, T.E., Clawson, R.A. & Oxley, Z.M. (1997) "Media Framing of a Civil Liberties Conflict and Its Effect on Tolerance", *American Political Science Review*, no.91, pp. 567-583.

Neuman, W.R., Just, M.R. & Crigler, A.N. (1992) *Common Knowledge. News and the Construction of Political Meaning*. Chicago: The University of Chicago Press.

Norris, P. (1995) "The Restless Searchlight. Network News Framing of the Post-cold War", *Political Communication*, no.12, pp. 357-370.

Norris, P. (2000) *A Virtuous Circle: Political Communication in Post-industrial Democracies*. Cambridge: Cambridge University Press.

Pan, Z. & Kosicki, G.M. (1993) "Framing Analysis: An Approach to News Discourse", *Political Communication*, no.10, pp. 59-79.

Patterson, T.E. (1993) *Out of Order*. New York: Vintage Books.

Patterson, T.E. (1998) "Political Roles of the Journalist", in D. Graber, D. McQuail & P. Norris (eds.) *The Politics of News. The News of Politics*. Washington, DC: CQ Press.

Price, V. (1989) "Social Identification and Public Opinion: Effects of Communicating Group Conflict", *Public Opinion Quarterly*, no.53, pp. 197-224.

Price, V., Tewksbury, D. & Powers, E. (1997) "Switching Trains of Thought. The Impact of News Frames on Readers' Cognitive Responses", *Communication Research*, no.24, pp. 481-506.

Reif, K. (1984) "Ten Second-order National Elections", in K. Reif (ed.) *European Elections 1979/81 and 1984*. Berlin: Quorum.

Rhee, J.W. (1997) "Strategy and Issue Frames in Election Coverage. A Social Cognitive Account of Framing Effects", *Journal of Communication*, no.17, pp. 26-43.

Riffe, D., Lacy, S. & Fico, F.G. (1998) *Analyzing Media Messages. Using Quantitative Content Analyses in Research*. Hillsdale, NJ: Lawrence Erlbaum.

Scheufele, D.A. (1999) "Framing as a Theory of Media Effects", *Journal of Communication*, no.49, pp. 103-122.

Semetko, H.A. & Valkenburg, P.M. (2000) "Framing European Politics: A Content Analysis of Press and Television News", *Journal of Communication*, no.50, pp. 93-109.

Severin, W.J. & Tankard, J.W. Jr. (1997) *Communication Theories. Origins, Methods, and uses in the Mass Media*. New York: Longman, (4th ed.).

Tuchman, G. (1978) *Making the News*. New York: Free Press.

Valkenburg, P.M., Semetko, H.A. & de Vreese, C.H. (1999) "The Effects of News Frames on Readers' Thoughts and Recall", *Communication Research*, no.26, pp. 550-568.

de Vreese, C.H. (1999) *News and European Integration. News Content and Effects in Cross-national Comparative Perspective*. University of Amsterdam.

de Vreese, C.H., Peter, J. & Semetko, H.A. (2000) *A Cross-national Comparative Study of Frames in the News*. Paper presented to the annual meetings of The International Communication Association, Acapulco, Mexico.

Weaver, D.H. (1998) (ed.) *The Global Journalist*. Bloomington: Indiana University Press.

Weaver, D.H. & Wilhoit, G.C. (1996) *The American Journalist: A Portrait of US News People and Their work*. Bloomington: Indiana University Press.

War News in Global Media

Globalisation of War News
Challenges for Media Research

Stig A. Nohrstedt & Rune Ottosen

Introduction

Mass media researcher Elihu Katz (1992) has raised an important question: is independent journalism possible in the so-called New World Order? Katz refers primarily to the experiences of the Gulf War and the way media news reporting was restricted, manipulated and managed by the authorities and military of the Coalition forces. His concern was mainly limited to the national level – to relations between domestic media and military authorities in this crisis. Here we have a wider focus: the international problems for war journalism in conjunction with transnational relations between the media and military propaganda. We intend to follow the development of these relations from the Gulf War to the Kosovo War. The purpose of this endeavour is to try to bring to the surface some important insights into what the de facto New World Order actually means for international communication during major crises.

Despite the many studies about the Gulf War since the armistice in March 1991, the full assessment of its historical significance is still to be made. Time is needed for research to grasp the complete picture of such an event. After all, even today, at the end of the 1990s, new and enlightening analyses of the Vietnam War are still appearing (e.g. Page, 1996; Patterson, 1995).

In the media and in the general public debate, the Gulf War and its implications were soon relegated to a less prominent position. Other urgent issues and new conflicts, such as the Balkan Wars, have replaced the Gulf War as the focus of political and journalistic attention. However, the legacy of the Gulf War continues to play a significant role in contemporary conflicts, within the UN and in all discussions on global issues. In popular culture, for example in films like *Courage under Fire, Independence Day* and *Air Force One,* propaganda images from the Gulf War proliferate, creating a collective memory of this conflict. But such important events should be consigned neither to oblivion nor to the mere myths of popular culture. Research can serve as a corrective, both to the short attention span of news media coverage and to popular culture's glorification of the war. The obligations of and challenges for media studies should be readily apparent here.

Indeed several media studies have been conducted on the Gulf War. One inventory from 1996 showed the number of such studies in the English language to amount to 39 books, 89 articles, 22 book reviews and 11 theses and dissertations (Weber, 1996). On the other hand, most of this reported research was conducted shortly after the war, and was usually restricted to media images in a single country. However important these studies are – and we are certainly dependent on them for our own analyses here – there is more to be said now than ever before about the implications of this conflict as a global media event.

Regarding the general understanding of the new global situation after the end of the Cold War, two contrasting perspectives have received considerable attention. The international political situation that US President Bush called the 'New World Order' has encouraged utopian as well as dystopian prognoses. The perspective represented primarily by neo-liberal and idealistic commentators has interpreted the disintegration of the Soviet Union and the Warsaw Pact as the beginning of a new era in which freedom, rights and morality will prevail in the world. The expansion of the market economy on a global scale, including China, has raised hopes for democratic reforms. Francis Fukuyama's thesis about the end of history is, of course, the best-known representation of this ideological trend (cf. Kegley, 1995). Without subscribing to Fukuyama's analysis of the global situation after the Cold War, David Held has argued that the time is right to elaborate the principles for a cosmopolitan democracy, i.e. a model for developing democratic elements in the field of international relations (Held, 1995).

In contrast to these more idealistic views, the realist school of international relations, represented by Samuel Huntington and his prognosis of future clashes of civilisations, provides a far more pessimistic, not to say horrifying, perspective – horrifying, since it may become a self-fulfilling prophecy (Huntington, 1996; cf. also Sørensen & Rose, 1997). In this view, the 'New World Order' will be marked not by peace and global understanding, but solely by new conflict lines primarily along the globe's cultural and religious fissures or 'fault-lines'.

With regard to the outcome of the Gulf War and the conflicts and wars in ex-Yugoslavia, the more pessimistic of the two perspectives would appear more significant, partly as result of an ideological hangover effect of the propaganda messages accompanying the military mobilisation of the Coalition during the former conflict. Slogans about a New World Order in which liberty and right should be protected were employed in propaganda and spread widely by the media. In retrospect, it has become clear that some of these expectations have not been met. Sovereignty was restored in Kuwait, but a proper democracy has not yet been established there. In Iraq, Saddam Hussein – the single individual who, according to the propaganda, was the main obstacle to the New Order – still heads a terror regime. Despite UN attempts to force him to destroy the Iraqi arsenal of mass destruction weapons, he has managed to stay in power, mainly through constant repression of the Iraqi people and continuous threats to neighbouring countries. By and large, the outcome of the war has been a blemish on the Allies' triumph chart, easy to forget for those who enthusiastically supported the 'irreconcilable' American line. The Gulf War will therefore remain as a mutilated memory of a 'Nintendo war' (Falk, 1994, p. 543) – as a recollection of a fantastic victory won by the high-tech warfare organised and led by the USA. This is the story told in popular culture versions of the war in movies, TV series and novels.

Even more frightening is the Western media's tendency to ignore the realities of the war, not least as understood in terms of arrogant attitudes towards the war's consequences for the Iraqi people, its civilians and children. There are also more directly media-related changes that make it urgent to consider the post-Cold War situation for transnational journalism. What impact does the new media technology have on the content and quality of the transnational news flow? The proliferation of new electronic media for news – primarily television channels, satellite distribution systems that connect newsrooms and audiences worldwide, and the 24-hour channels with 'instant coverage' – has dramatically changed the conditions for the journalism of international war and crises. No longer can media influences on opinion formation be comprehended solely within national borders: they must be understood in a global or at least transnational context. Moreover, public relations and media management now find themselves operating under different conditions. Successful attempts to control the media have given military circles new experience, at the expense of media integrity and independence.

In this paper, we will first address some general theoretical questions concerning the media's role in international conflicts today, in the New World Order. Second, we will discuss some methodological demands on research, and, third, present some findings from an international project on the media Gulf War. Finally, the paper brings up some more hypothetical reflections with respect to the media's role in the Kosovo War as compared to the Gulf War.

The Gulf War, Globalisation and US Dominance?

From a theoretical as well as empirical point of view, it is fair to say that the Gulf War was a global media event if there ever was one. In terms of Anthony Giddens' globalisation dimensions (Giddens, 1990), this conflict involved at least three of the four main institutional dimensions:

1. First, from an economic point of view, the conflict between Iraq and Kuwait concerned access to certain oil wells in the border area between the countries, and the world market price for oil.

2. Second, Iraq's occupation of Kuwait was a serious offence against the nation-state system and the rules of collective security that had been established after World War II. Iraq had attacked and annexed a sovereign nation, a member of the UN.

3. Third, for the world military order, and the power balance in the region in particular, Iraq's provocative action could have led to dramatic displacements

and instability, both in relation to other countries in the region and to the Western powers even beyond the Gulf area itself (Farouk-Sluglett & Sluglett, 1994; Telhami, 1994).

Thus, seen in light of the globalising processes that have come to characterise international development during recent decades, and especially after the end of the Cold War, the Iraqi occupation of Kuwait was truly a global event.

This does not mean that the conflict was interpreted in the same way throughout the world. Certainly, when assessed in relation to the outcomes of the Gulf War for the most affected region, the glorification of the war in the West had no broader resonance elsewhere:

> It was becoming readily apparent that in the Middle East this new world order of harmony and peace was only the surface of an order that consecrated the hegemony of the winners of the Cold War. (Ismael & Ismael, 1994, p. 14)

In order to acknowledge experiences of this kind, and also to balance the euphoric connotations linked to the notion of a New World Order with some realism, the concept of 'uneven globalisation' seems particularly apt. Even if the Gulf War were a global event, there are reasons to expect differing degrees of globalisation in the centres and peripheries of the international system (cf. Holm & Sørensen, 1995).

The Gulf War was also a global *media* event, not least because of the enormous media exposition of the war in practically all parts of the world. This is a challenge to media research. It has becoming increasingly obvious that an in-depth understanding of the role of the media cannot be obtained from studies limited to single national media systems. If researchers are not to be overtaken by the development of media technology, studies will have to be directed towards the transnational processes in news journalism. We will return to the challenges for media researchers that are implied here. But before doing so, we will elaborate somewhat further on the notion of globalisation.

Globalisation has become a major theme in the current theoretical debates on cultural and social tendencies in the 1990s. This notion has even been described as a sign of a paradigm shift in the field of international communication (Sreberny-Mohammadi et al., 1997; cf. Ekecrantz, 1998). Others, however, seem to be somewhat uneasy with the concept of globalisation, because it tends to be linked to taken-for-granted values and standpoints while also referring to almost any relations that cross national boarders. A less demanding and problematic terminology may then be to talk about transnational processes (Hannerz, 1996, s. 5-6).

Why is 'globalisation' such a central theme in current research? The answer is clearly related to a basic feature of today's 'post-modern' society – increased emphasis on the general awareness of other parts of the world. More and more, the world is being recognised as 'a single place' (Robertson, 1992, p.6). This cognitive aspect is referred to, at least implicitly, in almost every contribution to the discussion. But some theorists reveal a special interest in exploring the mental and cultural dimensions of globalisation. That makes them especially interesting for media studies asking: how does transnational news affect international relations when worldviews and self-understandings from different national cultures are circulated globally?

After the end of the Cold War, some immediately envisioned a New World Order that they diagnosed as 'the end of history' and characterised as a relatively homogenous global community. Later analysts, however, have noted not homogeneity but heterogeneity, and the conflicts emerging in this new situation. Mike Featherstone, as one representative of the second orientation, responds in the negative to the question of whether there is a 'global' culture similar in nature to national cultures. For him globalisation consists of transnational cultural processes that need not have homogenisation effects on national cultures, nor represent any threat to them (Featherstone, 1990). Other authors have presented similar arguments for why globalisation is not the same as increased cultural homogeneity in the world (e.g. Appadurai, 1990; Robertson, 1990; Smith, 1990). In yet another contribution to the discussion, Marjorie Ferguson argues that the notion of globalisation is linked to myths about an irresistible process towards global cultural homogeneity, which becomes 'increasingly problematic' (Ferguson, 1992, p. 82). The French communication theorist Armand Mattelart has discussed globalisation and culture primarily in terms of the worldwide diffusion of corporate and management ideologies and cultures. He highlights the way in which this variant of globalisation dismissed large parts of the world as irrelevant (Mattelart, 1994). With a somewhat similar view of the international communication research field, Hamid Mowlana finds it necessary to avoid some of the reified meanings of the term 'globalisation' (Mowlana, 1996, p. 194).

Although we are witnessing a compression of the world, there seem to be good reason to question overly simplistic assumptions about a historical development towards increased global homogeneity, unification and harmony. Contrary to the exaggerated promises of globalisation bringing about a 'global village', we suggest that opposite tendencies are just as important and should be examined carefully: fragmentation, complexity and differences in the expressions of globalising processes in various regions and countries, along with increased heterogeneity and contradictions. We suggest that the conflicting interpretations with respect to the globalisation tendencies, whether they are homogenising or heterogenising, should be settled through empirical studies of specific cases of global events.

For this purpose, both the Gulf War and the Kosovo War would seem to be good choices. Central to such a study is understanding – to what degree and how – national, foreign and security policies are affected by globalisation during the conflict. Are national policies 'relativized', i.e. reconsidered and reoriented, as a result of what the conflict reveals of the new post-Cold War international situation? 'Relativization' is a notion developed by Roland Robertson in the context of a theory of globalisation. Robertson's theory is explicitly introduced as an alternative to economic interpretations of globalisation, whether of neo-Liberal or neo-Marxist kinds. Accordingly, globalisation is not only an 'objective' development process of economic nature, but also a matter of understanding and conception: 'Globalisation as a concept refers both to the compression of the world and the intensification of consciousness of the world as a whole' (1992, p. 8). This intensified awareness of the global dimensions initiates relativization processes in the 'global field', with consequences for how we as social and human beings understand ourselves, our national societies, the world system and humankind – and the interrelations among these components of the field. In this context, 'relativization' refers to the challenges to traditional 'worldviews' and patterns of participation in the interactions with other cultures, countries, etc., that are brought to the fore by the processes of globalisation (p. 29).

What this means is further developed by Robertson as regards the mutual relations between tendencies of universalization and particularization in today's historical situation. Universalism and particularism are roughly conceived as two sides of the same coin. Robertson aims at a non-reductive understanding of this relation, which should '...preserve direct attention to *both* particularity and difference *and* to universality and homogeneity'. And further: ' ...we are, in the late twentieth century, witnesses to – and participants in – a massive, twofold process involving *the interpenetration of the universalization of particularism and the particularization of universalism...* (Robertson, 1992, p. 100; italics in original).

Thus, as we become increasingly aware of cultural differences, we also continuously have to face the fact that some perspectives are promoted with universalist claims – with pretensions to represent a single comprehensive and valid understanding of the world, including how all these cultures and peoples are related to each other globally. Although globalisation means increased understanding of the complexity and relativity of much of our conceptions, it does not necessarily make cultural and political hegemony a thing of the past.

Robertson's approach is methodologically open and flexible, and this is what makes it so valuable. For understanding war propaganda, the globalisation theme encourages increased attention to how propaganda intervenes in and stimulates ongoing relativization processes, and the ways it influences the conceptions of various national societies and their relations within the wider international system. The level of globalisation reached in the present historical situation makes it both possible and necessary for actors with international strategic aims to conceive of propaganda in a global context. In our analyses we should do likewise.

This brings us to a related theme in the current research on transnational news, namely what can be called relativization within the system of global news exchange. In research on the globalisation role of the media, it is acknowledged that coverage of the very same events, as well as interpretations of event-related images, will vary among the different national media systems and usually also among the different types of media. Although media products have global diffusion, their appropriation or reception is local and characterised by the differing cultural, linguistic and ideological preconditions of the audiences in question (e.g. Cohen et al., 1996; Thompson, 1995).

Making a distinction between media content and the decodings of the audience is an important step for research in this field. It has also provided the basis for a well-founded critique of older theories and analytical models, which had held that the effects exercised by the media on the views, attitudes and behaviour of receivers were linear, direct and irresistible. These new insights have in turn made valuable contributions to media research (e.g. Jensen, 1986; Liebes & Katz, 1993; Radway, 1984). At the same time, however, media research has tended to concentrate more on audience reception than on content – which is natural as long as the objective is to explore how the media affects receivers' worldviews, opinions, etc. But, we would argue, news-flow studies and content analyses have more to offer in their own right – provided one takes care not to draw immediate conclusions about the impact on the audience.

Furthermore, we would emphasise that the notion of local appropriation or domestication does not exclude research on global dominance or hegemony. Whether the former contradicts the latter is dependent on the degree to which the modifications of news meanings passing national or cultural boarders are part of a system of dominance relations. In the cultural imperialism perspective, it is assumed that the only remaining superpower will heavily influence the transnational news flow, and that the images constructed in Washington, particularly from a conflict in which the US is involved, will proliferate globally. However, it is not necessarily so that US dominance is based on the mechanical copying of American images in other countries' media. It is not inconsistent with the dominance or hegemony thesis that in fact recontextualisation and local appropriation of US propaganda images strengthens their impact globally.

Media and Relativization of Opinions and Policies Transnationally

The symbolic production of meanings associated with the Gulf War took place *not only* in the immediate centre of the events – where the actors involved in propaganda, decisions and practical actions like military mobilisation competed as to how this conflict should be understood – *but also* in more distant quarters – in political circles of nation-states that were not active participants in the war, and even in local public interactions and exchange of views on the war, whether in pubs or community media. We will argue that media, as a key factor for the globalisation of politics and opinion formation, have crucial importance for the production of meaning in both these respects, and that media provide the connections between these dual symbolic processes.

In terms of propaganda, the enormous media attention and the involvement of the general public were crucial for strategies to influence public opinion. Along with the compression of space and time in conjunction with instant satellite media coverage, the media and public attention were '...another rationale for governments to control and censor war news' (Hachten, 1996, p. 156). The US, as the leading force behind the alliance against Iraq, developed a global strategy of 'public diplomacy' to strengthen its leadership with the media's assistance.

Real-time broadcasts of President Bush's speeches and co-operation with the major media, primarily the CNN, were central components in this propaganda strategy. This campaign was designed to raise support for US policy also in foreign countries and cultures, although US opinion was the main target.

Another globalisation effect of the Gulf War was that it brought about a re-evaluation of prior conceptions both about the international system and the national position of one's own country in that system. This can be described as relativization of the nation-states' positions and identities partly in relation to the 'world system of societies' and partly to 'humankind' (cf. Robertson, 1992, p. 27). We will concentrate here on the relativizing processes that took place between the international and the national levels in connection with the Gulf War. On both levels, actors appeared in public with proposals for how the conflict should be conceived, what the opposite positions were, and why their own policy was right. The conflict discourse in this respect – internationally as well as nationally – concerns the definition of this new reality and at the same time the actors' own identities. For the US, part of what was at stake in the conflict discourse was the construction of the meaning of the New World Order (NWO) and its own leadership in this process. For other countries, such as the Nordic countries, the conflict discourse was – at least partly – about reconsidering traditional security and foreign policies and taking up a position in relation to the US claims as leader of the war campaign against Iraq. The security policies in Finland, Norway and Sweden after 1945 have been rather different. Finland has considered it necessary to avoid close collaboration with NATO and the Western countries in order not to disturb the sensitive relations to its Eastern neighbour. Finland has also been restricted to less sensitive sectors of Nordic co-operation than defence and security. Norway, as a member of NATO, has developed close co-operation with the US and the UK in both its security policy and its defence strategy. Sweden has, throughout the 20th century, officially relied on its non-alignment policy, aimed at remaining neutral in case of military conflicts in the surrounding region, and therefore claimed to be independent in relation to the two super-powers during the Cold War. Recent historical findings have, however, documented that the linkage between the Swedish and US governments was far closer than the official neutrality position should indicate. Especially in Finland and Sweden, the end of the Cold War and the Gulf War gave rise to substantial uncertainty about the position and role of both nations in the NWO.

We return below to the media's role regarding influences on the reconsiderations of national policies in the Gulf War. Suffice it here to note that the media are simultaneously arena and motor in these relativization processes. As Martin Shaw has argued, in at least some international crises, the media are more important than traditional civil society institutions in connecting distant problems and human needs with national government policy (Shaw 1996). Furthermore, the media might have had a more independent role in the countries not directly involved in the conflict than in those that were members of the coalition against Iraq. In the latter countries, national leaders had the initiative and defined the policy, but in the former, the political situation was more open and gave other actors, including journalists and media commentators, more chance to influence the re-orientation of the nation's policy. Thus the globalisation of Gulf War policies should be seen as an uneven process also with respect to the media in different countries.

The ways in which the globalised diffusion of media content influences the audience's views and opinions have at least tentatively been elaborated by John B. Thompson, who argues that the appropriation of such symbolic material will always depend on local cultural, political, etc. conditions. Such appropriation is further characterised by 'symbolic distancing from the spatial–temporal contexts of everyday life' and is also a 'source of tension and potential conflict' (Thompson, 1995, pp. 175, 177). This means that even media content that is distributed worldwide will not generate identical interpretations and mental effects everywhere. The impacts of transnational media activities in local reception contexts should instead be understood as increased reflexivity concerning the taken-for-granted beliefs, norms and mores. Moreover, since the distancing processes are rarely smooth and painless, they will frequently lead to political and ethical ruptures.

This analysis seems also to offer a relevant framework for conceptualising the way global media interact with national policies. For our analytical focus, this suggests studying not only the similarities and variations in content among media in different countries, but also that the coverage should be understood as a process of propaganda and conflict images flowing between national media systems – a process whereby propaganda and images become discursively transformed. Our approach has made it particularly interesting to study in detail the symbolic transformations of some key events as they 'move' from one national communication context to another.

Previous Research

We have not found much empirical research applying this kind of approach in cross-national media studies. Of course, there is some research that has general bearings on the present project, though not dealing directly with the Gulf War. For example, 'The Global Newsroom' project has focused on the consequences of television technology for transnational relations within the Eurovision News Exchange (EVN). Its main conclusion is that the 'global newsroom' is far from realised, despite a shared international professional culture: 'Thus, while the images may have global currency, the meanings given to them may not necessarily be shared globally.' (Gurevitch et al., 1991, p. 214) Domestication of foreign news takes place in journalists' decoding of the events, in their encoding of them for the purpose of making them understandable for the receivers, and in the audience's interpretation of the media content. Only a small group of the EVN news co-ordinators are actually detached from their original national identities (Cohen et al., 1996, pp.152–153).

Another study of EVN news output, conducted by Stig Hjarvard (1995), shows that of the total material, 19% deals with Western Europe, 16% with Eastern Europe, 19% with the Soviet Union and 13% with the US. In this project, specified figures are also presented for the TV-agency material distributed by EVN: 20% Soviet Union, 24% USA and 15% Africa, incl. north, middle and south Africa. For the sake of comparison, only 1% deals with the UN (calculated from table 11, p. 238). When compared with studies from the early 1970s, Hjarvard found no substantial differences with respect to geographical distribution, except a minor increase in proportions for the Soviet Union, Eastern Europe and Latin America (p. 247). In sum, Hjarvard's results do not reveal a remarkable US dominance in the EVN-news. There is some concentration on the US scene in the TV-agencies' material, which counts for about half of the total material, but the general picture is that every eighth news item is about the US, and that is hardly alarming. Thus, Hjarvard's general conclusion is not dramatic: There are reasons to believe that the international news system is not, at least, developing towards more inequality and imbalance (Hjarvard, 1995)

Some previous studies of the Gulf War, although limited to single countries, have examined the way national media 'domesticated' the US and allied propaganda, albeit without using this exact concept. Studies available so far seem to indicate a similar pattern in several countries, a pattern of hesitation and reluctance to support the policies advocated by US President Bush and his associates. In early autumn 1990, the Canadian and Spanish media, for example, did not cover the US policy affirmatively. Then, partly as a result of the successful propaganda campaign, with its links between Hussein and Hitler, and its extensive references to the UN for legitimation, media opinion gradually converted to support of the war policy – not, however, without some remaining signs of refusal to acknowledge US leadership. A particularly interesting finding in these studies is how national myths served as effective symbolic devices that made allegiance to the US policy more acceptable to the domestic general public (Kirton, 1993; Rojo, 1995).

A comparative analysis of the first weeks' television coverage of the Gulf War in seven countries revealed not one Gulf War story, but seven different stories, each of them conditioned by specific 'national sentiments and affinities' (Swanson & Smith, 1993, p. 190). Another television study, in this case of the coverage of the al-Amarya incident, looked at twelve different services in five countries. It draws slightly different conclusions: that the bombing of this alleged shelter for civilians in Baghdad was narrated as basically the same story in all channels, although with different angles depending on the national media culture (MacGregor, 1997, p. 170 ff.).

What these studies at least make plausible is the conclusion that the media constructions of the conflict were important in the shift of public opinion in these countries, and furthermore, that the media had an active and partly independent role, which went far beyond that of non-selective and passive transmission of US propaganda. In fact, these findings indicate that the de- and re-coding of the propaganda, which the media pursued within the respective national political and cultural contexts, were adapted to country-specific cultural codes and myths. In this way, the propaganda contributed to the mobilisation of the general public in several different countries. This makes it misleading to assume, as some media scholars apparently do, that such decodings of messages from the superpower are irreconcilable with the notion that this superpower has a hegemonic, dominating influence over international opinion. On the contrary, we would argue that it is precisely this recontextualization and accommodation to the variety of local cultural conditions that makes the propaganda effective globally.

Media research concerning the thesis of superpower dominance still suffers from a lack of empirical testing. One major line of research has concentrated on studying heterogeneity and variety in the news flow, but only in synchronic analyses (e.g. Cohen et al., 1996; Kirton, 1993; MacGregor, 1997; Rojo, 1995; Swanson & Smith, 1993). In the present project, the dominance hypothesis is tested in greater depth through convergence analysis based on diachronic data (cf. Ekecrantz, 1998). The notion of 'dominance' does not refer to a situation of more or less total unity among conflict images in various national media systems at any particular point in time. It rather relates to a *process* by which the image promoted by the hegemonic power is spread to and further conveyed by media in other countries. Another conclusion from previous studies is that dominance in the field of international communication should be studied in situations where the interests of the hegemonic power can be assumed to be at stake. From our point of view, testing the dominance thesis on normal news reporting without considering whether the hegemon's vital interests are affected is basically irrelevant.

Project Design

The "Journalism in the New World Order Project" has been conducted as a joint research effort by a team of scholars from five countries and with multi-disciplinary backgrounds. Two volumes are forthcoming, published by Nordicom in winter 2000 and spring 2001 respectively (Nohrstedt & Ottosen, forthcoming; Kempf & Luostarinen, forthcoming).

The design of the project's main sample aims at systematic comparisons between four types of news media in five main countries during the period August 1990 to January 1993. These five countries are Finland, Germany, Norway, Sweden and the US. Within this period, news reports in ten specific sample periods – 3-day-long on average – have been selected, amounting to 31 days of news coverage in each medium. The sample of media from each country comprises one leading quality paper, one provincial paper, one popular or tabloid paper and one major, prime-time television news programme. Besides the media from the main countries, one Iraqi paper and two Ethiopian papers have also been included in the material, to allow comparisons on certain points with media representing the Iraqi view and the views from a Third World country not involved in the conflict. In total, the material amounts to approximately 4,100 news items.

Basically the same sample has been used for various content analysis methods, both quantitative and qualitative. With respect to quantitative content analysis, both traditional and latent class analysis (LCA) methods have been applied[1]. On specific parts of the material more in-depth analysis has been accomplished using qualitative approaches.

The following media are represented in the material for the quantitative analyses (the Iraqi newspaper *the Baghdad Observer* has been excluded because it is not represented for all sample periods):

Figure 1. The media sample

	Prestige papers	Popular papers	Local papers	Television
Ethiopia	*Addis Zemen* *Ethiopian Herald*	–	–	–
Finland	*Helsingin Sanomat*	*Ilta-Sanomat*	*Turun Sanomat*	YLE 1, 20.30 News
Germany	*Süddeutsche Zeitung*	*Bild-Zeitung*	*Südkurier*	Heute
Norway	*Aftenposten*	*Verdens Gang*	*Bergens Tidende*	Dagsrevyen
Sweden	*Dagens Nyheter*	*Expressen*	*Nerikes-Allehanda*	Rapport 19.30
USA	*The Washington Post*	*The New York Post*	–	(ABC;CBS;NBC)*

* Sampled from Sky World News at 23.00 hours to 23.30 hours.

Our ambition to match the samples from each country has been realised in most cases, but there are unfortunately some imperfections. Practical restrictions made it impossible to include a local US paper. The US television material is limited to the 'hot' war period, i.e. to five sample periods (see below) between January 12, 1991 and February 28, 1991. Lacking access to material from a prime-time programme transmitted to the US audience, we decided to use the news items from the major US television channels conveyed to Europe by the late evening news programme 'Sky World News'.[2]

The ten sample periods have been selected to cover particularly important events before, during and after the war between the Coalition forces and Iraq. Thus the material should be sufficiently comprehensive to allow comparative and diachronic analyses. The periods covered also include the autumn of 1990 and some later war events in the aftermath of the war. The sample periods are as follows:

Sample period 1: August 2–7, 1990
The Iraqi invasion of Kuwait; President Bush's declaration that Iraqi aggression 'will not stand'; UN Security Resolution 661 (mandatory sanctions on Iraq); US troops and aircraft sent to Saudi Arabia.

Sample period 2: November 28–30, 1990
UN Security Council's decision to sanction the use of every possible means to liberate Kuwait.

Sample period 3: January 12–14, 1991
The US Congress votes to support President Bush's request to use the armed forces; US pressure on Israel not to respond if attacked by Iraq; UN Secretary-General Perez de Cuellar's visit to Baghdad and the failed attempt to persuade Saddam Hussein to withdraw from Kuwait.

Sample period 4: January 17–19, 1991
'Operation Desert Storm', the Coalition air campaign; the first Iraqi Scud missile attack on Israel and 'the call for Patriots to defend Israel'.

Sample period 5: February 13–15, 1991
The bombing of the Amirya bunker.

Sample period 6: February 21–23, 1991
Iraqi acceptance of the Soviet peace plan; President Bush rejects the plan; news about 'death road' to Basra; US and other major Coalition members reject Gorbachev's request to delay ground offensive; Coalition ground offensive begins.

Sample period 7: February 27–28, 1991
Liberation of Kuwait City; letter from Raiq Aziz to UN Security Council accepting Resolutions 660, 662 and 674; Security Council permanent members demanding unconditional acceptance of all resolutions relevant to the crisis; temporary cease-fire after Iraqi acceptance of conditions.

Sample period 8: 26–28 April 1991
The Kurds and Shias rise up against the Iraqi regime as recommended by President Bush; the US, the UK and France proclaim that they will protect Kurd territory against attacks from Iraqi airplanes.

Sample period 9: August 25–27, 1992
Shias are given the same kind of protection by the Allies as the Kurds, except humanitarian support.

Sample period 10: January14–15, 1993
US forces with assistance from France and Great Britain bomb Baghdad with the aim of forcing Iraq to follow up the UN resolutions and to respect the no-flight zone in the north and south of Iraq.

The design chosen for the quantitative content analyses makes the results strictly comparable and combinable, since the basic sample is the same with respect to media and sample periods irrespective of method used, i.e. latent class analysis or traditional content analysis. This enables cross-validity checks and provides a broad foundation for the conclusions reached.

Some Results from the
"Journalism in the New World Order Project"

Two major conclusions deserve emphasis as we sum up the project results, since they relate to the heart of the matter of the media's role in globalisation processes and their institutional context within international politics. To the degree that news media reports are important for the long-term consequences of international conflicts, this impact – in connection with the Gulf War – is revealed in the extension of the following observations:

Media reporting from the Gulf War was largely about conveying information on the US policy to a global audience. Since the US was seen as the driving power in the conflict process, coverage focused on considerations, decisions and comments on the US political agenda. The leading superpower therefore exercised international or global leadership partly due to the contribution of the media. This leading and driving role was all the more obvious because the political elite in several countries took a wait-and-see attitude, without expressing any marked positions of their own as to how the conflict should be resolved.

This does not mean, however, that US policy in the conflict is described in exactly the same way or equally favourably in all news media worldwide. Although US views are widely covered and moreover depicted as decisive for conflict development, the perspectives and the angles in the various media differ due to local historical circumstances in each country. The news has become 'domesticated' in the sense that the image of US policy is presented in different lights through the narrative devices in the priority-setting and comment-making selection process of every single medium. In some instances, these differences can be ascribed to a particular type of medium or media genre. More important in this context is that the reporting generally seems to be marked by national patterns of apprehension and domestication. We will soon exemplify this in connection with our summary of the effects of propaganda on news coverage. Suffice it here to note that these national variations do not entail any given conclusion as to the question of US power over media coverage. The variety of interpretations in different national news discourses as to the US role in the game could mean that the superpower has not succeeded in controlling media coverage through its propaganda. But whether this is valid will depend on the character of these variations – whether they support or oppose US propaganda interests, and whether the variations remain stable over time. The question of dominance has been discussed widely among media researchers, especially in relation to the theory of media and cultural imperialism. It has then usually referred to US export of media products to other parts of the world. In this project, the issue of dominance has another and more precise meaning in relation to propaganda theory: here it is treated as an empirical question whether US propaganda managed to influence the news media, not only in the US, but also in other countries.

Thanks to Laurien Alexandre's analysis of the 'Voice of America' editorials in one of the sub-studies, confirmed by previous studies as well, a clear picture emerges of how US propaganda was constructed in this conflict. The actions taken by the Coalition were, according to US propaganda, taken exclusively on behalf of the UN, and dictated by the sole objectives of liberating Kuwait from the Iraqi occupation and establishing a New World Order in which freedom and justice should prevail. This propaganda image either neglected the economic sanctions or dismissed them as irrelevant. The haphazard interest in peace initiatives from third parties or even refutations of them on the pretext that these third parties were running Saddam Hussein's errands are another part of this picture. A final crucial element in this US propaganda was the accusation that the Iraqi dictator was as dangerous for world peace as Hitler had been (Alexandre, forthcoming).

To what extent was this one-dimensional propaganda image conveyed by news media in different countries? As underlined above, the approach we pursue does not assume that US views are automatically transmitted without any modifications in the transnational news flow. On the contrary, we assume that recontextualization and domestication entail transforming propaganda to adjust it to local views, which implies that its influence may be either strengthened or counteracted.

Our results confirm the assumption that historical ties between the homeland and the US with respect to foreign, defence and security policy are important for national media coverage. The more a country's security has been based on close co-operation with the US, primarily within NATO, the more the media promote active support of the US Gulf War policy in both national and local media. Additionally, some specific national conditions were observed to make their mark on reporting from the Gulf War. This was the case for the constitutional controversy in Germany, as well as for Finland's 'liberation' from previous sensitivity to the views of Moscow as reflected in the Finish media discourse.

In another sub-study, Wilhelm Kempf, Michael Reimann and Heikki Luostarinen analyse New World Order rhetoric. They find that the central element in US propaganda – the historical parallel drawn between Hitler and Saddam Hussein, or the so-called 'German factor' – on the one hand had the strongest impact on US media coverage as compared to coverage in the European countries. On the other hand, they also find substantial variations among the European media. The Hitler–Saddam parallel is more frequent in Norwegian and German media than in the Finnish and Swedish. Concurrently, both Norwegian and German media are found to contain relatively much critique of the NWO rhetoric, which in conjunction with the strong impact of US propaganda indicates a cross-pressure situation in the media discourses of these countries. By contrast, the US media hardly convey any such critique of the proclamations of a NWO (Kempf, et al., forthcoming).

Kempf's second sub-study deals with conflict escalation as symbolic constructions in the media. This study, as well as one conducted by Stig Nohrstedt, documents that the Finnish and Swedish media devote more attention to the UN than do the other media groups. This is particularly evident in comparison with the US media, which in general show the least interest in the international peace organisation. It is also the Finnish and Swedish media that tend to idealise the UN as an instrument for peace and maintenance of international law. Moreover,

Kempf shows that media from these two countries are more prone to pay attention to initiatives from third parties than are the other media groups (Kempf, forthcoming).

Nohrstedt's sub-study reveals that the US media have the most propagandistically polarised coverage of all the analysed groups. The conflict is depicted in black and white: In terms of attitudes and in comparison to media elsewhere, the US media are far more positive towards the US, President Bush and the coalition, and more negative towards Iraq and President Hussein. They focus somewhat more on military aspects in the early stage of the conflict, and more often neglect or play down negotiation initiatives and the UN. As to the European media groups, despite their internal variations, when compared with the US media they deviate so consistently that we can see a clear division between the US and non-US media in the sample. But among the European media, Nohrstedt also finds variations that indicate a correlation between the homeland's foreign policy tradition and the penetration of media discourses by US propaganda. This is perhaps most apparent in the results of the convergence analysis which indicates that media in traditionally non-aligned countries – here Finland and Sweden – initially took a reluctant attitude towards Bush, but later gradually became more and more pro-American. Moreover, the convergence analysis supports the conclusion that Norwegian and German media experienced cross-pressures during the initial stage of the war. These pressures were eventually replaced by a strong relief – in the later stages (sample periods) of the conflict, i.e. after the liberation of Kuwait. This was even more evident when the US, along with the UK and France, forced Iraq not to attack the Kurds and Shias from the air. German and Norwegian media reacted with the strongest pro-US attitudes of all media, including even those within the US (Nohrstedt, forthcoming).

The project's studies have documented that European media focused heavily on the US scene in their coverage of the Gulf War. Given the leading role of the US in the Coalition and in the development of the conflict, this might seem natural and inevitable. But irrespective of how this is understood from a journalist point of view, it surely stands out as a crucial factor for understanding the importance of news reporting for international politics during and after the Gulf War. Through this US-centric media coverage, the US approach was established as the reference point for opinion formation also in a global sense. As observed, this meant that US policy gradually received greater acceptance in the European media during the later stages of the Gulf War. Concurrently, this also seems to have meant that the UN's image became increasingly framed by a perspective already apparent in US media discourse from the very beginning of the conflict. The hegemony of the world's sole remaining superpower was thus reinforced by transnational co-operation and mutual dependency among the media actors.

Let us now think of media coverage not just as a mirror of 'reality', but rather as a part of the opinion-creating processes whereby media discourses are connected to and interact with political and cultural discourses in society. From this perspective, these findings may carry crucial implications for the future. We could hypothesise that the journalistic tendency to adjust the focus of coverage in international conflicts to the hierarchical power structure of nation-states is an advantage for the foreign policy ambitions of the US (and of other big powers). According to the same logic, however, this is a disadvantage for the UN – because political processes that do not fit well into this pseudo-realistic framework, such as UN policy and the role of NGOs in international politics, will be disfavoured by journalistic routines. In this way, the transnational news system, in connection with the Gulf War, prepared the ground for the foreign and security policy reorientation that was to take place in Europe during the 1990s. These changes had a relatively dramatic character in Northern Europe and particularly in the former non-aligned countries, Finland and Sweden. Collective security, both in Europe and elsewhere in the world, has tended towards a Pax Americana upheld through US military strength. To a lesser degree it is also an issue for the UN and non-military peace work. The media, with their capacity to symbolically construct the available possibilities, simultaneously create history – both instant and more persistent history. Which direction history takes is, of course, not the result of an isolated media effect, but something that evolves – at least partly – out of the reciprocal interactions between journalism and politics. We can dispute the extent to which politicians' thoughts and actions in the field of international relations depend on the media's reports, and – vice versa – how dependent journalists are on authoritative information sources in their reporting. In any case, we may conclude that the result of this mutual influence is what creates the opinion conditions for the political players and their legitimacy. This in turn means that the media inevitably have great importance for the national and local political reorientation taking place in conjunction with global events.

The Kosovo War and the Media: Some Impressions

As during the Gulf War 1990-91, the US is the focus of media attention also in connection with the Kosovo War 1999. Thus, both at the level of actions and at the level of discourse and signification, US dominance or at least hegemony is apparent. As an example, it is President Clinton who explains the motives behind the bombings of Serbia in the Swedish TV4 story when the bombing campaign started.

Thus, the Western media largely become channels for US and NATO propaganda surrounding the Kosovo conflict. But this should not blind us to the fact that national and local variations in media coverage are substantial. On Swedish TV4, the studio reporter announced a news item about the onset of bombing, on the evening of March 24, in the following words:

> The NATO-attack on Yugoslavia has started. And it is a broad onslaught /.../ In NATO's 50-year history, this attack is the first to be made against a sovereign state without UN authorisation.

After this announcement, the secretary-general of NATO, Javier Solana, explains that NATO is not at war with Yugoslavia, and that "we have no quarrel with the

213

people of Yugoslavia". What follows is (after some information about the attack targets) a statement by President Bill Clinton, in which he explains the objectives. The first objective is: "...to demonstrate the seriousness of NATO's opposition to aggression and its support for peace." In the Swedish translation presented in subtitles the quotation is: "Det första är att visa allvaret i NATO:s motvilja mot vapenmakt..." In English this would be: "to demonstrate the seriousness of NATO's dislike of the force of arms". Against the background of our findings from the Gulf War, this slant of meaning attached to the Clinton statement is hardly coincidental. We believe that it could not have happened in, for example, the Norwegian media.

Among at least Swedish journalists, there was an ambition in conjunction with the Gulf War that they should depict the "true face" of the war, meaning that they regarded it as their professional task to describe the consequences for civilians. After the Gulf War, they admit that they failed in this respect. Only the suffering of the Kuwaiti refugees was covered. In the Kosovo War, however, the situation was different. Media had access to thousands of civilians who had escaped from the province. And perhaps as a sort of delayed compensatory act for what they failed to do in the Gulf War, journalists now pursued something of a campaign for the UCK side by giving extensive attention to the refugees' atrocity stories in which they blamed the Serbs for all their suffering. The natural effect was that NATO and UCK propaganda was given even more support by the media. Later, when the bombings had ceased, and when the UCK and Kfor had taken over control of the Kosovo province and terror against the Kosovo-Serbs surfaced occasionally, the reports were rather restrained and less open to propaganda.

Another important observation regarding both the Gulf War and the Kosovo War has to do with the media's role as initiator of and forum for debate. These two cases seem to confirm a key conclusion in Daniel Hallin's study of the Vietnam War, namely that, in war situations, the media are generally incapable or unwilling to develop crucial critique against the government and the political elite unless the establishment is divided with respect to the rationality of pursuing the war policy (Hallin, 1986). Naturally, a "rallying around the flag" reaction can also be expected from the media when their own country's troops are involved, but the interesting thing is that even in a non-involved country like Sweden, something similar or at least a related pattern emerged in these two conflicts. It was rare that the media really penetrated the more critical issues concerning the legal basis for the US led alliance's operations, for example the no-fly zones in the northern and southern parts of Iraq during the Gulf War or the actual content of the proposed Rambouillet agreement that the JFR refused to accept or the bombing of the TV house in Belgrade. Certainly, these issues were mentioned in some media and even discussed in letters to the editor, but they were nothing that an ordinary journalist would invest time, effort and pages or hours of airtime to investigate. We suggest that this can be explained by two factors: (a) the hegemonic influence of the US view on "world opinion" as constructed by the media, and (b) the reluctance among national politicians, in for example Sweden, to debate the NATO/US policy in the conflict, which in the end equals accommodation to the strategy pursued by the latter.

In Sweden, this is all the more remarkable considering the non-alignment security and foreign policy tradition dating back to the beginning of the 19th century, and also the heritage of the former Prime Minister Olof Palme, who strongly opposed US bombardments of Hanoi during Christmas 1972 and who compared them with the Fascists' bombings of Guernica during the Spanish Civil War. In connection with the NATO attacks on Belgrade, the only comment from the Swedish government was that they were "understandable". And in the Swedish parliament, hardly any discussion about Kosovo took place. But the media's low profile in terms of promoting discussion is not simply a matter of them mirroring the political elite's relative silence. As Peter Berglez has shown in a study of the leading prestige paper's, *Dagens Nyheter*, coverage of the Bosnia conflict, in some instances the parliamentary debate that actually takes place, for example, on the issue of putting Swedish troops under NATO command, is discursively marginalised in the media (Berglez, 1999).

The lack of political discussion in the Swedish public sphere about the Kosovo policy is not much different from the situation in Norway, notwithstanding the fact that Norway took an active part in the military NATO operations. But an important difference is that, in Norway, one leading newspaper remarked on the policymaking process. On April 17, the largest morning paper, *Aftenposten*, published an article focused on the decision-making process before Norway decided to join the warfare. *Aftenposten* showed that the Norwegian parliament (Stortinget) joined the bombing campaign without any written information from the government to Parliament, without a formal vote and almost without a political discussion.

The media could also have focused more on the legacy from the Gulf War and on what impact it had on the Kosovo War in terms of US/UN relations. Operation Desert Storm had a UN mandate, but in the post-Gulf War period, this mandate has been replace by a diffuse follow-up mandate. The US and Great Britain, as the leading military powers in the old alliance, chose to define the UN mandate in their own terms. The left-wing media criticism was that the clear mandate from resolution 678, giving the Coalition the right to pressure Iraq out of Kuwait with "all necessary means", was misused to continue to bomb Iraq on several occasions as a part of the new post-Gulf War "New World Order". Later UN resolutions (like 687) do describe the terms for a cease-fire, but do not define the consequences if Iraq refuses to fulfil its obligations. Thus, when the US and Great Britain have continued a "low intensity warfare" by bombing Iraq on several occasions (in January 1993, June 1993, September 1996, December 1998 and on several occasions in 1999), these actions have not had a UN mandate. Neither was the implemented no-fly zone in the northern and southern parts of Iraq authorised by the UN. The critical media saw the preparation for a NATO attack on Kosovo as the logical follow-up to the leading NATO powers' role as a self-proclaimed international police force. Since NATO consciously avoided UN treatment of the issue of using military force against Serbia, this was

215

treated in the left-wing press as evidence that the Western powers wanted to avoid a open debate on the legality of the bombing campaign against Kosovo, but this was given little mention in the mainstream press (Ottosen 1999b).

On May 10, *Dagbladet* published an open letter from the Norwegian section of the Red Cross to Stortinget and Prime Minister Kjell Magne Bondevik where the question was raised of whether Norwegian participation in the war could be a violation of the Geneva Convention. The letter referred to point 52 in the convention, which demands that any military attack should be limited to military targets. According to the Geneva Convention, it is the duty of the national branch of the Red Cross in each country to determine whether its own government lives up to the charter. This letter was therefore historical and of great principle interest. The Prime Minister's reply to the letter in *Dagbladet* was that Norway had not violated the Geneva Convention. The Red Cross initiative died with this general statement before the debate had even started. This was possible because none of the other mainstream media followed up on the issue. None of the broadcasting companies challenged the government on this issue. The very same day that the letter was published, the most influential television news programme, *Dagsrevyen* (NRK), interviewed the Prime Minister who was asked generally about the refugees' situation, but no reference was made to the letter from the Red Cross.

The issue of media restrictions should also be dealt with in summing up the recent experience from the Kosovo conflict. The new authoritarian press law introduced by the Milosovic regime is well documented (IPI-Report First Quarter 1999). The threat from NATO was used to prohibit rebroadcast of "foreign propaganda". The law also allowed the courts to levy fines on media ignoring the new restrictions, so high that few if any media would be able to pay them. If the fines are not paid within 24 hours, the authorities may confiscate the properties of the given media. This new law was already used to silence critical media before the bombing started, targeting the weekly *Evroplljanin*, the independent dailies *Dnevni Teelgraf*, *Nasha Borba* and *Danas*.

After the bombing began, correspondents from the countries involved in the bombing were expelled and other restrictions, such as censorship and banning journalists from certain areas, were implemented. Critical Yugoslavian journalists covering the war have been attacked and accused of "high treason" by extreme nationalists and media loyal to the government.

On the NATO side, there have also been restrictions such as the banning of use of names or photos to identify Norwegian military personnel taking part in the military operation over Kosovo. This was justified by the consideration for the safety for the soldiers and their families.

The NATO decision to bomb a television installation in Serbia was even more controversial. The very idea that media could be considered legitimate military targets caused some critical debate in the Norwegian media. The incident raised the issue of whether journalists and the mass media need special protection under international law (Ottosen, 1999). There is no doubt that the government-controlled media in Yugoslavia serve as an integrated part of the aggressive propaganda machine. But the other side of this picture is that these media, in their propaganda effort, also show parts of the reality of warfare that the NATO "spin machine" would rather see unpublished. The civilian casualties and suffering after NATO bombing are among those stories that could potentially trigger something like the "Vietnam syndrome", a complex that President Bush said the US had finally got rid of after the Gulf War.

War Journalism:
A Challenge Both for Journalists and Media Researchers

In order to analyse war journalism it is important to use an historical approach. In all major conflicts since the Vietnam War, media-military relations have been subject to heated debates on issues of media management, censorship and other forms of restrictions. In many ways, the military establishment seems to have a better collective memory than the press corps. However, after experiences from major conflicts like the Gulf War and the Kosovo conflict, a common understanding is developing, even in the media community, that the propaganda war is an integrated part of modern warfare. All parties in a conflict will try to manipulate the media through media management, disinformation and propaganda. To avoid the propaganda trap, one must be conscious of the nature of modern media management on a global scale.

War journalism is a challenge: for those who want to understand the mechanisms behind conflict escalation, and for those who consider it important that the debate on journalism ethics is constantly pursued. These two issues are closely related: if the media can be a contributing factor in the aggravation of conflicts – to the extent that the result is military confrontation – then there is certainly a reason to be concerned about ethical questions in war journalism. Our results indicate that media are easily drawn into conflicts, where they can end up as an instrument for propaganda. Thus, the media may be a factor promoting military solutions by making them seem acceptable to the public. But our findings have also shown that the media's receptivity to propaganda influences varies, and should be related to different phases of the conflict processes (cf. also Shaw & Martin, 1993) and also to different political and cultural contexts.

Let us finish with an appeal for cross-national co-operation among researchers and concerned journalists in the field of war journalism. It is, we believe, evident that the public – citizens in general and civilians trapped in war zones in particular – is deceived by the way the major media operate today. The New World Order seems to us to require independent and critical analyses of the way media are exploited by war propaganda, which furthermore seems to entail militarisation of international peace policies and collective security.

Notes

1. LCA has emerged from the empirical social research proposed by Paul F. Lazarfeld, who formed his basic views as a psychologist in the 1920's and 1930's. The meaning of the word "latent" in the "Latent Structural Analyses" indicates the "latent space" described by the theoretical concepts. It also points to mathematical relations implicit in empirical data. The method is based on coding specific discourse structures in a news text, and is further explained in Kempf (1994) and (Reaunanen & Suikkanen 1999).
2. Access to this television material was kindly allowed by Professor David Morrison of the University of Leeds, UK.

References

Alexandre, L. (2000) "Voicing the Gulf: The Voice of America Constructs the Gulf War", in Nohrstedt, S.A. & Ottosen, R. (eds.) *Journalism and the New World Order. Gulf War, National News Discourses and Globalization*. Göteborg: Nordicom.

Appadurai, Arjun (1990) "Disjuncture and Difference in the Global Cultural Economy", in Featherstone, Mike (ed.) *Global Culture. Nationalism, Globalization and Modernity*. London: Sage.

Bennet, W. Lance & Paletz, David (eds.) (1994) *Taken By Storm: The Media, Public Opinion, and US Foreign Policy in the Gulf War*. Chicago, Ill: The University of Chicago Press.

Berglez, P. (1999) *Bilder av FN och NATO*. Örebro: Örebro universitet (Studier i kommunikation och medier, nr. 15).

Cohen, Akiba A.; Levy; Mark R.; Roeh, Itzhak & Gurevitch, Michael (1996) *Global Newsrooms, Local Audiences. A Study of the Eurovision News Exchange*. London: John Libbey & Company Ltd.

Ekecrantz, J. (1998) "Modernitet, globalisering och medier", *Sociologisk Forskning*, no.3-4.

Falk, Richard (1994) "Democracy Died at the Gulf", in Ismael, Tareq Y. & Ismael, Jacqueline S. (eds.) *The Gulf War and the New World Order*. Gainesville, Fl.: University Press of Florida.

Farouk-Sluglett, Marion & Peter Sluglett (1994) "Iraq and the New Word Order", in Ismael, Tareq Y. & Ismael , Jacqueline S. (eds.) *The Gulf War and the New World Order*. Gainesville, Fl.: University Press of Florida.

Featherstone, Mike (ed.) (1990) *Global Culture. Nationalism, Globalization and Modernity*. London: Sage.

Featherstone, Mike (1990) "Global Culture: An Introduction", in Featherstone, Mike (ed.) *Global Culture. Nationalism, Globalization and Modernity*. London: Sage.

Ferguson, Marjorie (1992) "The Mythology about Globalization", *European Journal of Communication*, vol.7, pp. 69-93.

Giddens, Anthony (1990) *The Consequences of Modernity*. Cambridge: Polity Press.

Golding, Peter & Harris, Phil (1997) "Introduction", in Golding, Peter & Harris, Phil (eds.) *Beyond Cultural Imperialism. Globalization, Communication & the New International Order*. London: Sage.

Gurevitch, M.; Levy, M.R. & Roeh, I. (1991) "The Global Newsroom: Convergences and Diversities in the Globalization of Television News", in Dahlgren, P. & Sparks, C. (eds.) *Communication and Citizenship. Journalism and the Public Sphere*. London: Routledge.

Hachten, William A. (1996) *The World News Prism*. Ames: Iowa State University Press (4th ed.).

Hamelink, C. (1997) "MacBride with Hindsight", in Golding, Peter & Harris, Phil (eds.) *Beyond Cultural Imperialism. Globalization, Communication & the New International Order*. London: Sage.

Hannerz, U. (1992) *Cultural Complexity*. New York: Columbia University Press.

Hannerz, U. (1996) *Transnational Connections. Culture, People, Places*. London: Routledge.

Held, David, 1995. "Democracy and the New International Order", in Archibugi, Daniele & Held, David (eds.) *Cosmopolitan Democracy*. Cambridge: Politiy Press.

Herman, E.S. & McChesnay, R.W. (1997) *The Global Media*. London: Cassell.

Hjarvard, S. (1995) *Internationale TV-nyheter*. København: Akademisk Forlag.

Holm, Hans-Henrik & Sørensen, Georg (1995) "Introduction: What Has Changed?", in Holm, Hans-Henrik & Sørensen, Georg (eds.) *Whose World Order? Uneven Globalization and the End of the Cold War*. Boulder: Westview Press.

Huntington, Samuel P. (1996) *The Clash of Civilizations and the Remaking of World*. New York, N.Y.: Simon & Schuster.

Ismael, Tareq Y. & Ismael, Jacqueline S. (1994) "Introduction", in Ismael, Tareq Y. & Ismael, Jacqueline S. (eds.) *The Gulf War and the New World Order*. Gainesville, Fl.: University Press of Florida.

Jensen, Klaus B. (1986) *Making Sense of the News*. Aarhus: Aarhus University Press.

Katz, Elihu (1992) "The End of Journalism? Notes on Watching the War", *Journal of Communication*, vol.42, no.3, Summer, pp. 5-13.

Kegley Jr., Charles W. (1995) "The Neoliberal Challenge to Realist Theories of World Politics: An Introduction", in Kegley Jr., Charles W. (ed.) *Controversies in International Relations Theory*. New York: St. Martin"s Press.

Kellner. D. (1992) *The Persian Gulf War*. Boulder, Col.: Westview Press.

Kempf, W. (1994) *Towards an Intergration of Quantitative and Qualitative Content Analyses in Propaganda Research*. Universität Konstanz (Diskussionsbeiträge no.27/1994 der Projektgruppe Friendsforschun, Projekt 13/85)

Kempf, W. & Luostarinen, H. (forthcoming) *Journalism in the New World Order. Volume II: Studying War and the Media*. Göteborg: Nordicom.

Kempf, W.; Reimann, M. & Luostarinen, H. (2000) "New World Order Rhetorics in American and European Media", in Nohrstedt, S.A. & Ottosen, R. (eds.) *Journalism and the New World Order. Gulf War, National News Discourses and Globalization*. Göteborg: Nordicom.

Kempf, W. (2000) "News Media and Conflict Escalation – A Comparative Study of the Gulf War Coverage in American and European Media", in Nohrstedt, S.A. & Ottosen, R. (eds.) *Journalism and the New World Order. Gulf War, National News Discourses and Globalization*. Göteborg: Nordicom..

Kirton, John (1993) "National Mythology and Media Coverage: Mobilizing Consent for Canada"s War in the Gulf", *Political Communication*, vol.10, no.4, pp. 425-441.

Liebes, Tamar & Katz, Elihu (1993) *The Export of Meaning*. Cambridge: Polity Press.

Mattelart, Armand (1994) *Mapping World Communication*. Minneapolis: Univ. of Minnesota Press.

MacGregor, Brent (1997) *Live, Direct and Biased?. Making Television News in the Satellite Age*. London: Arnold.

Mowlana, Hamid (1996) *Global Communication in Transition. The End of Diversity?* London: Sage.

Nohrstedt, S.A. (2000) "US Dominance in the Gulf War News? The propaganda Relations Between the News Discourses in Amerian and European Media", in Nohrstedt, S.A. & Ottosen, R. (eds.) *Journalism and the New World Order. Gulf War, National News Discourses and Globalization*. Göteborg: Nordicom..

Nohrstedt, S.A. & Ottosen, R. (eds.) (2000) *Journalism and the New World Order. Volume I: Gulf War, National News Discourses and Globalization*. Göteborg: Nordicom.

Nohrstedt, S.A. & Ottosen, R. (2000) "Summary and Conclusion: Globalization and the Gulf Conflict 1990-98: Challenges for War Journalism in the New World Order", in Nohrstedt, S.A. & Ottosen, R. (eds.) *Journalism and the New World Order. Gulf War, National News Discourses and Globalization*. Göteborg: Nordicom.

Ottosen, R. (1999) "Trenger mediene et særskilt rettsvern i krig?". *Mennesker og rettigheter*, no.3.

Ottosen, R. (1999b) "In Crossfire Between Serb propaganda and the NATO Spin Machine", in Goff, Peter (ed.): *The Kosovo News and Propaganda War*, International Press Institute.

Page, Caroline (1996) *U.S. Official Propaganda During the Vietnam War, 1965-1973*. London: Leicester University Press.

Patterson III, Oscar (1995) "If the Vietnam War Had Been Reported Under Gulf War Rules", *Journal of Broadcasting & Electronic Media*, vol.39, Winter, pp. 20-29.

Radway, Janice A. (1984) *Reading the Romance: Women, Patriarchy, and Popular Literature*. Chapel Hill: University of North Carolina.

Reunanen, E. & Suikkanen, R. (1999) *Latent Class Analyses: Wandering in the Latent Space*. Universität Konstanz (Diskussionsbeiträge no.44/1999 der Projektgruppe Friendsforschun, Projekt 13/85 & 590/95).

Robertson, Roland (1990) "Mapping the Global Condition: Globalization as the Central Concept", in Featherstone, Mike (ed.) *Global Culture. Nationalism, Globalization and Modernity*. London: Sage.

Robertson, Roland (1992) *Globalization. Social Theory and Global Culture*. London: Sage.

Rojo, Luisa M. (1995) "Division and Rejection: From the Personification of the Gulf Conflict to the Demonization of Saddam Hussein", *Discourse & Society*, vol.6, no.1, pp. 49-80.

Shaw, Donald L. & Shannon, Martin E. (1993) "The Natural, and Inevitable, Phases of War Reporting: Historical Shadows, New Communication in the Persian Gulf", in Robert E. Denton (ed.) *The Media and the Gulf War*. London: Praeger.

Smith, Anthony D. (1990) "Towards a Global Culture?", in Mike Featherstone (ed.) *Global Culture. Nationalism, Globalization and Modernity*. London: Sage.

Srebreny-Mohammadi, et al. (1997) "Editors' Introduction – Media in Global Context", in Srebreny-Mohammadi, A.; Winseck, D.; McKenna, J. & Boyd-Barrett, O. (red) *Media in Global Context . A Reader*. London: Arnold.

Swanson, David L. & Larry D. Smith (1993) "War in the Global Village: A Seven-Country Comparison of Television News Coverage of the Beginning of the Gulf War", in Denton, Robert E. (ed.) *The Media and the Gulf War*. London: Praeger.

Telhami, Shibley (1994) "Between Theory and Fact: Explaining U.S. Behavior in the Gulf Crisis", in Ismael, Tareq Y. & Ismael, Jacqueline S. (eds.) *The Gulf War and the New World Order*. Gainesville, Fl.: University Press of Florida.

Tomlinson, John (1994) "Mass Communications and the Idea of a Global Public Sphere. The Political Agenda of Globalization", *International Journal of Communication*, vol.1, no.2, December.

Thompson, John B. (1995) *The Media and Modernity. A Social Theory of the Media*. Cambridge: Polity Press.

Tomlinson, John (1997) "Cultural Globalization and Cultural Imperialism", in Mohammadi, Ali (ed.) *International Communication and Globalization*. London: Sage.

Weber, Tracy A. (1996) "Media Coverage of the Persian Gulf War: A Survey of Literature". Washington D.C.: American University, (MA diss., mimeo).

Østergaard Sørensen, Søren & Flemming, Rose (1997) "Kloden har tømmermænd", *Berlingske Tidende*, 2. (sektion, 15, juni).

An 'Insight' into CNN's Coverage of NATO's First War

Daya Kishan Thussu

This chapter examines the role of global television news channels, specifically Cable News Network (CNN – 'the world's news leader') in legitimising a change in the remit of NATO, the United States-led Western military alliance from a defensive to an offensive, 'peace-enforcing' organisation. It analyses CNN's coverage of NATO's bombing of Yugoslavia in March-June 1999, the first conflict in which the world's most powerful military alliance intervened in the internal affairs of a sovereign state. The chapter argues that the strategic implications of NATO's precedent-setting action were largely ignored by CNN's treatment of the crisis in Kosovo, which was framed instead as a 'humanitarian' intervention by the West, led by the United States, to protect the human rights of citizens in a region of the world which was outside the remit of the North Atlantic alliance and where the West did not have any apparent geo-strategic or economic interests.

The coverage, the chapter argues, tended to follow the news agenda set by NATO, ignoring alternative views. The legality of NATO's action was rarely questioned in CNN's framing and most importantly, a fundamental change in the nature of NATO – from a relic of the Cold War to a global peace-enforcing organisation – was not covered. Finally, the chapter assesses the international implications of such framing, arguing that, given the global reach and influence of CNN, its version of NATO's war also shaped the wider view of what CNN called the 'Strike against Yugoslavia'.

NATO's 78-day bombing of Yugoslavia between 24 March and 10 June 1999, the last military campaign of the twentieth century, christened *Operation Allied Force*, was arguably one of the most significant geo-political developments of the post-Cold War era, one that will shape strategic thinking in the twenty-first century. NATO's first war was an unprecedented action in several respects: the alliance 'won' the conflict without a single life lost in combat operations on its own side. The war also had the distinction of being the first conflict in the history of modern warfare in which the victory was achieved by air power alone (Cook, 1999). In addition, it was also the first time since 1945 that Germany used its planes on a bombing mission. However, these issues were not pursued in the media coverage of the crisis. The questions raised were not concerned whether this was an appropriate action for NATO but in terms of, for example, should the bombing be intensified? Should ground troops be used? Should a naval blockade be imposed to stop Serbia's oil supplies? There was unending speculation about the irrationality of the Serbian leadership and whether and how the Serbian President Slobodan Milosevic should be removed from power.

Unlike the 1991 Gulf War, where clear geo-strategic and economic interests were involved, TV networks such as CNN found it more difficult to characterise the conflict in the former Yugoslavia. The general impression that most of the Western media projected of the decade-old conflict was that it was an intractable problem of the Balkans, with its history and 'traditions' of ethnic hatred and only Western military intervention could resolve the crisis (Ali, (ed.) 2000).

That there was large-scale and systematic ethnic violence taking place in Kosovo was undeniable and once the Yugoslav Federation started to break up in the early 1990s it was not surprising that the Albanian majority in Kosovo demanded the same rights to nationhood as Bosnia. Yet the West has not encouraged its claim to independence; instead it has established a NATO protectorate in a geo-strategically significant part of Europe.

The Evolution of a New NATO

As it celebrated its 50th birthday, the North Atlantic Treaty Organisation (NATO), was involved in the first offensive action in its history, intervening in the internal affairs of a sovereign country that was not threatening any of its member states and was outside its area of deployment. The action, in fact, violated the charter under which NATO was established in 1949 as a defensive organisation – protecting Western democracies from the apparent threat from Soviet communism. In addition, NATO showed no respect for international law which does not permit military intervention by a group of countries in the internal affairs of another. Furthermore, what made NATO's bombing legally dubious was the fact that the United Nations Security Council had not approved the action. It could have used the relevant provision of international law for humanitarian intervention if satisfied that the situation posed a threat to international peace. However, NATO's bombing was consistent with its efforts in the post-Cold War years to find a new role for itself.

With the dismantling of the Soviet Union and the end of communist threat to European democracies in the wake of the fall of the Berlin Wall in 1989, NATO's status came under scrutiny as it was in danger of becoming an anachronism. In defence and political circles – both in Europe and the United States – questions had been raised about the relevance of a military alliance at a time when its counterpart Warsaw Pact had been dissolved, with three of its members (Hungary, Poland and the Czech Republic) formally joining NATO in 1999, while many other Eastern European and Baltic nations were queuing to come under the security umbrella of the Western military alliance. The US, which contributes about 60 per cent of NATO's annual budget, was able to use the civil wars in Yugoslavia as a new field of action for the defence alliance: NATO planes were used in Bosnia in 1995 as part of a UN operation and a NATO-led force – SFOR (Stabilisation Force) continues to monitor the 'peace' there. Though the ostensible reason for US involvement in the former Yugoslavia through NATO was toguarantee peace in the troubled country, its motives may additionally have been to check the emerging German influence in central and eastern Europe.

In its new 'peacekeeping' and 'peace-enforcing' mode, NATO created a Rapid Reaction Force to police the world's hotspots and to deal with 'humanitarian emergencies.' By 1997, this flexible and highly mobile force was already undertaking military exercises in Central Asia. This choice of NATO's first ever out-of-area deployment, in a region outside the remit of the alliance, was geo-strategically and economically significant, given the oil and gas resources in the Caspian basin (Meek and Whitehouse, 1997). A year later, the geographical expansion of NATO's area of activity was implicitly recognised by the US Secretary of State Madeleine Albright who described the alliance as 'a force for peace from the Middle East to Central Africa'. Others like US Senator Richard Lugar were cautioning that if NATO 'does not go out of area, it will go out of business' (quoted in Buchan and Fidler, 1999).

This line of argument was given intellectual justification in a prestigious foreign policy journal, as one senior commentator argued: 'The stakes for NATO in constructing a viable peace-operations mission are large. At a time when many citizens in the developed world hardly think about security at all in traditional military terms, maintaining and using armed forces of any size and expense requires public justification and some demonstrable impact on policy outcomes with which people can identify. Peace operations could meet at least some of that need' (Lepgold, 1998:106).

It was not surprising then that at its 50th birthday party in Washington in April 1999, NATO spoke of an extended role for the organisation. The final communiqué issued after the summit argued that NATO had to tackle 'uncertainty and instability in and around the Euro-Atlantic area and the possibility of regional crisis at the periphery of the alliance, which could evolve rapidly' (quoted in *International Herald Tribune*, April 26, 1999). Seen within this perspective, NATO's military action in Kosovo was the logical step for a military organisation which was in the process of changing its character.

NATO Intervention and the Media

Television coverage of NATO's action in Kosovo was not couched, however, in terms of changes in the role of NATO but in the language of human rights and humanitarianism. Most reports on international news networks such as CNN were framed in this way, with little concern being expressed about the legality of the bombing. The TV networks were also silent about the implications of

NATO's military action for the concept of national sovereignty, which has defined international relations since the end of Second World War. Instead they presented the position articulated by the United States President Bill Clinton and British Prime Minister Tony Blair, that defending human rights could override national sovereignty, thus creating a precedent in international relations and legitimising what came to be known as 'humanitarian intervention'.

One of the main arguments presented by NATO (Solana, 1999) and repeatedly reproduced by CNN and other Western television networks, was that the Yugoslav government had caused a humanitarian crisis in Kosovo. This situation undermined regional security and posed a serious threat to international peace. Accusing the Yugoslav authorities of indulging in a genocidal campaign against the ethnic Albanian population of Kosovo, the US and its NATO allies insisted that compelling humanitarian considerations had prompted them to take military action. It was forcefully argued by NATO governments via the media that they had no geo-political and economic interests in Kosovo and were undertaking the largest military operation in Europe since the ending of the Second World War for merely humanitarian reasons. One former US National Security Adviser, Anthony Lake, went to the extent of arguing that the NATO bombing of Yugoslavia was an example of the 'saintly glow' of US policy (quoted in Chomsky, 1999: 14).

The ostensible reason for NATO action was the failure of the peace talks between the Yugoslav government and the representatives of the Kosovo Liberation Army (KLA) at Rambouillet outside Paris in February and March 1999. It is now known that the Yugoslav government was willing to sign until a secret appendix was handed to them at US behest on the last day, demanding, in effect, they surrender all of Yugoslavia to NATO occupation. Particularly controversial was Appendix B of the Agreement which said that NATO should enjoy 'free and unrestricted passage and unimpeded access throughout the FRY (Federal Republic of Yugoslavia) including associated airspace and territorial waters' (quoted in Chomsky, 1999: 107). The Clinton administration also summarily rejected a Serbian National Assembly resolution passed on 23 March (the day before the NATO bombing started) which included a proposal for 'political autonomy' that could have been the basis for a peaceful resolution of the crisis. These issues remained largely unreported by television news at the time, (although the leading French newspaper *Le Monde* leaked Appendix B on the Internet) while networks such as CNN continued to project the Serbian opposition to the Rambouillet talks as intransigent and even unreasonable.

This was typical of television reporting which continued to frame the conflict within an 'us vs. them' dichotomy. In the era of the 'information society', targeting messages has acquired a very high degree of sophistication, as two of its leading proponents suggest: 'Precision-targeting information is just as important as precision-targeting weapons...' (Toffler and Toffler, 1993: 171). In a coverage dominated by NATO and other Western officials through the sheer volume of information, half and quarter truths were presented with speculative if not false information (Fisk, 1999; BBC, 1999a; Goff (ed.), 1999). Reports whose veracity was later doubted included claims that NATO bombers had destroyed hundreds of Serb tanks and personnel carriers. Quoting a report from the US Air Force, *Newsweek* reported (a year after the bombing) that out of the 744 'confirmed' strikes by NATO pilots during the Kosovo war, the US investigators found evidence of just 58. The number of targets verifiably destroyed, the *Newsweek* investigation revealed, was a tiny fraction of those claimed by NATO information machine: 14 tanks, not 120; 18 armoured personnel carriers, not 220; 20 artillery pieces, not 450 (Barry and Thomas, 2000).

Similarly, media reports unquestionably reproduced the often wildly exaggerated figures of the number of people killed as a result of alleged Serbian atrocities provided by the leaders of the US and Britain and NATO military commanders. At one point, the claim was made that as many as 100,000 Kosovars had been executed and thrown into mass graves by Serb paramilitary and regular soldiers. After NATO troops moved into Kosovo in June 1999, suspected massacre sites were scoured for evidence and bodies exhumed under the supervision prosecutors from the UN's International Criminal Tribunal for the former Yugoslavia (ICTY). By November 1999, according to ICTY's chief prosecutor Carla del Ponte, 2,100 bodies had been exhumed. However, leading up to the bombing and during the NATO air campaign the Serbian atrocity stories, many emanating from KLA sources, formed an integral part of most CNN news bulletins.

CNN tended to present 'collateral damage' as unfortunate exceptions, ignoring the regularity with which civilian targets – hospitals, television studios, housing estates, factories and power sources – were bombarded, sometimes with 'anti-personnel' cluster bombs. One major mistake, according to reports on CNN, was the 'accidental' bombing of the Chinese embassy in Belgrade on 7 May 1999, blamed on old maps provided by the CIA. It was subsequently reported in a joint investigation by the London *Observer* and the Danish newspaper *Politiken*, that the bombing was a deliberate act and not an error, as NATO's electronic intelligence had detected signals being sent from the embassy to the Yugoslav army (Sweeney et al, 1999).

CNN's Coverage of NATO's War

As the world's most influential television news organisation – reaching more than 150 million television households in over 212 countries and territories, 24-hours a day – CNN is a particularly significant news network in an international crisis (Flournoy and Stewart, 1997; Volkmer, 1999). During the height of bombing of Yugoslavia, CNN had 70 journalists and other crew in the Balkan region and the network was spending an estimated $150,000 a day to cover NATO's first war (Gibson, 1999).

CNN's *Insight*, a regular 30-minute programme offering analysis of topical subjects, including interviews with experts and commentators, was analysed. During the weeks of bombing CNN ran a two-part *Insight* programme on NATO at 50, broadcast on 22 and 23 April 1999, to coincide with the half-century celebrations of the Atlantic alliance. Unlike a CNN news report which only has at the most 3-4 minutes to make a complex story accessible and interesting to an increasingly heterogeneous global audience, a programme such as *Insight* aims to provide in-depth analysis of a given issue. Of the two programmes analysed for this study, the first one largely focused on NATO expansion eastward and how it was creating strategic and political unease in Russia, which boycotted the Washington summit. Though NATO's bombing of Yugoslavia was mentioned in the programme, it was not given any detailed treatment.

The second part of the programme, broadcast on 23 April 1999, almost exclusively looked at the implications for NATO as a military alliance in the wake of its first offensive action against Yugoslavia and therefore is worth analysing in greater detail for the purposes of this study. *Table 1* gives the running order of the programme.

Table 1.   CNN Insight, 23 April 1999: NATO at 50

Time	Speaker	Designation	Location	Content
00.11	Jonathan Mann	CNN presenter	NATO summit, Washington	Introduction
00.59	Patricia Kelly	CNN reporter	Washington	Bombing continues; Jamie Shea and Robin Cook addressing summit
03.34	David Ensor with Jonathan Mann	CNN reporter	Washington	NATO summit/goals
05.49 08.34	Brent Sadler	CNN reporter	Belgrade (live via phone)	Serbian view of NATO Anti-NATO protests Role of Greece
	BREAK			
10.53 16.42	Jamie Shea with Jonathan Mann	NATO spokesman	NATO summit	Summit overtaken by Kosovo; campaign being intensified; NATO forces there to protect refugees
	BREAK			
18.00	Andrea Koppel	CNN reporter	NATO summit	Ivo Daalder, Brookings Institute: NATO under threat – being marginalised Madeleine Albright, US Secretary of State: NATO's fundamental purpose is unchanging Jeremy Rosner, former US State official: NATO still relevant-threats remain
20.20	Charles Kupchan with Jonathan Mann	Council on Foreign Relations	NATO summit	NATO must meet new threats
25.22-25.36	Jonathan Mann	CNN presenter	NATO summit	Round-up

The programme was anchored by Jonathan Mann, a regular presenter of *Insight* and was broadcast live from the NATO summit in Washington. The programme had three main reports and live discussion with experts. After an introduction on the evolution of NATO and its role in European security, the first report by CNN's Patricia Kelly focused on NATO's bombing of Kosovo, arguing that the military campaign in Kosovo would continue until Milosevic capitulated and a NATO-led military protection force entered the Yugoslav province to ensure the return of refugees. Listing NATO demands, which included withdrawal of Yugoslav army from Kosovo, the report said further air strikes were likely to continue. It quoted Jamie Shea, the NATO spokesman, justifying the bombing of communication facilities including radio and TV stations as an 'instrument of war' which were 'more responsible than Serb army' for atrocities. The report ended with the view that the sustained bombing might weaken Milosevic but was unlikely to remove him from power.

This was followed by comments from David Ensor on the NATO summit. These concentrated on how the summit had succeeded in projecting a public show of unity but admitted that some cracks in alliance over use of ground forces were visible, with the US heading the doubters camp. Jonathan Mann raised the question of the role of new NATO members in the conflict, especially Hungary which had emerged, Ensor reported, as a key player only 10 days after joining the alliance, allowing a base to be used by air operations for refuelling. Hungary has interests in former Yugoslavia as 300,000 ethnic Hungarians lived in northern Serbia.

The second report in the programme came from Brent Sadler, based in Belgrade. Sadler, a veteran war correspondent, reported live by telephone how the Serbian media covered the NATO summit, relegating it to the end of the bulletin and reporting it in a matter-of-fact manner, without comment. Sadler also talked of anti-NATO protests in Serbia and the Greek position on the war, as a NATO member with close economic and cultural ties with Serbia.

The second part of the programme began with an interview with Jamie Shea. Replying to questions from Mann, the NATO spokesman summarised how the Kosovo crisis had affected the summit and why it demonstrated the relevance of NATO in the post-Cold War world. Shea also discussed the issue of the oil embargo against Serbia and suggested that NATO's strategy was to use air power alone to force the Serb army to leave Kosovo. Once this was achieved, he argued, ground troops from NATO countries would go in, indicating a shift from the aim of having the voluntary presence of an international force to troops from NATO countries going in uninvited to protect returning refugees. Shea's emphasis was very much on the humanitarian aspects of the crisis.

Refugees also formed the backdrop to the third report of the programme by correspondent Andrea Koppel. Interspersed with pictures of Kosovar refugees fleeing the Serbian army, Koppel maintained that NATO was fighting in former Yugoslavia to protect the ethnic Albanians in Kosovo. The report then quoted Ivo Daalder of the Brookings Institute, who argued that the Western military alliance was under threat: 'NATO's future is very much at stake. NATO may in fact no longer be the instrument of European security and will become increasingly marginal in the foreign policy of its major members.'

However Madeleine Albright, the US Secretary of State reiterated that NATO's fundamental purpose, was 'safeguarding the ideals, interests and territory of its members, is unchanging'. Having provided the framework for NATO's role, Koppel then commented: 'Kosovo is the litmus test of NATO's mission in the 21st century, a mission that began to evolve earlier this decade from one that was entirely defensive to a more aggressive alliance when NATO troops entered Bosnia, a non-NATO member as peacekeepers.'

This line of argument was given authority by quoting Jeremy Rosner, former US State official who believed that NATO 'remains our best shield against external aggression. Just because the Soviet Union has gone, we should not think that any threat of aggression has gone forever.' With pictures of refugees on the screen, Koppel finished her report with the words: 'the future of NATO is not likely to be decided at this summit but rather on the battlefield in Yugoslavia. As one US official put it, 'the alliance cannot lose this war, otherwise you can kiss NATO goodbye.'

The last part of the programme had an interview with Charles Kupchan from the US Council on Foreign Relations. Claiming that NATO's strategy was 'not working' Kupchan argued that the US should 'up the ante'. Kupchan maintained that NATO was a beacon of peace in a world full of dangers, arguing that the 'real threats are nationalism, fascism, the Kosovos of this world'. Rounding up the issues discussed in the programme, the anchor Jonathan Mann raised the question why should the US bail Europe out?

A close examination of this particular edition of *Insight* gives an interesting insight into the ideological underpinning of a network such as CNN. All those interviewed on the programme belonged to the US government or NATO. The experts quoted were Americans, of a right-wing orientation, more often than not 'hawks' rather than 'doves', none of whom were critical of the NATO bombing. No alternative views were aired and no questions were raised about the legality of NATO action. It is indicative of the approach of the coverage that by far the longest airtime was given to the NATO spokesman, Jamie Shea (nearly 6 minutes). Although this is a small sample of CNN's output over this period, it reflects the general editorial position adopted by the network.

The coverage, in the tradition of war reporting since the 1991 Gulf War, focused on the military success of 'allied' efforts and tended to provide moral justification for the bombing. The alliance was projected as getting involved in the Balkans crisis in fulfilment of its ideals. The fact that NATO was intervening in a strategically significant part of Europe – at the cross-roads of Western and Eastern Europe and close to the strategically vital Middle East and Central Asia – was rarely mentioned. The subsequent events, the building of one of the biggest NATO bases in Kosovo (largely ignored in international media) shows that the intervention was carefully planned and executed with a long term view of security in the region, a view shaped by Western strategic priorities rather than humanitarian concerns. The news discourse did not really address the key issues raised by the

NATO bombing, namely the precedent of military intervention in the internal affairs of a sovereign nation, thereby changing the rules of international relations, undermining state sovereignty and the UN system.

The Global Impact of CNN Framing

Such framing of a war has a global impact, given the international reach of US-dominated Western media. The world's three main news agencies Associated Press (AP) (US), Reuters (UK) and Agence France Press (AFP) (France) are Western and they dominate the global flow of news, with AP alone putting out 20 million words per day. AP and Reuters are also the two main providers of international television news material. Reuters Television (formerly Visnews) is one of the world's two largest television news agencies, while its rival, Associated Press Television News (APTN) is another major supplier of news footage to broadcasters worldwide (Tunstall and Machin, 1999).

Particularly significant in the global television journalism are channels such as BBC World and CNN – the two major 24-hour news networks with global reach and influence. The CNN Group, part of AOL-Time Warner, one of the world's biggest media and entertainment corporations, is the largest and most profitable news and information companies in the world. In 2000, it was available to more than 800 million people across the globe. The group includes six cable and satellite television networks (*CNN*, *CNN Headline News*, *CNN International*, *CNNfn*, *CNN/SI* and *CNN en Español*), two radio networks (*CNNRadio* and a Spanish version *CNNRadio Noticias*), eleven web sites on *CNN Interactive* and *CNN Newsource*, the world's most extensive syndicated news service, with more than 200 international affiliates. This media power gives CNN the capacity to set and then build the global news agenda.

The overwhelming US/UK dominance – what British media scholar Jeremy Tunstall called the 'US/UK news duopoly' (Tunstall and Machin, 1999) in the supply of raw news footage and news reports – can result in imbalances in the way the world is covered by television news. Although Western news organisations employ international staff and produce high quality news reports, consciously or unconsciously they pursue a Western or more accurately an American news agenda, particularly on stories which impinge upon Western geopolitical or economic interests. For obvious reasons, journalists contest such charges, arguing that they present news in a professional manner, without fear or favour to any particular perspective. Yet there is enough evidence to show that Western media, as indeed any media, offer perspectives influenced by political and economic elites. Subservience to the dominant ideology by mainstream media organisations has been well documented by academic studies of the US media's coverage of Vietnam (Hallin, 1986), of East Timor and Central America (Herman and Chomsky, 1988) and of Iraq (Mowlana et al 1992).

If anti-communism defined Western attitudes in international reporting during the Cold War years, in the post-Soviet era and an age of round-the-clock global news, military intervention in the world's hotspots to protect new types of security, has dominated the foreign news agenda. To a large extent, the world's view of US military interventions in various parts of the globe has been moulded by the US-supplied television images. There appears to be a consistency in US-dominated Western television's coverage of *Operation Just Cause* in 1989 in Panama; *Operation Provide Comfort* (in Northern Iraq, following the Gulf War in 1991); *Operation Restore Hope* in Somalia in 1992 and *Operation Uphold Democracy* in Haiti in 1994 (Seib, 1997). More often than not, media reports have echoed Washington's diplomatic position and interventions been framed in terms of how they fit into an American view of the world. Critical questions have been largely ignored in media reports while a justification has been found to legitimise new versions of what may be a new type of imperialism.

Basing his analysis of the coverage in the US elite media of US military interventions in Grenada (1983), Panama (1989), Iraq (1991) and Somalia (1992), Jonathan Mermin concludes that such elite media as the *New York Times*, ABC's *World News Tonight* and the *MacNeil/Lehrer Newshour*, the most in-depth news programme on US television, have contributed little to the foreign policy debate in the US. 'The spectrum of debate in Washington, instead,' he writes, 'has determined the spectrum of debate in the news.' (Mermin, 1999: 143). Mermin's research shows that journalists generally marginalise what he calls critical perspectives.

Given the limited critical engagement by the media with foreign-policy issues it is likely that the coverage of international topics may be further reduced to simplistic narratives of the benevolent West and the 'evil Other,' personified by Manuel Noriega (Panama), Saddam Hussein (Iraq), General Mohammed Aideed (Somalia) and Slobodan Milosevic (Serbia). As Islamic 'fundamentalism' and other 'Third World threats' – narco-terrorism, the spread of weapons of mass destruction among 'rogue' states – replace communism as a major foreign policy concern, it is important that other perspectives, especially those from the global South, are included onto the international news agenda. This is particularly important given the expansion and consolidation of Western investment in the South – site of many a 'failed state' and ethnic tensions and religious conflict. However, in the absence of a credible global news alternative, the CNN-type of framing continues to set the terms of debate in international media, given its capability to shape global public opinion. In the end, it remains a question of power and it is likely that the perspectives of the dominant international players will continue to set the global news agenda.

More NATO Interventions?

The Kosovo precedent raises many important questions relating to the conduct of international relations in the twenty-first century. Apart from conferring legitimacy to NATO's offensive action and its intervention outside the alliance's area of operation, the action further marginalises the UN. The moral of the tale is simple: no UN authorisation is required for military intervention as long as the major powers undertake it. The action has given a new dimension to the US strategic thinking by changing NATO's mission to address issues such as the proliferation of weapons of mass destruction, drugs and terrorism (Guicherd, 1999; Haass, 1999).

The potentially most significant legacy of *Operation Allied Force* is likely to be the legitimisation of so-called 'humanitarian intervention'. Unlike the news media, global security and international relations journals are full of the debate about the new role of NATO (Rubinstein, 1998; Lepgold, 1998; Daalder and O'Hanlon, 1999; Deutch et al, 1999; Rodman, 1999). The general tone and tenor of these analyses is for a enhanced role for NATO in the twenty-first century, as the UN becomes further marginalised in international affairs. Two prominent US analysts have even suggested that the world body is not equipped to handle the new humanitarian crises. 'Actual military interventions are best left to regional organisations, such as NATO, or to coalitions of the willing that, for now at least, will generally have to have the United States at their core' (Daalder and O'Hanlon, 1999).

Already, within months of the ending of the NATO bombing, humanitarian intervention was being hotly discussed within the UN, where during the 1999 session of the General Assembly, Secretary General Kofi Annan advocated the need for humanitarian intervention wherever civilian populations were at risk. Humanitarianism has also come to dominate Western academic and journalistic discourse, with calls to abandon the rigidities of existing international law, within which the concept of national sovereignty has a crucial position. The debate in the UN about the right of 'the international community' (a euphemism for the West) to intervene to defend human rights was also echoed at other international forums. A major development was the Charter for European Security adopted by the 54-member Organisation for Security and Co-operation in Europe (OSCE) in Istanbul in November 1999, which incorporated a 'principle' that takes interventionism a step further. Among the security risks the Charter included international terrorism, violent extremism, organised crime, drug trafficking, the spread of small and light weapons, acute economic problems, environmental degradation, as well as instability in the Mediterranean basin and central Asia (Ghebali, 2000).

The close relationship between OSCE and NATO, the former being a more respectable and political face of a military alliance, was in evidence during the Kosovo crisis and may be used to expand the remit of NATO to intervene in the geo-strategically significant areas of the globe such as Central Asia. However, in much media coverage these issues do not appear to receive much attention or critical scrutiny. Alternative sources of information – few and far between and many based on the World Wide Web – are of interest only to a small minority. For most of the audience, however, the television news networks remain the key source of information, globally (Hoge, 1994; Schreiber, 1998; Hachten, 1999).

The NATO bombing of Yugoslavia, apart from the human tragedy, cost $11 billion in warfare alone, while further $60 billion of damage was inflicted by the bombing (BBC, 1999b) and yet it was labelled as a humanitarian intervention, couched in moral tones and presented by the media as a great victory for human rights. What historian Bruce Cumings wrote, in the context of the Gulf War, also rings true for CNN's coverage of NATO's first war: 'High technology rendered the weapons smart, and the medium deaf, dumb and blind' (Cumings, 1992: 2).

References

Ali, Tariq (ed.) (2000) *Masters of the Universe? Nato's Balkan Crusade*. London: Verso.

Barry, John & Thomas, Evan (2000) "The Kosovo Cover-Up", *Newsweek*, May 15.

BBC (1999a) "How the War Was Spun", *Correspondent Special,* British Broadcasting Corporation, BBC2, 10 October.

BBC (1999b) "An Audit of War", *Correspondent Special*, British Broadcasting Corporation, BBC2, 17 October.

Buchan, David & Fidler, Stephen (1999) "An Uneasy Anniversary", *The Financial Times*, 23 April, p. 21.

Chomsky, Noam (1999) *The New Military Humanism: Lessons from Kosovo*. Monroe, ME: Common Courage Press.

Cook, Nick (1999) "War of Extremes", *Jane's Defence Weekly*, 7 July.

Cumings, Bruce (1992) *War and Television*. London: Verso.

Daalder, Ivo & O'Hanlon, Michael (1999) "Unlearning the Lessons of Kosovo", *Foreign Policy*, Fall, pp. 128-140.

Deutch, John; Kanter, Arnold & Scowcroft, Brent (1999) "Saving NATO's Foundation", *Foreign Affairs*, vol.78 no.6, pp. 54-67.

Fisk, Robert (1999) "Taken in by the NATO Line", *The Independent*, 29 June, p. 12.

Flournoy, Don & Stewart, Robert (1997) *CNN – Making News in the Global Market*. Luton: University of Luton Press.

Ghebali, Victor-Yves (2000) "The OSCE's Istanbul Charter for European Security", *NATO Review*, vol.48, no.1 , pp. 23-26.

Gibson, Janine (1999) "CNN Counts Costs of War", *The Guardian*, 14 May, p. 4.

Goff, Peter (ed.) (1999) *The Kosovo News and Propaganda War*. Vienna: International Press Institute.

Goldgeier, James (1999) *Not Whether But When – The US Decision to Enlarge NATO*. Washington: Brookings Institution Press.

Guicherd, Catherine (1999) "International Law and the War in Kosovo", *Survival*, 41(2), pp. 19-34.

Haass, Richard (1999) *Intervention: The Uses of Military Force in the Post-Cold War World*. Washington: Brookings Institution Press (2nd ed.).

Hachten, William (1999) *The World News Prism – Changing Media of International Communication*. Ames: Iowa State University Press (5th ed.).

Hallin, Daniel (1986) *The Uncensored War: The Media and Vietnam*. Oxford: Oxford University Press.

Herman, Edward & Chomsky, Noam (1988) *Manufacturing Consent – The Political Economy of the Mass Media*. New York: Pantheon.

Hoge, James (1994) "Media Pervasiveness", *Foreign Affairs*, vol.73, no.4, pp. 136-144.

Lepgold, Joseph (1998) "NATO's Post-Cold War Collective Action Problem", *International Security*, vol.23, no.1, pp. 78-106.

Meek, James & Whitehouse, Tom (1997) "Where Madness Seeps Out of the Earth", *The Observer*, 23, December.

Mermin, Jonathan (1999) *Debating War and Peace – Media Coverage of US Intervention in the Post-Vietnam Era*. Princeton: Princeton University Press.

Mowlana, Hamid; Gerbner, George & Schiller, Herbert (eds.) (1992) *Triumph of the Image: The Media's War in the Persian Gulf.* Boulder, CO.: Westview Press.

Rodman, Peter (1999) "The Fallout from Kosovo", *Foreign Affairs,* 78 (4), pp. 45-51.

Rubinstein, Alvin (1998) "NATO Enlargement vs. American Interests", *Orbis,* Winter, pp. 37-48.

Schreiber, D. (1998) "News World", *Cable and Satellite Europe,* November, pp. 16-17.

Seib, Philip (1997) *Headline Diplomacy – How News Coverage Affects Foreign Policy.* Westport: Praeger.

Solana, Javier (1999) "NATO's Success in Kosovo", *Foreign Affairs,* 78 (6), pp. 114-120.

Sweeney, John; Holsoe, Jens & Vulliamy (ed.) (1999) "Revealed: NATO Bombed Chinese Deliberately", *The Observer,* 17 October, pp. 1-2.

Toffler, Alvin & Toffler, Heidi (1993) *War and Anti-War – Survival at the Dawn of the 21st Century.* New York: Little, Brown,

Tunstall, Jeremy & Machin, David (1999) *The Anglo-American Media Connection.* Oxford: Oxford University Press.

Volkmer, Ingrid (1999) *News in the Global Sphere – A Study of CNN and Its Impact on Global Communications.* Luton: University of Luton Press.

About the Authors

Daniel Biltereyst, Ph.D., Associate Professor in Film, Cultural Media Studies and International Communication at the University of Gent, Belgium (1997-). He has been publishing in various international journals such as the 'European Journal of Communication', 'Communications', 'Cultural Policy', 'Asian Journal of Communication' and 'Media, Culture & Society', mainly about topics at the crossroads of international and global communications on the one hand, and more culturalist perspectives on the other hand. His recent research is on foreign/international news and global citizenship (funded by the Belgian National Research Council, 1999-2002).

Stig Hjarvard, Ph.D., Associate Professor at Department of Film & Media Studies, University of Copenhagen. He is head of research programme "Global Media Cultures", financed by the Danish Research Council for the Humanities, 1999-2001. Among his research interest are journalism, international communication, political communication, media history and the relationships between mediated and face-to-face communication. Recent books are *Internationale tv-nyheder* (1995) [International tv news] and *Tv-nyheder i konkurrence* (1999) [Tv news in competition]. Co-editor of *Audiovisual Media in Transition* (together with Thomas Tufte, 1998).

Hans-Henrik Holm, Jean Monnet Professor in International Relations and Head of Department at the Danish School of Journalism. Latest books are *Verden paa tilbud* (With L. Kabel et al., 2000) [On media foreign coverage], *Whose World Order?*, (With G. Sorensen, 1996), *And Now What. International Politics After the Cold War* (1999).

Klaus Bruhn Jensen, Dr. Phil., Associate Professor, Department of Film and Media Studies, University of Copenhagen, Denmark. Professor II, University of Oslo, Norway. Recent publications include *The Social Semiotics of Mass Communication* (1995); *News of the World: World Cultures Look at Television News* (editor and contributor, 1998); and *A Handbook of Media and Communication Research: Qualitative and Quantitative Methodologies* (editor, forthcoming).

Stig A. Nohrstedt, Ph.D. in Political Science (University of Uppsala, Sweden). Professor of Media and Communication, University of Örebro. Books include *Tredje världen i nyheterna* [News Coverage of the Third World, 1986]; *En nyhetsdag* [A Newsday, 1994]; Journalistikens etiska problem [The Ethical Problem of Journalism, 1996, with Mats Ekström]; *Risker, kommunikation och medier* [Risks, Communication and Media] (co-editor and contributor, 2000).

Rune Ottosen, Professor of journalism at Oslo College. He graduated both in journalism (1973) and in political science (1984) and has previously worked as a journalist and as a Research Fellow at the International Peace Research Institute, Oslo (PRIO). From 1994-1996 he worked as a research fellow at the Norwegian Journalist Federation writing the professional history of Norwegian journalists. He has published several books and articles in the field of journalism, cultural history, environment-problems and international conflicts.

Chris A. Paterson, Ph.D., is Assistant Professor at Department of Media Studies of the University of San Francisco, USA. He has worked in television production in the US, where he received his doctorate from the University of Texas. He is currently writing a book about television news agencies and co-editing a book about the sources of international news.

Tore Slaatta, dr.polit., is Researcher at Department of Media and Communication, University of Oslo, presently working as research coordinator for media and communication research within the national project "Power and Democracy in Norway" (1998-2003), funded by the Norwegian Research Council. Related publications are *Europeanisation and the Norwegian News Media: Political Discourse and News Production in the Transnational Field*, (doctoral thesis, 1999) and *Media and the Transition of Collective Identities* (editor, 1996). The working title of his present research project is "Symbolic power in the politico-economic field", which include empirical research on financial news production and reception in Norway.

Daya Kishan Thussu is a Senior Lecturer in Mass Communications at the University of North London. A former Associate Editor of Gemini News Service, a London-based international news agency, he is co-author of *Contra-Flow in Global News* (1992), editor of *Electronic Empires – Global Media and Local Resistance* (1998), and author of *International Communication – Continuity and Change* (2000).

Ingrid Volkmer is Visiting Scholar at MIT (Comparative Media Studies Program). She has been Professor of Media Studies at the University in Augsburg and is also a part time lecturer at the New School for Social Research, New York. Her publications focus on global communication issues, such as *News in the Global Sphere* (1999) and "Beyond the Global and the Local: Media Systems and Journalism in the Global Network Paradigm" in *News and Digital Journalism* (Thorburn, David, ed., 2001).

Claes de Vreese is Ph.D. Candidate and Research Associate in The Amsterdam School of Communications Research *ASCoR* at the University of Amsterdam, the Netherlands. He is working on the research project "News and European Integration. News Content and Effects in Cross-national Comparative Perspective" supported by the Danish Research Academy and the Netherlands Organisation for Scientific Research [NWO]. Recent publications include articles in *Communication Research* and *West European Politics*.

Norbert Wildermuth is a Ph. D. student at Copenhagen University, Dept. of Film & Media Studies. As a student of social and cultural anthropology he has been visiting and studying India regularly since 1980. Over the last decade he has been involved extensively in journalistic work as well as media research with regard to India, spending in all more than three years on the Indian subcontinent. Since April 1998 he is working on a dissertation with the title *The Cultural Economy of Indian Satellite Television*, which is due to be finished by April 2001.